Improving School Go

About the first edition:

> 'School governors will find this a sound and practical guide to the nature of their responsibilities and the process of managing their workload. It is well researched, based on vast experience, illustrated from the best practice, free from jargon – and always interesting.'
>
> *Joan Sallis*

> '[D]efinitely a "must" for your bookshelf.'
> *National Association of Governors and Managers*

> 'An essential guide to help governors.'
> *Times Educational Supplement*

This book is about governing schools – about how a governing board made up largely of 'ordinary' people with no professional educational experience, working in partnership with professional leaders, can help to make schools better. It is intended for governors in schools in England and Wales, in other parts of the world where lay people engage in school leadership, and for people who work with governors.

Improving School Governance examines:

- how school governors got to be where they are today
- how governing boards do their jobs
- how individual governors can best contribute to their schools
- governors' accountability
- the nature of governors' meetings
- the rights that governors have
- the relationships between governors and the headteacher
- the role of governing boards in school inspection
- governors' relationships with parents and the wider community
- how to evaluate the performance and impact of governing boards
- what the future might hold for state-funded schools and their governance
- what national strategic issues will need to be addressed by governing boards in the next five to ten years.

Nigel Gann is an independent education consultant working with school governors and headteachers and has been involved in managing and governing schools for more than thirty years. He has written, spoken and trained on school leadership for the Department for Education, Ofsted, the British Council, BBC TV and Radio, the National College for Teaching and Leadership, the Universities of Leicester and Southampton, CfBT Education Trust, the National Governors' Association, Governors Wales, Worklife Support, most of the local authorities in England and Wales, and in Russia, the Middle East and Cyprus. He has been a governor in eight schools, including spells as chair in three of them.

Improving School Governance

How better governors make better schools

Second edition

Nigel Gann

Routledge
Taylor & Francis Group

LONDON AND NEW YORK

Second edition published 2016
by Routledge
2 Park Square, Milton Park, Abingdon, Oxon OX14 4RN

and by Routledge
711 Third Avenue, New York, NY 10017

Routledge is an imprint of the Taylor & Francis Group, an Informa business

First edition published by Routledge 1998

British Library Cataloguing in Publication Data
A catalogue record for this book is available from the British Library

Library of Congress Cataloging-in-Publication Data
A catalog record for this book has been requested

ISBN: 978-1-138-83284-8 (hbk)
ISBN: 978-1-138-83285-5 (pbk)
ISBN: 978-1-315-73575-7 (ebk)

Typeset in Bembo
by Swales & Willis Ltd, Exeter, Devon, UK

This book is dedicated to five inspirational women:

Cathy Wood, Emma Gann, Olivia Gann, Alex Lewis and Eleanor Gann

The future of Finley, Jack and Jesse Lewis, Summer and Callum Theobald, and their contemporaries depends on our schools and their governance being at their best.

Contents

List of figures and tables   ix
Foreword   x
Preface   xii
Acknowledgements   xiv

Introduction   1

1 People and their schools: how lay governors, after a
  long history, came to have an important role in
  school governance   9

2 The revival of school governance: how governing schools
  came to make a meaningful contribution to school
  improvement   29

3 The strategic governing board: how the governing
  board brings about school improvement   52

4 The responsibilities, roles and rights of governors:
  in which we look at some ideas about governing   80

5 Governance, leadership and management: being an
  investigation of the relationships that governing
  boards have with their headteacher and staff   109

6 School governance and school inspection:
  a consideration of the impact inspection has on
  school governance   134

7 Schools, parents and the community:
  in which we consider the relationships of schools
  with parents and other local people   150

 8 Evaluating governance: how do we know how well
    we are governing the school?   168

 9 Schools in uncertain times: what the present looks like and
    what the future might hold; the state of the nation and its
    schooling   173

10 The future of governing schools: future proofing the school   189

    Reading list   206
    Bibliography   209
    Appendices   218
    Index   241

Figures and tables

Figures

3.1 The school continuum 67
4.1 Role descriptions 96
4.2 A strategic cycle 100
4.3 Chair's meeting guide 101
4.4 A good meeting 102
4.5 A meetings charter 103
7.1 Criteria for ease of parental access 161

Tables

6.1 Inspection outcomes 2013: secondary schools 144
6.2 Inspection outcomes 2013: primary schools 145

Foreword

In the current turbulent times for education in England, it is extremely important that schools remain secure and stable as proper institutions in our communities. The role of school governors has therefore never been more important because ensuring the institutional legitimacy of schools is in effect what they do and what they are responsible for. There is then a paradox between the importance of school governing and its nature. Important though it is, school governing is largely hidden from view. The work of governing is very much a 'behind-the-scenes' activity. It's hard to see it in action in an everyday sense and to see the direct effects of good governing in the rich busy-ness of life in schools. Governors themselves tend to be modest in nature – ready to let others in schools receive praise and stand in the spotlight. Nonetheless, the effects of 'good governing' are felt deeply by all those connected with a school. Good governing provides a secure foundation for a school, an underpinning of what happens in a school on a daily basis, and an overall framework within which the work of teachers and learners can take place.

Another consequence of the hidden nature of governing is that it can make learning how to be a good governor very difficult. What do they do? Yes, we've all had the 'apprenticeship of observation', we all know about schools because we've spent years in them as students. But unless you have worked in a school you will have no real sense of what goes on in the 'other side' – the staff side. Again much of that is hidden from sight. Again that can make learning to be a governor difficult.

All of that is for me an important rationale for this book and why I am delighted to commend it to you. Written by a highly respected expert in education at all levels, Nigel Gann, the book explains the nature of school governing – where it sits in the education system, what it means, and how to do it. Unusually for books of this kind, the text not only explains the current roles and responsibilities of school governors, it locates it in time. The book explains the historical context, which is very important, and the present landscape, and it does some future gazing too. Importantly, Nigel Gann does all this in a very lively and engaging way. You may not agree with everything he says but you will enjoy how he says it, and it's a demanding read in places too.

In many ways, the book reflects what so many governors say about governing: 'Well, we have some serious disagreements on our governing body, and sometimes governing is very taxing but do you know what, I really enjoy it.' I hope and think you will gain a lot from reading this book as indeed I hope and think you gain a lot from being a school governor.

Professor Chris James
University of Bath
March 2015

Preface to the second edition

This book would not have been written without the thousands of school governors I have met and worked with over some thirty-five years, in England, Wales and further afield. I am grateful to all of them for the ideas they have had and to the organisations which have enabled me to work with them, including: Leicestershire County Council, the University of Leicester School of Education, the University of Southampton School of Education, the BBC, Ofsted and the Department for Education in its various guises, CfBT Education Trust, the British Council, Dorset County Council, the National Governors' Association and its consultancy service.

The work that has led to this book could not have happened without the inspiration, support and tolerance of Cathy Wood. All of us who work with, or serve as, school governors owe an incalculable debt to Joan Sallis, the forerunner and inspirer of all of us.

I have been fortunate to have served as a governor at eight schools over thirty-five years:

Solway Community School, Cumbria (1984–1986)

Hightown First School, Southampton (1988–1992)

Woodlands Community School, Southampton (1988–1998)

Norton-sub-Hamdon CE Primary School, Somerset (2000–2015)

Stanchester Community School, Somerset (2004–2011)

Sandwell Academy, West Bromwich (2006–2008)

Archbishop Cranmer Primary School Interim Executive Board, Taunton, Somerset (2012–13)

Norton-sub-Hamdon/West Chinnock Federation of CE Primary Schools, 2010–2015

I have worked in teams of inspirational governors and headteachers who have taught me everything I know about governance – including headteachers like Val Down and Paul Burke in Southampton, Kathy Foot and Glyn Ottery in Somerset. Earlier, I learnt about schools from colleagues in Inner London, Leicestershire and Cumbria, including the late Tim Rogers and Roger Seckington in Leicestershire.

For this current edition, I am particularly grateful to Professor Chris James of the University of Bath, a key player in the academic and practical study of school governance today. Also, to Clare Collins, lead consultant with the National Governors' Association and Don Walkley, Executive Director of the Australian Institute for School Governance.

Nothing could be much better than spending a working lifetime in and around schools. They are some of the most important and exciting places to be. That looks likely to continue to be the case.

Acknowledgements

I am grateful to the following for permission to reproduce materials:

The National Governors' Association, for permission to copy the Agreement on Roles (Appendix 6), the eight elements of good governance and the common themes of governance in practice, and to quote from the Framework for Governance in Chapter 8.

Forum (Journal for promoting 3–19 comprehensive education, published by Symposium Books) for extracts from Volume 53 Number 3, 2011, and Volume 56 Number 3, 2014.

Darlington, Hinds and Holt (1988) for the characteristics of a good meeting (Figure 4.4).

Norton-sub-Hamdon Church of England Primary School, Somerset, for the letter to parents in Chapter 7.

Jackie Walters and Colin Richardson of the Bradford School Governor Service for their work based on Carver, 1990.

Introduction

What could be more unlikely – or extraordinary – than the governing of schools? Schools, like hospitals and the police and railways and roads, are provided by 'the state'. We pay for them in our taxes, if we're lucky enough to have work and money, and there they are. Nobody really wants to know what sort of roads or medical care we want, so the people who constitute 'the state' give us what they think we want, or should have or what they want us to have. If it isn't – well, we can complain, or vote them out next time, can't we? That's an advanced democratic capitalist state for you. Very sensible, very practical, and not too much bother from the electorate. Who would want to spend hours every year talking about roads or doctors or the police? No one, except politicians.

We send our children and grandchildren and nieces and nephews to school. Mostly, we don't pay anything for it, and unless we choose to do it ourselves at home, our children are taught what other people want them to be taught – mainly politicians these days, though it used to be teachers – in a way that other people decide they should be taught, at times and in places when other people think it should happen. And, when the children come home, we say, 'How did you get on in school today?' or 'What did you learn in school today?' as if it's nothing much to do with us.

Clever university professors and politicians and schoolteachers spend their lives arguing about what the answers to these questions might be, but, as in all these other areas of our lives, we leave them to it (though we often moan that they get it all wrong). Our lives are filled up by the demands and requirements and expectations of other people, and we do what we're told, what's expected of us, and life goes on, full and demanding and largely dictated, and nobody much takes much notice of what we think about it all.

Except in schools. In schools, someone seems to care. Perhaps it's only a token, but headteachers and politicians and schoolworkers spend hours and hours talking with, and maybe listening to, people who aren't experts. Not just talking, but actually making themselves subject to these people in a whole lot of areas of their work.

How extraordinary! That 350,000 or so people, almost all of them past school attenders, and many parents or grandparents of current school attenders, should be involved in sitting down with all those clever people engaged 24/7 with 'schooling' and deciding with them, as equals, or even as their bosses, how the school should go on. When do ordinary people ever get the chance to say to a doctor or an architect or a railway company 'Why did you do that? Why do you do it that way? What's the outcome of you doing that? Can't you do it better?'

But in schools we do that. And the teachers (and sometimes the politicians) listen, and have to explain, and have to do it better. This is unique, isn't it? The remarkableness of, several times a year, a group of people walking into a school and saying 'How well are you doing? How can you do even better?' leaves us gasping when we think about it. But it happens. It's embodied in the law, and the teachers, especially the headteachers, go along with it and the best ones welcome it and enjoy it. The politicians support it and strengthen it. And the people who engage with it spend hours and days, often late into the night after a day of their own work, trying to do it better.

What a model this might provide for everything else we do. Why not meet occasionally with our doctors and talk about how they might do better? And our roadbuilders and transport providers and waste collectors, and our bankers? And our politicians?

What a nation we might be if we did that about everything that affects us.

Meanwhile, in schools, we must keep trying to engage more people in this conversation. We know from plentiful research that children do best at school when their parents support the school and share the role of educator with it. But what do most parents think of schools? And most children? And the people who live in the neighbourhood, the part of the city, the bit of town, the village, where children who go to school live? The danger with the model we have is that only people who are already successful, confident, 'educated', know about 'meetings', know 'how to talk to people', will engage with the governing conversation. But the conversation about schools should welcome and embrace everyone, because education is a universal experience – pretty well everyone went to school. Like a city festival or a village fair, there should be some place for everyone in this 'multilogue', and what everyone says should be heard, respected, valued and responded to.

At its best – and many people seem to be forgetting this – schooling is a magical thing. For a few short years, Ofsted, the school inspection body, asked its inspectors to report on moments of 'awe and wonder' in the schools they visited. What a magical notion! When we look back on our own schooling, it's those moments we remember: unpredictable instants when we were sparked into life by a physical experience, a piece of music, a scientific insight, a poem. In one school, early in the twenty-first century, an inspector accompanied a primary class to walk up a hill near the school. A girl, running ahead, sat astride a stile and looked about her and cried: 'Cor, Miss, you can see the whole of the world from here.' And the inspector thought it worth recording! That's awe and wonder and it happened as part of a formal education. It's the moment we remember, and the moment teachers never forget, either.

For the most part, schools are squared off, ruled, fixed and rigid things. What people are told to judge them by are numbers, statistics and data; by the way everyone behaves the same, doing just what they're told; by the way teachers and other schoolworkers follow rules, obey government diktats, produce measurable results.

But curvy things like awe and wonder, things more difficult to pin down and measure, happen in schools all the time, too. Jokes and stories force their way in and people do unexpected, not always welcome, but always rounded human things.

School management is often about producing these measurable things – getting the data right, building the numbers up, attaining and achieving and progressing. School leadership, and, in particular governance, must be about the rounded things, not just about 'How many . . . ?' and 'How much . . . ?', but about why and how and who. Governance brings people into schools who will not be slaves to calculations, whose careers will not be blessed by annual percentage increases, or blighted by disappointing numbers.

Ever since ordinary people inserted themselves into the provision of schools, first, through the philanthropic process of establishing voluntary, usually faith-based, schools, then in the school boards of the late Victorian age, governments have tried to marshal and control them. In 1902, they did it by handing education over to the new local authorities, and allowing school governors only a very peripheral role. The revival of individual and meaningful school governance in the 1980s brought not just the middle-class great and good (though they came in large numbers) but parents and other ordinary people who saw schools as expressions of the strength of their local communities. So government sought to tie them down. It said it wanted governing bodies to be more 'business-like'; it tried to define what it thought governors should be doing, making them more efficient, making them more like those great and efficient institutions like banking and investment and currency manipulation that had made this nation what it is today. It brought in inspectors to tell governors what to do and to judge how well they do it; it kept saying that governors needed to be more skilled, more focused, more directive – that governing bodies should be smaller, so that they didn't have time to be distracted from their primary task – to make the school get better results.

Maybe governors will go on resisting these pressures. Perhaps school governors are a genuine and rare example of democratic participation in action, the voice of ordinary people.

Welcome to this book, which is about where we are today in this history of the role ordinary people play in the leadership of schools.

This is a book about school governance – about the network of structures and patterns created by legislation, custom and practice that determine the way schools operate and how they are led. It is also a book about governing schools – about how a governing board consisting predominantly of 'ordinary' people with no professional educational experience can make a positive contribution to the leadership of schools. The book seeks to explain how both the governance and the governing of schools can be improved.

The first edition of the book, published in 1998, appeared at a time when, with a very small number of exceptions, English state-funded schools were overseen by local education authorities, comprising a large and experienced band of professional educational administrators and advisers, most of them former teachers, under the direction of a committee of locally elected politicians. The newly-elected Labour government of the time brought an element of local oversight to the grant-maintained schools and city technology colleges created by the previous Conservative government, an early experiment in the creation of state-funded schools independent of their local authorities.

In the intervening seventeen years, but especially since the coalition government of 2010 took office, the picture has changed radically. At the time of writing, more than 60 per cent of all state-funded secondary schools in England have academy or free school status, untrammelled by any significant relationship with, or accountability to, local government. While the conversion of primary schools has proceeded at a far slower pace (some 13 per cent at the time of writing), there are indications of increasing government pressure to 'free' all state-funded schools of their local government links, and there are many local authorities (LAs - no longer 'local education authorities') that are hurrying that process along.

So the context of this edition is very different from that of its predecessor. Education – once a party political free zone – is now an arena for ideologues and polemicists. The shrinking of the state, both at central government and local government levels, is now part of every major political party's agenda. Lines of responsibility for previously state-provided services, and chains of accountability, are increasingly blurred. Ownership of services has taken on a new set of meanings.

But this book has not changed its primary perspective in these intervening years. It is based on the belief that people have a right (and a duty) to run the organisations that impact on their lives. And one thing all state-funded schools in England and Wales share in common, as well as many independent schools, and thousands of schools in other countries, is that the body with ultimate legal responsibility for their performance is a governing board.

In order to discharge this responsibility effectively, it is helpful to understand the *context* in which governing boards as they work today have come about. This means that the *history* is important. Governing boards were once described as having 'responsibility without power'. This can surely no longer be said. Governors exercise enormous powers over their schools, and some would argue that this can be without significant channels of accountability. Without knowing why there were lay governors in the early days of state education, how they became disempowered, why the major political parties in England eventually became committed to lay governance, 'ordinary people' may feel overawed by the systems, and so less effective as a result.

Context is not the only reason why we need to know the history. For those of us lucky enough to work in this field, one of the things we still hear from some governors is 'Why me? What have I got to offer?' The history suggests that lay governors do have the capacity to significantly improve the ways that schools operate – but only where governors feel that they have an absolute right to do so.

So the history leads to the current legislative and social context, determining how lay governors feel about schools, and how schools feel about lay governors. This is a considerably more complex issue than it was before the turn of the twenty-first century. Consequently, the nature and conduct of school governance is considerably more contentious now than it was then.

It is now recognised, however, by both the Department for Education (DfE) and the Schools Inspectorate (Ofsted) that the majority of governing boards in state-funded schools in England make a positive contribution to their schools' performance. That many governing boards could do better, and that pupils would benefit if they did, is also true.

So, in this book, we will be considering why some governing boards are not as effective as they might be, and how they might operate more effectively. This is the kernel and the main purpose of the book. It will, I hope, be read by many of the 350,000 or so governors of the 24,000 state-funded schools in England (and Wales, where many of the same circumstances prevail, although not the wide range or large number of schools unaccountable to their local authorities) whether they are lay governors, or headteachers or other educationalists, whether they serve on a traditional governing board, a multi-academy trust or a local governing board, or anyone else who works with governors, with a view to helping them to improve the quality of education offered to young people in the early years of the twenty-first century.

This book does not need to be read from cover to cover. You can dip into it as it suits you, although there is a logic to the shape. Chapter 1 deals with how school governors got to be where they are today. This is important, because our past legitimises, and offers possible narratives for, our present and our future. There are political, social, cultural and ideological reasons why governors have such an important place in today's schools.

Chapter 2 shows how the governing boards set up in 1988, and only tinkered with since, do their jobs. It describes the different types of school we now have in England and the roles that governing boards play in them. It considers the other roles of governors in independent state-funded schools such as academies and free schools, and the relationships between trusts and local governing boards. It also considers who governors are, what they do and what their impact on the school might be. It also reflects on what governors might be for, and the possibility of there being two main political views of predominantly lay governing boards: a conservative or consumerist model, and a radical or ownership model. It concludes by considering the new small-state model of the delivery of public services and the strategy put in place by the 2010 coalition government to achieve it.

Chapter 3 considers the current statutory duties and responsibilities of governing boards and the expectations held of them by the DfE and Ofsted. We will look at what is meant by the division between strategic and managerial responsibilities, and the challenges offered by actual practice and by government requirements. We will look at models of school improvement and development planning, at vehicles for monitoring school performance, including what governors should – and shouldn't – monitor. The critical question that governors need to address is 'How do we know how well the school is doing?' We will address that question here.

Having thought through what governing boards are for, Chapter 4 looks at who governors are and how they do their jobs. We consider the difference between the traditional 'stakeholder' view of school governance and the more recent skills-based approach. We look at governor behaviour and how it can be monitored. We will also consider a new element in school governance – the issue of probity. It is only since 2010 that serious doubts have been raised about the motivations of some governors and trustees, and we will look at some examples of questionable practice. This will lead us into looking at the role of volunteers in what is now seen by many as the market-place of education. We will also consider here some of the best practice of meeting behaviour, recruitment and retention of governors, the skills needed of individual governors, the rights that governors have of support, and the professional clerking of governing boards.

Chapter 5 looks at the key relationship that governors have with the professional leadership of the school. What are the respective roles of governors and headteachers? How do governors go about appointing a headteacher? We will look here at some of the different models of school leadership and management, especially at the thorny issue of 'superheads' and how the fashionable 'distributive leadership' of the first decade of the century impacts on governance.

Chapter 6 is about the inspection of schools and of governors. The regulations concerning school inspection are subject to frequent and substantial change. However, one element that has held true since the inception of Ofsted in England and Estyn in Wales has been the growing importance of governance in the process. Some practical advice will be offered, alongside the usual warnings about the likelihood of changes to the detail.

Chapter 7 considers the relationship between schools and their communities, especially with their parents. The brief history shows that the world of education had to do a lot of work to catch up with current demands for explicit engagement and accountability. This has by no means been ameliorated by the capacity of parent groups to open their own state-funded schools. We will look at some of the ways in which schools have overcome this, and how governors have a crucial role in helping to develop strategies towards a real partnership with the community.

Chapter 8 tackles the thorny question of how to know that the governing board itself is doing a good job. Increasingly we are seeing a demand for evidence of the impact that governors have on school performance, and how it enables continuous improvement. We will look at the induction, training and development of governors, and at a number of models for governing board self-review. We will also consider the range of accountabilities that governing boards have. We will consider the various aids and obstacles to the effectiveness of governing boards, and how they can be efficient, effective, democratic, accountable, transparent, challenging and supportive.

Chapter 9 will introduce the debate about what constitutes a 'good' school and, therefore, a good governing body. It will lay all caution to one side and dare to make some projections about the future of education – or, at least, what we might like that future to be.

Chapter 10, in conclusion, concerns itself with the current state of the nation and the role of school governance within it. Some readers might find it overly 'political'. But politics is about the governance of the state, and schooling is largely a state provision, so it cannot be avoided. Within it, though, we will look at what issues are around at the moment, and still likely to be around in five years' time, and the need for governors to consider these in their strategic planning.

There is a very extensive bibliography attached to the book, but I have followed the practice of the first edition and selected – on a purely subjective basis – some books or documents that I have found particularly useful, interesting or inspiring.

You will find scattered throughout the book a number of 'frames'. These are mainly stories or statistics which shed some light on the book's arguments. The anecdotes are all, as far as we can establish, true. But they should not be taken as necessarily representative.

You will notice that the book uses two ways to describe the full collective of governors – the governing body and the governing board. A further complication is the occasional use of the archaic 'managing body'. The term 'manager' was used for primary school governors until the 1986 Education Act (No. 2) regulated the position, so that all governors became 'governors'. The term 'governing body' was in common usage until 2014. The non-statutory guidance given in 2014 by the DfE reads as follows:

'The governing body provides non-executive leadership. Its role is to operate as a board akin to the board of trustees of a charity, or the board of directors of a company. In all matters, the "board of governors" should operate at a strategic level, leaving the headteacher and senior school leaders responsible and accountable to it for the operational day-to-day running of the school. To emphasize this point, this advice will refer to the governing body as "the board" ' (DfE, 2014a).

I have followed this advice, and for generally up-to-date references I refer to the board of governors.

Finally, this book is about school governance in England and, with some important differences, Wales and Northern Ireland. Some of the administrative arrangements for decision-making and funding are different for Welsh schools and, at the time of writing, the Welsh government has not embraced the academies and free schools increasingly common in England. School governance is organised altogether differently in Scotland, as it is elsewhere in the world. However, other commonwealth countries such as Australia, New Zealand and South Africa have been developing lay participation in their schools' management; the United States has a history of lay control of school administration at school board level, and has pioneered the development of charter schools which are the model for English academies, as well as developments in schooling elsewhere, particularly in the Middle East; and a number of European countries are developing systems of lay governance and/or participation. There are, I hope, valuable ideas in this second edition for lay and professional people who are working together, whatever the context, to get the best out of their schools for the benefit of our children.

Chapter 1

People and their schools

How lay governors, after a long history, came to have an important role in school governance

This is the story of governing schools. Governors have a longer history than you might think. You don't have to read this history in order to make up your own mind as to how we should exercise our oversight of schools today, but you might find it useful to know some of the background to where we find ourselves in the first quarter of the twenty-first century.

The history of governing schools is the story of how ordinary people got to have a say in the running of their schools. But the main conflict within education has been – and in many ways still is – between politicians and professional educators. This conflict has been about who should have ownership of the education system.

The administration of education operates, in simple terms, on three levels: First, *school governance* – people with the responsibility for an individual school or group of schools. They delegate some functions to the professional staff they employ, specifically, the day-to-day running of the school with a view to enabling the best possible learning of the pupils. These governors (and we now have different levels of governors in some schools, where a board of trustees might appoint a local governing board) carry the legal responsibility for what goes on in the schools. Secondly, the *local level of school administration*, with more, less or in a growing number of cases, no control over the first level. Only for a comparatively short time in our history, in the last quarter of the nineteenth century, have the people at this level been elected to deal solely with education. For almost all of the twentieth century, local government was elected to provide directly a range of services, of which schooling was by some distance the most expensive and the most labour-intensive. Only in the 1990s did a small number of state-funded schools take the opportunity then on offer to break away from their local education authority and to receive their funding from, and become directly responsible to, the national government. From this time on, and with increasing rapidity, the army of professional support provided to schools by local authorities began to shrink. Thirdly, *national government* exerts its influence in a number of ways, through acts of parliament, through the actions and preferences of ministers responsible for education, and through the more or less independent actions of civil servants employed by the department responsible for education.

There is no simple division here between policy and implementation, between theory and practice. For many years, state education in England and Wales was described as a national system, locally administered. This can no longer be said, even as the broadest generalisation. Except for a brief period towards the end of the nineteenth century, the voice of the community, the voice of ordinary people who pay for education through their local taxes, the voice of 'the consumer', has rarely been heard – until recently. What we saw, between 1839 and 1988, was a professionalisation and bureaucratisation of education at both central and local government levels; and the neutralisation of school governance by a failure to define specific areas of responsibility for lay people. The outcome was the overarching control of schools from 'above' by local education authorities and their officers; and from 'below', by their headteachers and other professional staff. Another factor which kept education largely away from the influence of politicians was the broad consensus between the two major parties of government about the purpose and structures of schooling. The trend towards providing ever-longer and more egalitarian state schooling to the entire population of young people dominated education policy throughout the twentieth century. Even debates about comprehensive versus selective secondary education were largely peripheral to the great aim of universal provision.

The 1970s saw the beginning of the end of this period, since when both the structures and the content of schooling have become deeply contentious. This turnaround has of course had its own impact on governance. In the early summer of 2014, what was almost certainly a hoax letter from a Birmingham school governor led to an impassioned debate in newspapers about the role of governors, exacerbated by the variety of types of school in existence throughout England, the confusing range of accountabilities and responsibilities of schools, the content of the curriculum, and the very purposes of schooling.

The history of school governing bodies

From the Dark Ages to Victorian times

The first school governing bodies were the boards of trustees responsible for setting up and running English schools from the sixth century on. These were originally church institutions, but by the fifteenth and sixteenth centuries more and more schools were being set up by groups of lay people, such as guilds and companies. Of course, these were almost exclusively for boys only, and aimed at a classical preparation for the increasingly secular universities. They were now being governed by 'respectable' people who were trustees of schools established by wealthy, philanthropic citizens, representatives of the newly emerging middle class. Everything the school did was in the hands of these trustees, including maintaining the buildings and appointing the teachers. While some governing bodies took an active and day-to-day interest, we know that many of them didn't take the job seriously, and left the running of the school to often incompetent, sometimes corrupt, headteachers.

In the late seventeenth century, there was a rise in 'associated philanthropy' (Owen, 1964). Wealthy people came together in what we now call voluntary organisations: 'One of the most shining testimonies to this new form of charity was the charity school movement. By 1729 there were over 1400 such schools in England catering for over 22,000 pupils' (Smith, 1995: p. 12). They were as much concerned with religious instruction as they were with secular education – as was the Sunday School movement from the 1780s, which attracted possibly '200,000 working class children by 1800, and 2 million by mid-century' (Smith, 1995: p. 18). Were such schools mainly a means of social control, or were they an extension of popular working-class culture? While 'middle-class' teachers and sponsors, for the most part, controlled the schools, some clergy attacked them as seditious.

Religious foundations, however, were the most likely to fund schools. Non-conformist schools were particularly likely to offer a practical education which suited the industrial and commercial expansion of the nineteenth century. It was these schools that grew into the public and grammar schools of the twentieth century.

People began to argue about what went on in schools. Should they just teach the basics, so that workers could function in the new machine age? Should they teach morals and religion? Were schools for 'keeping people in their place'? Or for developing individuality? Could they foster social mobility, seen by many as essential for a vibrant growing economy? In this debate – which is not unfamiliar today – the development of state funding of schools added a third element to those already in place, the governing body and the headteacher.

1839–1870

Most of the schools providing elementary education in the country in the 1830s were established by the National Society (of the Church of England) and the British and Foreign Schools Society (of the non-conformist churches). The government awarded grants to set up these schools, and to run them. In 1839, the Government Education Office was created as an adjunct to the Privy Council Office, and presided over by the Lord President, to distribute these grants to the two societies. The Secretary of Education ran the office. He was the first civil servant to devote his time entirely to education.

The Education Office appointed two inspectors, one Church of England, one non-conformist, to decide the size of the grant to be given to each school. But these inspectors had no *controlling* brief. The first Ofsted inspectors in 1993 were reminded that they 'should recognise that the appropriate authority (i.e. the governing board) has ultimate responsibility for executive action' (Ofsted, 1993: Section 3, p. 18). Nowadays, inspectors tell schools what they have to do to improve – but not how to do it. In 2014, on the publication of some reports on schools which implied otherwise, Ofsted hurried to deny that they favoured particular styles of teaching. There are 170 years of history behind this. The first Guidance for Inspectors, published in 1840, read: 'You are in no respect to interfere with the instruction, management or discipline of the school, or to press upon them any suggestion that they may be disinclined to receive' (quoted in Gordon, 1974). So they had very limited powers. In 1857, for example, a committee of school 'managers' (until the 1986 Education Act, all elementary and later primary school governors were called, deceptively, managers) said to HMI Blandford of their schoolmaster: 'He is very incompetent, but we like him for he gives us no trouble, and is very civil'. The power of inspectors was perhaps more in what people thought they could do, than what they actually could do.

Lina Waterfield (1961) tells how Matthew Arnold – son of the great Rugby headmaster, part-time poet, and school inspector – was once invited by her parents to visit her when she was 6 years old and still not reading:

'"Your mother tells me that you do not know how to read, and are refusing to learn. It surprises me very much that a little girl of six should not know how to read, and expects to be read to. It is disgraceful, and you must promise me to learn at once; if you don't, I shall have to put your father and mother in prison." I was startled and frightened by this threat, and at the very same time very puzzled that a poet could put people in prison. I asked father whether he could put him in prison. Father hesitated: "No, I don't think he could, although he *is* a Government Inspector of Schools".' The threat, though baseless, worked. The little girl was reading *Grimms' Fairy Tales* within a few weeks.

The church school managers, therefore, were not inclined to take orders, just as long as the grant kept coming. Some boards probably developed some interesting practices in order to do this, including inaccurate reports of the moral and professional qualities of teachers and pupil teachers, disregard for the Department's health regulations, and manipulation of attendance figures. Refusing to pay the grant became the only sanction that the government could impose on schools, while the responsibility for the provision of schools remained in the hands of the churches, charitable bodies and local – almost exclusively middle-class – people.

A report by HMI Norris, visiting church schools in Cheshire, Shropshire and Staffordshire in 1858, showed that:

- 37 per cent of schools were managed entirely by clergy, the management committees being active or non-existent;
- 43 per cent of schools were managed by clergy with a management committee;
- 9 per cent were managed by clergy and the local squire;
- 5 per cent entirely by the squire and his family;
- 3 per cent by a local industrialist;
- 3 per cent by a local lay committee.

The first serious Education Act

The 1870 Education Act was the first serious legislation in progress towards universal education. It didn't do much to alter the management of existing schools, but it did introduce a structure of local government responsible for providing and administering schools and it was, by the standards of the times, directly accountable to the people (or those who could vote). W. E. Forster, as Vice-President of the Privy Council, faced what we would now call a postcode lottery. Fewer than one third of school-age children were in state-aided schools, fewer than a quarter in other, voluntary, schools, and at least two million had no schooling at all. The lead-up to Forster's bill set the tone for parliamentary debate on education for the next 75 years. At no time does the secular curriculum of education appear to have been regarded as a matter for politicians. What they talked about was the place of religious instruction and worship, and the ownership of schools between church and state.

The 1870 Act and its successors brought some 5.2 million children into compulsory elementary education by 1895. The universal provision of education was a radical step – although Gladstone was not convinced of its benefits, and H. G. Wells described the act as 'an Act to educate the lower classes for employment on lower class lines, and with specially trained, inferior teachers who had no universal quality' (Wells, 1934). At the same time, deciding who would administer schools involved a very democratic system for its time.

The country was divided into School Districts, along the lines of boroughs or civil parishes. School Boards were created where there were not already enough schools. The size of these boards varied between five and fifteen members according to the population of the district, and members were elected every three years by cumulative vote (that is, every voter having as many votes as there were seats, and distributing them among the candidates). The electoral roll was the same as the burgess roll in a borough, or ratepayers in a parish, so, unlike parliamentary elections, it included single women and widows with property. However, there were none of the usual restrictions on eligibility to stand for election: 'the school boards created under the Elementary Education Act were the most democratically constituted of all elected bodies of local government. Members, who sat for three years, required neither a property nor a residential qualification. Although voters had to be ratepayers, they were all treated equally' (Hurt, 1979: p. 75). A further significant blow for women's rights at the time occurred when Victorian feminist, journalist and educator Florence Fenwick Miller won the right to be elected to her school board under her birth name rather than her married name, which led the way for married women later to stand for parliament under their birth names. Elections were by secret ballot, and the boards were able to pass bye-laws making school attendance compulsory for children between the ages of five and thirteen.

The 1870 Act had enormous political significance. Indeed, Hurt suggests that the debate 'was not predominantly an educational one about the need to extend the existing provision of elementary schooling, on that point there was by now a substantial consensus of opinion; it was a political one about how this extension should be made, the extent to which the schools should be under popular control, and how they should be financed. *Essentially, it was a conflict between protagonists of differing visions of society*, for whosoever controlled the schools could influence the education of the rising generations in a state that was moving slowly, albeit unwittingly, towards parliamentary democracy' (Hurt, 1979: p. 76, my italics).

And so, we might add, it is today. The debate about school governance in the 2010s is just as much about who should have control over the education system in both its academic and its socialising roles.

The debate on Forster's bill was largely about who should be responsible for managing schools. Some thought it should be only 'the great and good': 'This business of education is of a peculiar character; it requires for its performance a special knowledge and an interest in the intellectual and moral improvement of the children', said the Rt. Hon. W. F. Cowper in defence of the established order (quoted in Hurt, 1979: p. 79). The National Education League stood for national, universal, free, compulsory education managed by elected lay people. The National Education Union, supported by a number of Her Majesty's Inspectorate, wanted the schools to remain, in the words of Sir James Kay-Shuttleworth, 'to a great extent under the influence of the superior classes of society', so protecting the teacher from 'the caprices of the least intelligent class' (quoted in Hurt, 1979: p. 78). The remnants of this debate could still be heard when some professional associations spoke about the impact of the 1986 Act.

Managers within the London School Board District, 1884

Leisured classes	31 per cent
Church	21 per cent
Ladies	19 per cent
Professional classes	10 per cent
Working classes	4 per cent
	(Gordon, 1974)

What was the outcome of the 1870 Act? Both the extended representation, and the considerable powers accorded to the new boards, did attract criticism from sections of church and state. They were 'considered to be breeding grounds for radical agitators' (Sutherland, 1973), and a strong case has been made for their effectiveness as vehicles of radical change.

'[T]o review the work of Socialist members of School Boards is to find them working on the practical plane to realize, step by step, the aims summarised in their programme as "state maintenance". . . . they pressed for the free use of swimming baths by school children, the right to take them on educational visits to museums and botanical gardens, the development of school libraries. They spoke up on School Boards for improved salaries for teachers, equal pay for men and women, the raising of the leaving age to fourteen and even sixteen. It was to make the work of the Boards better known to electors that they pressed for the policy of displaying minutes of the Board's meetings in the city libraries, of changing the time of meetings to the evening and of allowing free use of the schools, to broaden education, and to realize in practice – even under the most difficult and distressing conditions in industrial cities – that broad view of the role and purpose of education which formed so essential an aspect of the socialist outlook.'

(Simon, 1965)

Already, the debate foreshadowed many of the issues around the lay governing of schools today:

- How much centralised state control of schools should there be?
- What should be the relationship between church and state, and what place is there for religious worship and instruction in schools?
- Is the purpose of education to serve the needs of the state, or to meet the needs of young people? Are these mutually exclusive?

- Are special qualities and skills needed for the lay governance of schools?
- Which elements of the school should be under the direction of lay people and which under the professional staff?
- Can and should lay governance impact on the context and content of schooling?

What the 1870 Act did

Despite the fears of the establishment and the hopes of the radicals, membership of the new school boards didn't come anywhere near to reflecting the social make-up of the country. In 1896, probably only 3 per cent of members (between 500 and 600) were 'working men'. By 1903, when the boards were disbanded, of some 18,000 members, about 370 were women (Simon, 1965). The 1870 Act brought about only limited change. Something more would be needed to make boards really 'representative'.

The foundations of modern school governing bodies were laid down by the 1870 Act. Chapter 75 section 15 stated: 'The School Board may . . . delegate any of the Powers under this Act except the power of raising money . . . to a body of managers appointed by them, consisting of not less than three persons'. Alternatively, one school management committee could be appointed to cover all the schools in a District – the origin of the grouping of schools that became common practice in some local government areas. Once again, of course, the majority of school 'managers' came from a fairly narrow range of the population. Board members – at least, the radical ones – had their own magazine. The *School Board Chronicle* campaigned for universal school boards and universal compulsory attendance for 5–13-year-olds. But in the face of working-class opposition, boards were not going to enforce such bye-laws even if they were passed: Boards in agricultural counties were not about to cut off the supply of cheap labour to farms, or to threaten the already subsistence level income or below that many families suffered, by enforcing school attendance.

So the freedom apparently available to school boards was not quite what it seemed. There was also increasing control by the state over the curriculum. Robert Lowe's system of 'payment by results' for teachers operated, with variations, between 1862 and 1895. It led to an almost entirely centralised curriculum. Lowe had wanted children to be educated so that they could cope with the democratic nation-state that was gradually developing, but this was at the cost of local lay power. 'All decisions except for those of the most trivial nature were made by higher authorities. For example, the decision to change the annual examinations from November to April was specified by Whitehall (1883). No longer . . . were the curriculum and form of education locally prescribed' (Ambrose, 1974). After 1874, the new Conservative government allowed local authorities to appoint School Attendance Committees in districts without school boards. Local and central government were closing in on the schools.

School governors in the nineteenth century

What do we know of what school governors (called 'managers') actually did in the years following the 1870 Act? Many managers played a very active role in their schools, in inspections, staff appointments, fund-raising, supervision of teaching, even paying daily visits to the school and teaching themselves (Gordon, 1974). But they were still seen, by many of the parents, as representatives of a system imposed from above. The Rev. Norris, referred to earlier, wrote in 1869 after his retirement from Her Majesty's Inspectorate, that the control over the administration of schools by such as the parson, the squire and the mill-owner, led to lack of parental commitment to the school: 'hence much of the evils complained of − apathy, want of co-operation with the teachers, irregular attendance, removal of their children for the most frivolous reasons' (quoted in Gordon, 1974). There is a familiar ring to this.

Not only were school managers 'unrepresentative', but there is some evidence that, where they were unskilled, they might have done more harm than good. As J. G. Wenham wrote in 1878: 'There is no training school or training for Managers. Many, indeed, have by great pains and application overcome this difficulty . . . but some do not see their deficiency, or trust to the light of Nature to make up for it, without any special effort on their own part; and much mischief is the result'.

(Hurt, 1971)

Growth brings bureaucracy, and bureaucracy brings regulations. The Mundella Code of 1880 made the inspectors more or less indispensible. Payment by results came to an end mourned by few, and inspectors started to descend on schools without warning. This meant that they became more distanced from the school 'management', just as many school governors in the 2010s have come to feel more alienated from their school's inspections as the period of notice has shrunk to one day or less. The increasing bureaucracy was less and less penetrable by lay people, and school managers left more to their headteacher. At School Board level, the profession was represented by the clerks. They formed an Association in 1893 − the forerunner of the Society of Education Officers and its successors. At all levels, professional staff were taking over duties which well-meaning amateurs had done for years. Local school inspectors were appointed by Boards, obviating the need for managers' inspections. So the last two decades of the nineteenth century saw the birth of the 'profession of education'. As the experience and confidence of the professionals grew, so lay people were squeezed out. Nobody thought to write down what their place, or their contribution, might be.

Local government takes over: 1902

In the last quarter of the nineteenth century, local government came to the fore. New forms of local authority had been established, but what should they provide? What would be the right balance between central and local provision and responsibility? The debate about the best methods of providing local services was concerned with the twin, but not always compatible, ideals of democracy and efficiency in administration. It was this debate that led up to the 1902 Act which did away with the school boards.

Despite opposition from non-conformists, liberals, radicals, and trades unionists, the duties of the local education authority were devolved upon the county and county borough councils created in 1888. The era of direct election of local lay education authorities had come to an end. The new authorities were compelled to take over all existing board schools, as well as taking on responsibility for the finances of church-owned voluntary schools.

The following years saw a series of regulations issued by the Board of Education which tried to clarify the relationships between teachers, managers (governors), local government and central government. In the school year 1902–1903 the regulations read: 'every school must be under the superintendence of a body of Managers responsible to the Board'. It was, however, possible for the Education Committee of a local authority itself to be the managing body of a school or group of schools. Many urban and Welsh authorities did just that, undermining the principle of local governance. In 1907–1908, the regulations demanded that governing bodies include a majority of governors appointed by the local authority 'or elected by local constituencies', an alternative which, as far as we know, was not taken up anywhere. The job of the governing body or management committee was to appoint and dismiss headteachers, subject to the approval of the local authority. In 1908 the Board of Education in Whitehall issued the first model instruments and articles of government for schools.

You can clearly see the evolution of the role of the school governor/manager under the control of central government. Any doubt as to their independence of the local authority could have been dispelled by reading A. J. Balfour's speech in Manchester in October, 1902, and reported in *The Times* (quoted by Hurt, 1971): 'I think some of the difficulty has arisen owing to a misunderstanding of one of the terms used in the Government Bill, the term "managers". I think it is very natural that anybody who saw the term "manager" in the Bill would say, "These are the people who have got control of the schools." It is a mistake, but it is a natural mistake. I do not think it is a mistake for which either the Government draughtsmen or the Government are responsible, because we have borrowed the term "manager" from the preceding Act of 1870: "management" and "manager" are terms which do not carry with them the idea of control.' If there was any concern about the confusion, it was not so great as to bring about disposal of the terms until 1986.

By the 1920s, a top-down structure of school administration dominated by professionals and local politicians had been constructed. It effectively excluded parents and school staff other than the headteacher from any participation in the governance and management of schools (teachers were barred from being managers or governors of their own schools by the 1918 Fisher Education Act). Neither did any school managing or governing body have to be accountable to anyone other than the local authority or Whitehall.

The relationship between the local authorities and the people who, as parents, supplied the raw material for their schools, was summed up by Professor J. J. Findlay, writing in 1923: 'for the very idea of elementary education sprang from pity for poor folk who could *not* organize, could *not* pay, could *not* realize what was good for their children. It is not surprising, therefore, that the organizers of schooling from the first compulsory Act of 1870 to the last of 1918 treated "the parent" as a prospective enemy, to be coerced by threat of summons and penalty'.

(Findlay, 1923)

After 1902, governing/managing bodies were effectively squeezed out of any significant role, sandwiched as they were between the overriding powers of the local education authority with its chief education officer, and the day-to-day handling of the school by its headteacher. The most famous of all education acts, the 1944 Butler Act, consolidated this. The Ministry of Education issued model instruments and articles of government for schools in 1945. 'Representative' governors were to be appointed by the local authority, and co-opted. No persons employed 'for the purposes of the school' were eligible. The articles specified three areas for which the governing body was responsible: the inspection of the school premises, and keeping the local authority informed of their condition; determining the use of the premises after school hours; appointing the headteacher, assistant teachers and non-teaching staff. The post-1944 governing body would be a combination of caretaker and employer. Paragraph Eight of the model articles went on to attempt to define the respective roles of the governing body and the headteacher:

a   The LEA shall determine the general educational character of the school and its place in the local education system. Subject thereto the Governors shall have the general direction of the conduct and curriculum of the school.
b   Subject to the provisions of these Articles the Headmaster (sic) shall control the internal organisation, management and discipline of the school, shall exercise supervision over the teaching and non-teaching staff, and shall have the power of suspending pupils from attendance for any cause which he considers adequate.

(Ministry of Education, 1945: p. 5)

The Ministry further recommended that there should be 'full' consultation at all times between the head and his chairman (sic) of governors, and that proposals and reports affecting the conduct and curriculum of the school should be submitted to the governors. The head should attend meetings of the governing body.

The vague definition of duties left the power in schools very much in the hands of the headteacher, in close professional co-operation with the officers of the local education authority (LEA). Although the conduct and curriculum of the school was nominally in the hands of the governors, any encroachment they might have made into the 'secret garden' of the curriculum would be fiercely resisted by the professionals of the school and LEA. In state secondary schools, anyway, which had been developing since the 1920s, and were now categorised in the tripartite system of grammar, secondary modern and technical schools, the curriculum was either dominated by the examination system, or left to the teachers. In addition, and most importantly, very few schools had control over any significant amounts of money; the powers of hiring additional staff and purchasing resources beyond a small annual 'capitation' fund stayed with the LEA. It is not surprising, then, that governing bodies found themselves ciphers – required to meet only three times a year in an arena where local community figures could gather to discuss matters which were largely peripheral to the real business of monitoring and improving the quality of education. That the governors of a boys' grammar school in West London in the 1960s met on Wednesday mornings, just before the regular Rotary lunch, betrays both the nature of the membership – male and professional – and the likely content and temper of the meetings.

In the 1970s

Of 45 counties:

- 22 (49 per cent) had individual governing bodies for each school
- 20 (44 per cent) had a mixture of provision
- 3 (7 per cent) had governing bodies for groups of schools only

Of 78 county boroughs:

- 21 (27 per cent) had governing bodies for each school
- 25 (32 per cent) had governing bodies for groups of two or three schools
- 12 (15 per cent) had governing bodies for groups of four or more schools
- 20 (26 per cent) had one governing body for all schools.

(Baron and Howell, 1974)

Changes in the role of school governing bodies from 1970

We now have access to a lot of information about school governors. The National Governors' Association and the University of Bath conduct regular surveys to establish who governors are, what they do and what they think of what they do. The way in which school governors are regarded now can be gauged from the amount of information we have about them. That the earliest and most comprehensive picture we have of school governing bodies in England and Wales dates back only to the late 1960s (Baron and Howell, 1974) shows how inconsequential they were once thought to be. At most, it would appear, only half of local education authorities regarded governing bodies as a significant tier in the administration of schools.

There were three elements which denied the governors any significant role. First, there were the full-time professional staff of education, in the local authorities and schools; secondly, there were the political elements of local government; thirdly, there was the failure of central government to define a discrete area of responsibility for the governors.

The professionals

As the bureaucratic army of education staff grew through the middle years of the twentieth century, and as teaching itself attracted all the trappings of a profession, so any scope for the meaningful participation of lay people began to vanish. Policy-making and the day-to-day running of the school were shared between the headteacher and the administrator. They bypassed not only the increasingly irrelevant termly meetings of the governing body, but also the LEA Education Committee itself, and the spiralling amounts of money available for administration gave more freedom to LEA officers, allowing them to augment – or sometimes override – political decisions. There was, however, by the end of the 1960s, some evidence that the education world recognised the limitations and the disadvantages of token governing bodies dominated by political appointees. In the evidence submitted to the Royal Commission on Local Government (1966), The Department of Education and Science, the Association of Education

Committees and the Association of County Councils all supported individual
(that is, not grouped) governing bodies of increased representativeness and influence. This view was not shared by the National Union of Teachers. Nor was it
supported by headteachers. The Taylor Report found

> little evidence that, at the time of the study [1975], the standard provi-
> sion in the articles that 'the governors shall have the general direction
> of the conduct and curriculum of the school' was taken seriously. Heads
> invariably maintained that they were entirely responsible for deciding
> what was taught, although they kept governors informed of any changes
> of note. Similarly, the most frequent response from governors was that
> they felt that the curriculum should be left to the head and his [sic] staff.
> [Furthermore] . . . involvement in financial matters was very slight indeed
> and seldom went beyond receiving and formally approving estimates
> drawn up elsewhere.
>
> (DES, 1977b: p. 7)

A modern school governor might wonder at this point what was left for the
governing body to do. When in 1970 the Labour council in Sheffield introduced an innovative scheme to extend the composition and influence of governing bodies, the response of headteachers was one of extreme concern. As
Bacon (1978) reports, they saw a threat to the professional control of schools,
and a potential danger to their role as the key innovators in education.

The politicians

The stranglehold that local political parties had on governing bodies, both by
their monopoly on appointments and by their control over policy-making, was
held onto by local authorities regardless of their political complexion. Until
the 1970s, party politics played little part in local government in many, especially rural authorities. But in urban LEAs, Labour or Conservative regimes
appointed only their own supporters to governing bodies.

> 'A large number of authorities would be very reluctant to give up political
> majorities and/or chairmanships. The reluctance seems even greater, on
> the whole, in Labour-controlled authorities . . . Conservative authorities
> can afford to be more relaxed about the actual formal majority control,
> because they are usually so good at exercising discipline by various gen-
> tlemanly means, such as chairmanship, cooption, links through common
> adherence to "circuits" of various kinds such as local firms, the Chamber
> of Commerce, the Rotary Club, sports clubs, etc.'
>
> (Sallis, 1977)

It did come as a surprise to a newly-appointed secondary school governor in a south Yorkshire town, as late as the early 1990s (that is, *after* the 1986 reforms), to be invited to a meeting, pre-autumn term, of the Labour members of the governing body and told he would be vice chair, before he had attended his first meeting. The chairship, of course, had already been settled amongst them.

It is pretty clear that governing bodies throughout the country, well into the 1980s, were in thrall to a paternalistic, party-led culture. Councillors of the ruling group, having the power to nominate most if not all the seats on governing bodies, reserved them either for themselves or for their supporters. To some professional politicians the demands for wider representation on governing bodies had nothing to do with the effective management of schools and everything to do with people wanting to join an exclusive club, part of the social network of the district: 'I do not think the present system has led to schools being managed or governed badly. The problem is much more one of giving an outlet for the aspirations of those who would like to become Governors; in other words, any need for a change in the system is not educational at all, but is a purely social demand' (letter from Toby Jessel MP, 21 March 1973, quoted in Sallis, 1977). Can there have been a more blatant acknowledgement of school governance as tokenism? There can have been few clearer statements that governing bodies made no actual difference to the running of schools.

Given these prevailing attitudes, we wouldn't expect parents and others to wield much power once they were on governing bodies. Parents had very little political or organisational muscle with which to oppose the representatives of well-established interests. In the most common arrangement by which LEA appointments were made, local parties put forward names in a ratio equivalent to the representation of parties on the council. Minor authorities (that is, district or parish councils), who had a statutory right to membership of primary school management bodies, normally behaved in the same way. Sometimes, however, agreements broke down and ruling parties ignored the custom:

In the London Borough of Haringey in 1979, three governors of Creighton Comprehensive School, including Harry Rée, former Professor of Education at the University of York, were removed from by the ruling Labour group after they refused to vote in support of a strike of school caretakers. Unfortunately, the party failed to observe such formalities as telling the governors of their dismissal, or having the decision ratified by the full council. The Local Government Commissioner reminded the council that 'only the Council can appoint and remove the governors of their maintained schools whatever informal arrangements may exist

(continued)

(continued)

between the political parties represented on the Council . . . it cannot be good administration let alone fair to the individuals concerned to appoint new governors before those they are to replace have been removed from office or even told that they are about to be removed'.

(Commission for Local Government, 1980)

Local party politicians, by 1980, had control over most of the composition and many of the activities of governing bodies, either from outside, through the Education Committee and its officers, or from inside, through control over the chair and the majority of members.

What was the governors' role?

The principal weakness from which governing bodies suffered before 1986 was the failure of the 1944 Act to leave them with any area of responsibility they could properly call their own. The most dramatic illustration of this was the case of the William Tyndale Junior School, in the then Inner London Education Authority in 1975. Here, a group of governors, mainly representatives of the new, broader-based Labour Party in the then newly-gentrified Islington, found themselves increasingly out of sympathy with the 'progressive' policies of the newly-appointed headteacher and deputy. Relationships between staff and governors deteriorated to breaking point. At one time, staff refused to allow individual governors access to the premises.

'Mr Ellis [the headteacher] said that he did not give a damn about parents, managers [i.e. governors] or anybody else, that teachers were "the pros at the game", and that nobody else had any right to judge them. Mrs Burnett [a manager] pointed out that, although parents were not "pros" in the field of education, they could recognize if their children were happy and interested in school, and that teachers could not ride roughshod over parents' feelings. In the course of the discussion that followed Mrs Burnett was horrified to hear Mr Ellis describe parents as either working class fascists or middle class trendies out for their own children.'

(Auld, 1976: para. 514)

In the subsequent inquiry it became clear that no-one knew whether a headteacher *could* legally order his chair of governors to leave the school. The Auld Report's most important finding was that the crisis need never have arisen had areas of responsibility and relationships between governors and staff been clearly laid down (Auld, 1976). Of course, the dispute was not as clear cut as it appeared to be in many accounts. Nevertheless, one interpretation of what happened is that a group of experienced middle–class activists who were able to enlist the support of bureaucrats and politicians got their way, against the majority of the teaching staff and the working-class parents who supported them. What is not in any doubt is that the William Tyndale episode encapsulated the key issues about the ownership of what went on in schools. Parents, teachers, local educational administrators and politicians lined up to vilify each other in the newspapers and in the official inquiry, because for some seventy years these areas of legitimate debate had been ignored.

During the 1970s, there were various attempts to strengthen the position of governing bodies, in line with the increasing influence of the consumer movement (see Chapter 2). The Campaign for the Advancement of State Education (CASE) agitated for more representative governing bodies, for example, in the greater London Boroughs of Richmond and Harrow. The National Association of Governors and Managers emerged as a pressure group, and to provide information and training; the first handbook for governors appeared (Burgess and Sofer, 1978); and the Advisory Centre for Education campaigned for more representative governing bodies. By 1977, there had been some significant progress in the development of governing bodies.

The ACE survey (Sallis, 1977) shows that, of the 108 authorities in England and Wales, 56 (52 per cent) had individual governing bodies for all schools; and 32 (30 per cent) had all or mostly individual governing bodies for secondary schools, while grouping primary school managing bodies to some extent. Representation too had broadened. Only 18 (16 per cent) had no formal representation of parents on their governing bodies, and 23 (21 per cent) no teacher representation. Non-teaching staff governors were allowed in eleven authorities; pupil governors in thirteen authorities. Sallis also reports some development in the issues discussed by governing bodies 'governors have gradually advanced from the formal and in most cases not very significant activity reported in the late sixties, to a much more direct involvement in the daily life and work of the school. Their concern with finance remains slight, though it is growing a little. They play a crucial part in the selection of headteachers and some part in the appointment of other staff. Above all, they are increasingly involved in discussion of general issues affecting all schools in their area and of the education provided at their individual schools'.

(1977: p. 38)

The Taylor Report, 1975–77

A key moment for the development of governing bodies towards a significant role in schools was the report of the Taylor Committee (DES, 1977b). The report was commissioned in 1975 in response to the growing pressures of the groups mentioned above, and the developments in some local authorities towards a stakeholder model of school governance.

The report identified five reasons for the increasing demands for wider involvement in school governance:

1   Local government reorganisation in 1974 had increased the size of local education authorities, bringing about a demand for greater involvement in decision-making at school level.
2   Reorganisation brought together authorities interested in giving a meaningful role to governing bodies with those who were not.
3   The advent of 'corporate management' into local authority structures, which took some independence away from LEA education departments, raised the profile of governing bodies as a voice for education.
4   The growth of comprehensive schools awakened public interest in the structures of education.
5   Voluntary organisations such as ACE, CASE, NAGM and PTAs brought pressure for change.

The report recommended representation on all maintained schools governing bodies, in four equal parts, of: (i) the local education authority (LEA); (ii) the teaching and non-teaching staff; (iii) parents; and (iv) individuals from the local community. The new bodies would be responsible for establishing the aims of the school, share in the formation of the curriculum, participate in budgeting, take an equal share with the LEA in appointing the headteacher, and the primary responsibility for appointing other staff. The new term of office was to be four years, with meetings to be held at least twice a term. The response from the Department of Education and Science (DES) in the Labour government was to endorse the proposals on composition but to resist any changes in their own powers. Certainly, the teachers' professional associations regarded these changes with suspicion.

The great debate, 1976

The collective impact of the changes in the way government and the public viewed education – the national economic crisis, the erosion of the post-war consensus on the purposes of state education, the move towards comprehensive education, local government reorganisation and the rising interest (and feeling they had a right to express opinions) of the increasingly well-educated public, especially the parent body, in what went on in schools – led to an unprecedented and definitive intervention of the new prime minister, James Callaghan.

The Labour government called for 'a greater awareness of the community at large; the needs of the nation as a whole; the working of a modern industrial society; and the role of an individual participating in a democracy' (DES, 1977a: p. 37). The green paper also considered the need for a core curriculum, for national monitoring of school performance, and a framework in which schools could be accountable to their communities – all of which would come into place during the next fifteen years.

It was left to the Conservative government, however, to enact legislation between 1980 and 1982 that brought parent and teacher representatives onto all state school governing bodies for the first time; made the agenda and minutes of governors' meetings available to the public; defined the governors' role in working towards 'a planned and coherent curriculum' (DES, 1981b) and required the publication of Her Majesty's Inspectorate (HMI) reports on schools. In 1984, the government proposed to restructure governing bodies with a majority of parents – a proposal which had to be dropped when parents' groups pointed out that they were asking for representation, not control. This tentative appearance of neoliberal market thinking in the provision of schools by a conservative government was probably intended to be a step towards the introduction of vouchers: 'the so-called "Voucher Men", who were keen to experiment with new and untried ways of organizing education, principally the notion that all parents should be issued with a free basic coupon, fixed at the average cost of schools in their area, to be "cashed in" at the school of their choice' (Chitty, 2014a).

While the shape of the Conservative government's proposals for school governance was not significantly different to those of the earlier Labour government, the reasoning – and therefore the language – are distinctive. Labour had talked about community and participation. The Conservative White Paper 'Better Schools' talked about schools serving 'their own and the country's needs and provid(ing) a fair return to those who pay for it' (DES, 1985: p. 4). The emphasis is on accountability to consumers and on value for money. In the event, the 1986–88 legislation provided a real job for governors to be elected by parents and staff, appointed by LEAs and co-opted by the governors themselves (see Chapter 2).

The Act also chipped away at the traditional role of the LEA. No longer was it to be the sole provider of funds for state schools, for the DES itself would in future identify its own priorities and provide some money. And the LEA would now be required to furnish the governing body with details of the expenditure on their school. While the 1986 Act caused a tremor in schools, the 1988 Education Reform Act initiated an earthquake.

From a marginal role in the party political debate, from a position of largely political and public consensus, education had shifted in the space of just over ten years to being one of two issues central to the political dialogue leading up to the 1987 general election: 'Just as we gained support in the last election from people who had acquired their own homes and shares, so we shall secure still further our political base in 1991–92 – by giving people a real say in education and housing' (Margaret Thatcher in *The Independent*, 17 July 1987, quoted in Simon, 1988: p. 12).

The 1988 Education Reform Act contained six major elements:

1   a National Curriculum, giving central government control over 90 per cent or more of the teaching content;
2   national standardisation of assessment and testing of all children at the ages of 7, 11 and 14;
3   open enrolment to schools;
4   the potential for existing schools to convert to a new breed of state school independent of its local authority, the 'grant maintained' school;
5   City Technology Colleges, also funded independently of the LEA, with an emphasis on technology and science;
6   the delegation of the major part of the school budget from the LEA to the governing body.

The new governors appointed and elected under the 1986 Act came into office in the autumn of 1988, just in time to face the beginnings of a revolution in educational administration and management. The coincidence of local management of schools with the new governing bodies had some unfortunate effects, as we shall see. But now there was no escaping the fact that they and no-one else were legally responsible for most of what goes on in schools: for the delivery of the National Curriculum; for the spending of the school's finances; for the effective employment of staff; and for the maintenance of the premises. Not only were they responsible, but also accountable, to parents and to the local education authority. After some 150 years of state education, the schools, though within a much tighter national framework, had become the responsibility of a body of who the majority were lay people with no professional experience of education. Was this a triumph of democracy, an advance in consumerism within the provision of public services, or a first step in the journey towards a neoliberal market in state education?

Chapter 2

The revival of school governance

How governing schools came to
make a meaningful contribution
to school improvement

New responsibilities and the new governing bodies in 1988

The year 1988 proved to be a significant watershed in the history of school governing in England and Wales. Whatever the range of motivations that politicians might have had, there was broad cross-party consensus that strengthening the role of governing bodies in all state-funded schools, and consequently weakening the role of local authorities, would be 'a good thing'.

The 1986 Education (No. 2) Act removed the built-in majority of local authority appointments on governing bodies, but not their overall responsibility and accountability for the performance of both school and governors. The 'new' governors taking office in the autumn of 1988 held a majority of places on county maintained and controlled schools. Depending on the size of the school there were between two and five elected parents, one or two elected teachers, between three and six governors to be co-opted by the governing body from the local community, between two and five governors appointed, as before, by the local education authority (including minor authority representatives in primary schools), and the headteacher if s/he chose. A small primary school might have a governing body of eight or nine, while a large secondary school could have nineteen governors. Voluntary aided schools retained a majority of 'foundation' governors appointed by the trustees or diocese, in the case of church schools.

Shortly, the 1988 Education Reform Act would be introducing new kinds of state-funded school altogether – the grant maintained school and the city technology college would be funded directly from the government department responsible for education, bypassing the local authority and excluding it from any responsibility for, or input to, the school's control. Although forming a very small proportion of state schools overall (there were about 1200 grant maintained schools by the time they were brought back into the local authority fold, and there were only ever 15 City Technology Colleges), they are important, as they were the forebears of academies and free schools.

The 1986 Act set down, for the first time, a detailed range of duties for governing bodies of maintained schools:

- to ensure that the curriculum produced by the LEA (from 1988, to be in line with the new National Curriculum), is implemented by the headteacher;
- to produce a statement of policy on sex education;
- to share responsibility with the LEA and the head for ensuring the teaching of religious education, and the arrangements for a daily act of collective worship (an undertaking observed more often in the breach than in the observance);
- to appoint a person responsible for seeing that the special educational needs of pupils are met;
- to receive a budget, decide how it is spent, and keep accurate accounts;
- to appoint staff in consultation with the LEA, and to require the LEA to dismiss staff, and to have disciplinary and grievance arrangements;
- to decide on the number and allocation of staff responsibility allowances;
- to offer the head a statement of principles on pupil behaviour and discipline, to reinstate excluded pupils where appropriate, and to keep attendance registers;
- to produce an annual report for parents;
- to conduct an annual parents' meeting;
- to control the use of premises outside the school day, and have a policy for community use of buildings.

There were a number of areas here that were new. Governing bodies now carried the legal responsibility for a number of activities within the school, with the LEA taking on a supportive and advisory role rather than one of control. This included accountability to parents; all financial matters (to be changed beyond recognition by the delegation of budgets following the 1988 Act); for all practical purposes, employment of staff (though the employer in maintained and controlled schools continued nominally to be the LEA); discipline of pupils; and the use and condition of buildings.

While the law was fairly clear on what was intended, there was an enormous variety of responses to this revolution in school management and leadership. Some local authorities embraced the changes, enabling governing bodies to take on their new responsibilities by offering advice and training to governors, with model policies and procedures. Others were more reluctant to let go, and found ways of implying that their advice was mandatory. Many years later, for example, some authorities were still sending out model agenda for governing body meetings, with the understanding that any deviance from the model might result in damaging legal consequences. Still others saw the new regime as an opportunity to begin the process of winding down the role of the local authority as provider of services, in order to merely 'ensure' the delivery of services. Broadly, these could be characterised from traditional left, through one-nation conservatism, to neo-con right. These fault lines continued well into the twenty-first century, with local authorities on the right of the spectrum contracting out as many of their legal duties as possible.

Headteachers also responded to the new order in different ways. Some (perhaps only a few, according to the professional associations), welcomed the new order, as a way of engaging in a true partnership with the communities served by their schools. These sea changes in school leadership coincided, of course, with the rapid growth in the application of new technologies. Headteachers, while suddenly finding themselves accountable to a new governing body, were grappling more or less enthusiastically with the computerisation of school records for attendance and for managing the delegation of all financial affairs to the school. Rarely has a traditional role – that of the local headteacher – undergone such rapid change. Their fears were summarised, somewhat pompously, by the leader of one of their professional associations:

> If I could believe that a school governing body would be a genuine reflection of overall parental thinking, I would not be so perturbed by the transition of power over school policy into the hands of lay oligarchs, but that benign outcome is highly improbable. I am, of course, comforted by the knowledge that the majority of parents prefer to repose their confidence in the judgement of teachers. I also believe that in many schools, even without the unifying benefit of Mr Baker's [Kenneth Baker, then Conservative Secretary of State for Education, whose reforms these largely were] specifications on testing and curriculum, the influence of teachers will inform and moderate governors' decisions. What scares me stiff is the knowledge that in some schools, governors' policy will be determined by a self-opinionated and wrong-headed group.
>
> (Smithies, 1988)

The relationship of headteachers with their governors, then, was just one element – and for some, one element to be resisted – of the new expectations being laid on them. Soon to come would be further accountabilities – that of regular inspection according to a national formula, the publication of reports and examination results, and the setting of national targets at the four stages of tests or examinations.

Looking back from the vantage point of twenty-five years on, we can see that not all these tensions have been dispelled. Although the overall legal responsibility of governing bodies is now pretty well undisputed, there are still tensions between governors and senior leaders in schools over who should be doing what, over what is strategic and what is day-to-day operational; between local authorities and governing boards over the support and/or 'control' exercised by LAs; and between school leaders (both professionals and lay governors) and the increasingly centralised control of the Department for Education and Ofsted.

Recruitment and training of governors

How did the schools and local authorities go about finding a body of some 350,000 people to serve as governors? These largely new categories of governor were to serve as the template for the governance of all state-funded schools except for grant maintained schools, city technology colleges and the new 'Labour' academies until 2010, when the shift towards academies accelerated.

Local authority appointments

The recruitment of large numbers of local authority governors has been an issue since 1902. Practice varied between the highly politicised (mainly urban) authorities, where the ruling party retained most or all appointments to members and supporters, and those (mainly rural) where any local interested party could be put forward, regardless of politics. Abuses of the old system were common. When the Conservative party won control of the Inner London Education Authority (ILEA) in 1967:

> The new ILEA leadership immediately faced a problem to which it had given no thought. The Conservatives were now entitled to appoint a majority of the governors for each of the authority's several hundred schools and colleges in inner London; in Labour Tower Hamlets as much as in Tory Westminster. These had to be found quickly, however, to vote when each governing body chose a new chairman in a few weeks' time.
>
> (Crick, 1996: p. 127)

The then newly elected member of the Greater London Council [GLC], later MP and writer Jeffrey Archer got the job of dragooning several hundred Tories into service: 'It was a formidable task. The Conservatives, naturally, were weakest in the inner-London boroughs, and party organization barely existed in some constituencies' (ibid., p. 127).

Both the ILEA and the GLC were disposed of by a later Conservative government, so that situation did not arise again. But even in 1988, both major parties in a number of authorities appointed only their own – Salford, Wolverhampton, Manchester, Wakefield, Dudley and Doncaster among Labour authorities; Barnet and Kent among Conservative LEAs. Some LEAs that changed hands removed existing nominees mid-term. The High Court confirmed that people appointed to governing bodies by the LEA could be removed for political reasons (*Times Educational Supplement*, 1989). But governors could not legally be removed for voting against the policies of their appointing body. Two inner London governors were removed from office for supporting an application for their school to become a City Technology College. The case of *Regina v ILEA*, ex parte Brunyate, showed that the ILEA had in fact exercised its powers for an unlawful purpose (Herbert, 1989). The

House of Lords found that, although the ILEA was apparently legally entitled to remove governors, in this case it had done so in order to enforce compliance with its own wishes, which was a usurpation of the governors' independent function.

By December 1989, the Local Government and Housing Act (1989) had encouraged LEAs to appoint governors in proportion to the party distribution on the council. Even so, it seemed that the number of LEAs appointing *only* from their own supporters was greater than before the 1986 Act – perhaps because there were fewer places available to them on governing bodies, and ruling groups wanted to be sure of filling all of them. A determined party group (see Chapter 1) could outflank other constituencies, especially naive and disorganised parents, by making an early bid for positions of influence.

Despite the difficulties and tortuous goings-on of political parties in some areas, LEA governors were actually among the easiest to recruit in the run-up to reconstitution in 1988. LEA governors were to make up about one quarter of governing bodies in county maintained schools, yet they constituted only 15 per cent of the vacancies reported in 1989 (Jefferies and Streatfield, 1989).

In terms of what type of people LEAs were appointing, they were the most likely of all the new governors to be white and over 60, and second most likely to be male. They were most likely to be retired or 'housewives', or in industry, education, white collar work, or the professions. Inevitably, a greater number of LEA appointments were likely to be experienced governors than any other category. However, they were of course experienced in governance under a set of wholly different rules, so perhaps they might also prove to be the most difficult to drag into the new era. Chairs of governors were most likely to be LEA governors. As time went on, however, it began to appear that LEA governors might not be so easy to recruit after all. Two years later, Baginsky et al. (1991) suggested that vacancies in this category were most common among the schools they studied.

By 2014, the role of LA governors had diminished almost to vanishing point. Quite apart from the recruitment issue, which led some LAs to invite governing boards to put forward their own candidates as LA governors, the growth of state-funded independent schools such as foundation schools, academies and free schools, meant that LAs had no part at all in the governance of the majority of secondary schools. In primary schools, where the large majority remained with their local authority, the number of LA governors would be as few as one. If LAs had ever expected their governors to represent or reflect the views of the ruling party, this had now become an irrelevant concept.

Parent governors

On the other hand, parent governors came to much greater prominence. In 1988, LEAs had feared that attempts to recruit parent governors would be met with apathy (Jefferies and Streatfield, 1989). This may have been a symptom of the patronising attitude of many educationists and politicians to community involvement in local decision-making structures. It would have been astonishing if parents, having been told for some 150 years that their children's education had nothing to do with them, believed that schools suddenly wanted to hear their views, and further, to give them real power. Some of this attitude had been reinforced by the early lacklustre response to the requirement that school governing bodies produce an annual report and hold an annual meeting for parents. Most schools, it seemed, decided that putting out rows of chairs in a large hall and offering to read out a report that had already been mailed to parents offered an enticing evening's entertainment. Unsurprisingly, these schools then blamed parents for their 'apathy' about their children's education. This phenomenon was noted: 'It is profoundly characteristic that responsibility for widespread non-participation is attributed wholly to the ignorance, indifference and shiftlessness of the people' (Schattschneider, 1960). Those (probably few), however, that offered a genuine session of information and open discussion were (and years after the legal requirement was dropped, still are) rewarded with much greater attendance and engagement.

Fortunately, LAs and others who predicted a low response were confounded. The total number of vacancies in the autumn of 1988 was very small and, of these, vacancies among parent governors were almost identical to those among LEA places. Nearly nine out of ten LEAs found recruitment of all types of governor as easy or easier than they had anticipated. Not only were there fewer vacancies than expected, the turnout among parent voters was encouraging. The average turnout in schools using pupil post for sending out and receiving the ballot paper was 41 per cent, while those using ballot boxes on premises only reached 21 per cent (Sutcliffe and Blackburne, 1988). There was wide variation between schools in the small sample in this study. While some schools attracted more than 70 per cent of eligible parents, others drew less than 10 per cent. Primary schools attracted marginally better voting figures (43 per cent) than secondary schools (39 per cent). The average turnout was 39 per cent – comparable to local election turnout.

If the recruitment of parent governors in pure numbers was something of a triumph, how 'representative' were they? One might hope that this group of governors, at least, should reflect the various constituencies. A number of LEAs stressed 'the need to recruit more people from ethnic minorities and from less privileged sectors of the community to ensure more balanced representation on certain governing bodies' (Jefferies and Streatfield, 1989). Among parent governors in their research, the single most common occupational group was – education! Perhaps teachers were responding to the National Union of Teachers' call to them to stand for election as parent governors in the schools their children attended (Parker, 1988). The small-scale survey conducted by the *Times Educational Supplement* in 1988 suggested that as many as one in eight in the first round of parent governors was a teacher (Sutcliffe and Blackburne,

1988), while Streatfield and Jefferies (1989) found that one in six of all governors worked in the education profession, with only just over 3 per cent of governors manual workers and 'an overwhelming majority' professionals. Golby and Brigley (1989) found that well over half of the parent governors surveyed were educated privately or at grammar schools. Deem, Behony and Heath (1995) found that slightly under one quarter of governors in 1994, apart from teacher governors, worked in some aspect of education.

Six years on, Earley (1994) showed that governing bodies had changed little in their composition: about 70 per cent of governors had GCE O Level; 44 per cent were graduates; 33 per cent had a professional institute final qualification; and 25 per cent held a teacher's certificate – not a typical cross-section of the population as a whole. Keys and Fernandes (1990) found that these percentages stayed constant even when teachers were removed from the sample.

Co-opted governors

The category of co-opted governors proved to be the arena where the issue of 'business governors' first began to be fought out. And the process of co-option brought about the first quasi-legal rows on the new governing bodies. The law required that the chair and vice-chair should be elected at the full meeting of the governing body of the academic year. By definition, this would exclude co-opted governors, who could only be brought on board by a full meeting. The Department for Education and Science (DES) originally advised that schools should hold elections for parent and teacher governors in the autumn of 1988, but that governing bodies should be fully constituted by 21st October. The department suggested that this meeting would not be a 'full' meeting, and that the election of the chair and vice chair could be postponed until co-opted governors were in place. This was not just a matter of form. Where LEA governors, newly in a minority, intended to make an early impact on the new body, they could do so at this first meeting by being better organised to nominate a chair from amongst themselves. At the same time, they could dominate the co-option process at a meeting where they would hold a larger proportion of the vote (40 per cent of the membership as opposed to 27 per cent). The new naive and less well-organised parents and teachers could be steamrollered. The potentially powerful position of chair, as well as a significant proportion of the governing body's membership, could already have been decided by a group of people well-known to each other and well-practised in political strategies.

How did schools go about co-opting governors in this first phase? Clause 6 of the 1986 Act told governing bodies to 'have regard to the extent to which (the governors) are members of the local business community'. Indeed, co-opted governors are often referred to as 'business governors', although there was never any requirement that they need be from that business community (see Chapter 4). LEAs placed advertisements in the local press, firms were circularised with glossy leaflets, and employers' networks were contacted.

Indeed, the large majority of governing bodies were successful in ensuring the representation of the business community through parent elections, LEA nominations or co-options (Jefferies and Streatfield, 1989).

Predictably perhaps, primary schools tended to recruit people from smaller local businesses, while secondary schools were more likely to attract the larger businesses, especially those with whom links existed through work experience schemes and the like. Some of the largest industries, such as IBM, laid on their own seminars for interested employees, and were surprised by the 'massive response' (Harrison, 1988), while the coordinating organisation 'Industry Matters' produced a pack for potential governors. British Gas produced a free specialist journal called, invitingly, 'Gas Governor'. Sainsbury, Shell, BP, British Telecom and Glaxo all became involved. The TUC also expressed interest, and wanted to make sure that all types of employee were allowed sufficient time off work to do their governing duties. Initially, at least, industry and business did dominate the co-options, with more than twice as many men than women in the group. This category had the largest number of inexperienced governors, suggesting that the campaigns to recruit wider representation from the business community were successful.

The law helped. School governors, like magistrates, councillors and other public volunteers, are entitled by the law to take a 'reasonable' amount of time off work, although what is 'reasonable' is not defined, and the employer is not required to give paid time off (though many do). How much time has to be agreed by employer and employee, based on how long the duties might take, how much time the employee has already taken, and if it will affect the business. The employer is entitled to refuse to grant the request if they think it is 'unreasonable'.

But many employers, small, medium and large, saw benefits for the school and for themselves in granting time off. Local banks, for example, saw their staff getting concrete experience in practical financial management through assisting in school budgeting – and maybe had an eye to picking up a few customers in the meantime. Schools did not always see the advantages, however. Many LEAs 'observed that "business" governors are among the worst attenders and often turn up late to meetings and leave early' (*TES*, 3 November 1989), although this is only an impression. An executive member of the National Association of Governors and Managers (NAGM) expressed a view common among educationists, especially at that time those suspicious of the possible impact of local management of schools, that the association had seen enough 'industrial' governors operating

> to know that they often have a different agenda to the rest of the governing body. They don't understand that schools aren't industries. It doesn't make them popular on governing bodies and it makes them very ineffective because they are not seen as part of a team.
>
> (*TES*, 3 November 1989)

The divide between the two cultures may have narrowed over the years since. Perhaps.

Co-option was not, however, synonymous with business or industry. Baginsky et al. (1991) report that, in their case-study schools

> the choice of co-optees was usually made with the intention of giving the governing body a range of expertise with which to cope with its roles and responsibilities. For this purpose, co-options included lawyers, accountants, architects and builders, administrators and business personnel whose knowledge and skills would be especially valuable when dealing with the legal, financial and structural aspects of the school. One governing body, for example, co-opted a solicitor, a bank manager, a retired diplomat and the managing director of a local printing firm, all of whom were chosen expressly 'to advise on or assist with LMS (Local Management of Schools)'.
>
> (1991: p. 15)

So the ground was prepared for the freeing of schools from their local authorities. It was largely schools with 'entepreneurial' heads supported by governors with such 'business' experience who took up the grant maintained option offered by this Conservative government, and the later much more popular (among secondary schools at least) academy option.

Teacher governors (and, later, staff governors)

Teacher governors were not a new phenomenon in the large majority of local education authorities. By 1977, 79 per cent of local authorities in England and Wales had arrangements for teacher representation (while eleven authorities had non-teaching or support staff governors) (Sallis, 1977). Teacher governors did not need the publicity provided for other vacancies (Jefferies and Streatfield, 1989) and there were fewest vacancies in this category. There were more women than men teacher governors overall (but then 80 per cent of primary teachers are women). Men predominated in the secondary sector (Streatfield and Jefferies, 1989), although they make up just half of all secondary teachers. In a few cases (2.5 per cent) the deputy headteacher was the teacher governor (almost inevitably in some of the smallest primary schools). Support staff governors, places that could be voted for and taken up by anyone working in the school full- or part-time on a regular basis, came into place in the school year of 1999–2000. The strong arguments in favour of support staff governors underlined the importance of the stakeholder model. Not only were the numbers of support staff growing in schools – a growth that would be further accelerated in the process of workforce remodelling which would dominate school organisation agenda in the early part of the next decade – but their role in the smooth and efficient running of the school was becoming indispensible. School secretaries were turning into business managers, caretakers were becoming premises managers, and teaching assistants were giving up the washing of yogurt pots for supporting individual and groups of children in the classroom.

Headteacher governors

Headteachers in County and Aided schools were given the choice as to whether to be a governor or not. About three-quarters chose to be governors in the new regime, while in other state-funded schools, it was common for the headteacher to be required to be a governor. Initially, the professional associations recommended that heads stand back from being actual governors, taking up a position of chief executive, advising and reporting to the governing body, as opposed to 'managing director'. However, this position has become less tenable and certainly less common, particularly since the professional associations joined with the National Governors' Association to endorse a document intended to clarify the distinctive roles of the head and the governors, in 2008, updated in 2012 and again in 2015 (ASCL, NGA and NAHT, 2015, Appendix 6).

Minority ethnic communities and governing bodies

Minority ethnic communities were under-represented on governing bodies. The DfE (Department for Education) survey (DfE, 1992) found that possibly only 2 per cent of school governors, against the 5 per cent of the population, were from such communities. An earlier survey (Community Development Foundation, 1990) looked at the recruitment and training of minority ethnic community governors in the twenty-six responding LEAs (out of sixty contacted). The poor return in itself suggests that few LEAs took positive action then to recruit from these communities. The report showed that only five LEAs translated recruitment leaflets into minority languages, while a further three took other action to identify target groups and individuals. Six LEAs 'made a clear effort to tailor training programmes to meet the needs of governors from minority ethnic communities'; seven monitored ethnic minority representation in some way; and only one reported the existence of a specific support group. Efforts to identify the presence of minority ethnic governors were therefore largely left to independent groups. For example, the Southampton Racial Equality Council identified 4.6 per cent of governors in Southampton as 'BME' (black and minority ethnic), of whom the large majority were Asian and who were largely concentrated in one school (Southampton Racial Equality Council, 1990). However, Hampshire, then Southampton's LEA, did not monitor ethnic origins in schools.

Since these surveys Muslim communities have become more established in school governance, publishing their own 'information, guidance, clarification and encouragement for increasing Muslim participation at all levels of

the consultative processes currently available within the education system'
(IQRA Trust, 1991). In the 1992 recruitment campaign, other LEAs such as
Birmingham went out positively to recruit from minority communities.

New schools for old

The landscape of school provision in England has changed completely since
1988 (but not in Wales, since the Welsh Assembly Government has retained
most of the features of the local authority centred model). In those days we
spoke of a national system of state schooling, locally administered. The local
authorities were central to the provision of schools, to the monitoring of their
performance, to the employment of school and centralised support staff, and
even to the effective determination of the curriculum. They also created the
dominant culture. Key figures were the directors of education, who set the tone
for the authority. Men (pretty well always men) like Alec Clegg in the West
Riding of Yorkshire, Henry Morris in Cambridgeshire and Stewart Mason
in Leicestershire, determined the nature and the priorities of their schools,
created bureaucratic structures to enact their ideas and, very often, personally
appointed the headteachers to further them. The personalised stamp of the lead
professional in these areas is hard to imagine these days.

Some of this culture, though, is still discernible today. Urban authorities
often had a paternalistic view of their role, encouraged by influential local
political leaders. This might be reflected in their attitude to governors, discour-
aging individual school initiative and micro-managing even such elements as
the governing body agenda. It is this type of authority to which national politicians refer when they talk about the 'control' over schools exercised by local
authorities restricting the freedom of movement of progressive headteachers
and governors. Most rural authorities, on the other hand, seemed to be much
more relaxed, seeing their role as supportive rather than controlling.

> Academies were born of the failure of comprehensivisation to achieve
> its goals . . . Academies were . . . intended to help overcome other fun-
> damental weaknesses of the comprehensive era: the rigid and damaging
> division between state and private schools; the low morale and appeal,
> and weak leadership, of the state teaching profession; the misconceived
> role of local education authorities as school managers; and the absence of
> sixth forms in the half of the country – mostly the more deprived half –
> where comprehensives stopped education at the age of sixteen.
>
> (Adonis, 2012: p. 11)

Those who believed that the entire system was in such disarray that
wholesale reform was the only answer were, of course, London–centred

politicians who felt they could provide answers to the undoubted challenges of urban comprehensives: underfunding, difficulty in recruiting large numbers of stable staff, huge issues of inner city poverty and low expectations, all leading to low performance in schools in terms of external examinations, alongside daily behaviour problems. In reforming the entire system, it was believed that the answer to over-subscribed, under-resourced urban schools would equally solve problems in the rural hinterland – issues of rural depopulation, high unemployment leading to lowered expectations and apathy about the rewards of advanced educational achievement – where country-dwellers on the whole had little freedom about which school their children would attend and the watchwords of the reformers, choice and competition, were largely irrelevant.

After Tony Blair's declaration that the three top priorities of his government after the 1997 general election would be 'education, education and education', he appointed Andrew (later Lord) Adonis to lead the reform. There were a number of false starts, at least partly due to Adonis' analysis of the current problems, which was highly personalised and subjective.

> All this came together in a plan for independent state schools, to replace failing comprehensives and to provide for entirely new schools, which Adonis proposed to Blair and David Blunkett, then prime minister and secretary of state for education, in late 1999.
>
> (Adonis, 2012: p. 59)

The new Labour government had already, ironically, taken back into the fold those schools which had been freed from local authority management by the 1988 Act, the 1200 or so grant-maintained schools. These were required to become 'foundation schools' and retained a limited form of the freedoms they had been given. At the same time, County and other maintained schools were renamed 'community schools'. The key principles of Labour education policy in principle were listed in their White Paper (DfEE, 1997a):

- Education will be at the heart of government.
- Policies will be designed to benefit the many, not just the few.
- The focus will be on standards, not structures.
- Intervention will be in inverse proportion to success.
- There will be zero tolerance of under-performance.
- Government will work in partnership with all those committed to raising standards.

With the focus on raising standards for pupils throughout the system, regular inspection, requiring LEAs to work with governors where problems with performance became apparent, and generally developing more immediate and urgent accountability of schools to their LEAs, Ofsted and the DfEE, the 1998

Act determined that there would be only three types of state-funded school: community, aided and foundation schools. However, the act also heralded the first engagement of private, non-local government management of education. Education Action Zones were created in areas of particular need and under-performance, and bids to manage them were invited from both public and private providers, including 'LEAs, TECs, Government Offices, Health Authorities, business, religious, community and other organisations' (quoted in Chitty, 1999). In the event, a number of companies backed successful bids, but as part of broader bids in which they played only a secondary role. But a more significant sign of things to come is cited by Chitty:

> Most worryingly, Surrey County Council took a decision in October 1998 to invite bids for the contract to run a 'failing' comprehensive school in Guildford. In a speech to the North of England Education Conference meeting in Sunderland in January 1999, Blunkett outlined a role for private companies and 'not-for-profit' organisations in providing services for 'failing' local authorities.
>
> (Chitty, 1999: p. 106)

The first seed of privatisation of state schooling had been sown.

What was the new government's aim here – an aim which, as we have seen, it appeared to share with the main opposition parties? The most obvious outcome of the developing academy programme has been the removal from LEAs of any significant responsibility for schools. But to do this without some sort of buffering would unreasonably strengthen the position of headteachers – a suspect lot, many of whom might be unreasonably disposed towards an inappropriately wishy-washy and liberal approach to schooling with insufficient focus on 'standards'.

This meant that governance was likely to be the best restraint on the education community – a community dubbed 'the blob' by a later Conservative secretary of state. Indeed, one of the strongest characteristics of the organisation of national education since the 1980s has been the unremitting mutual contempt in which the political and educational establishments have held each other.

Sadly, as academies developed over the following fifteen years, sometimes, the governors had their own agenda, their own ideas about education without the capacity to advance them, or just got signed up to a professional agenda – maybe one about standards or about children's well-being, or about schools knowing best.

The privatisation of schooling

A DfEE Green Paper of 2001 (DfEE, 2001) established the principle of privatising the supply of schooling. The actual themes of the paper, designed to start the process of transforming secondary education, were summarised (in Chitty, 2014a) as:

- a rejection of the principles underpinning the era of the 'one-size-fits-all' comprehensive;
- a concern to see the promotion of diversity among secondary schools and the extension of 'autonomy' for 'successful' schools; and
- a desire for private and voluntary sector sponsors to play a greater role in the provision of secondary schooling.

The outcome was a new type of school, the City Academy, independent of its local authority, sponsored by an organisation contributing a substantial sum and managed by a board of trustees acting as the governing body, usually but not always set up to replace inner city secondary schools identified by Ofsted as 'failing'. This enabled the new board to start with a new staff, a new school name, (usually) brand new and (usually) very expensive purpose-built buildings. In actual fact, sponsors, it turned out, brought very little money in, and the department for education bore the brunt:

> The academy programme was, in fact, a highly managed and supported kind of privatisation, in which central government handed over control of schools to enthusiastic industrialists or church bodies in exchange for relatively small amounts of capital, and in some cases – when the sponsorship money was not forthcoming – none at all. The programme also proved to be much more expensive than it was first thought. Initially, academies were projected to cost £10 million each, but the first twelve cost approximately £23 million each and one, the Bexley Business academy, eventually cost just over £35 million.
>
> (Benn, 2011)

These academies had accountability directly to the secretary of state and to the newly established Funding Agency. The author experienced governance in one of these:

> A modernistic temple to education as business, sited in the middle of one of the country's most blighted areas, with an ethnic minority population of around 80%, the academy's governing body comprised 16 governors, all relentlessly white, all with one exception male, with one Lord, one Dame and one Sir. The academy stuck to the letter of the law, and there was just one (white) parent governor.
>
> (Gann, 2011)

In terms of privatisation, the academy programme ran alongside a national initiative which was designed to defray the immediate costs of rebuilding or substantially refurbishing existing schools. The Private Finance Initiative was a Labour wheeze which required private companies to provide the buildings for schools (and other public buildings, especially hospitals) at their own immediate cost, clawing back the expenditure through an extended period of loan repayment taken on by the institution itself, usually also requiring them to engage the company as building managers. So it was that maintained 'community' secondary schools found themselves occupying buildings staffed by premises workers answerable only to their own organisation rather than to the governing body, and, through them, the local authority. The minutely detailed management contracts for these schools, designed to last through at least six generations of students, often proved to be the major issue impacting on efficient school governance and management.

By the time of the 2010 general election, there were 203 academies throughout England, and plans for a further 60. The coalition government taking office in May 2010, through its new secretary of state, Michael Gove (formerly a journalist for newspapers owned by Rupert Murdoch, the Americanised global media magnate), quickly pushed the act through parliament using a loophole introduced to enable the swift passage of anti-terrorist legislation. The niceties of green and white papers foreshadowing legislation and inviting consultation were by now things of the past. The 2010 Academies Act gave existing maintained and foundation schools the opportunity to convert to academy status. Initially this was confined to secondary schools designated by Ofsted as 'outstanding'. But further developments could be enacted by the secretary of state without the need to go through parliament, and very soon 'good' schools, then any secondary, then primary schools were not just enabled but encouraged, by rhetoric and a lot of hard cash (even more for eager early converters), to apply for conversion with very little risk of being turned down. Simultaneously a new category of 'free school' was introduced. These were, in fact, academies but were established by community groups as new schools, particularly where current provision was over-subscribed. It was also possible for an independent school to convert to being a free school – provided it stopped charging fees, of course. Most tellingly, local authorities, though still tasked with ensuring the adequate provision of school places, had removed from them the key power to provide new schools themselves.

Visitors to the secretary of state's office in the spring of 2012 reported seeing three maps on his wall: one showed the applications for free schools, the second showed existing academies, and the third applications for academy status. 'Freeing' schools from their local authorities clearly had a high priority. A case of 'structures, not standards'?

(Gann, 2011)

Importantly, and eventually highly controversially, the DfE took the power to instruct 'failing' schools to convert to academy status under a sponsor without the option.

The range of schools in England in 2015 and their governance arrangements

Community and voluntary controlled schools

The 2014 regulations emphasise that a 'key consideration in the appointment and election of all new governors should be the skills and experience the governing body needs to be effective' (DfE, 2014b).

The majority of schools in England remained with their local authorities although there was enormous variation between regions and local authorities. Some of this variation was down to the attitude of the LA – many Conservative-dominated authorities encouraged their schools to seek independence, and ran down the services they provided for schools. Some saw themselves eventually with purely an 'ensuring' role, buying in all children's services from outside suppliers. In other authorities, often traditional Labour ones, academies were still a rarity. These community and controlled schools retained the familiar governance model, although the reconstitution required of schools in 2014–15 shifted the emphasis from a stakeholder to a skills-based model (DfE, 2014b). The department also expressed a strong preference, though familiarly with no supporting evidence, for small governing bodies, from as few as seven upwards. This preference was based on the apparent effectiveness of interim executive boards (IEBs), the body appointed by a local authority to a school when it removed an ineffective or disagreeable governing body. The IEB's usual task was to oversee conversion to academy status, and their life-span was very limited. Indeed, the clue is in the title. IEBs were both interim, lasting for a few months rather than years, and took on executive powers in order to manage the conversion process. They were hardly models for permanent governing bodies with extensive monitoring and evaluating responsibilities. The DfE also felt that governing bodies should be called 'governing boards' to emphasise their business-like characteristics (DfE, 2014a).

The 2014 regulations required a governing board of at least seven, comprising at least two elected parents, one elected staff member, one local authority, the headteacher (ex officio), and two others, probably co-opted. Despite the stated preference for small governing boards, no upper limit was fixed.

Foundation and voluntary aided schools

These comprised the former grant maintained schools and schools run under a foundation trust, largely those of a religious foundation which had retained an element of independence under the deal done with the Church of England and the Roman Catholic dioceses in 1944.

These retain a majority of governors appointed by the foundation. They are also required to have a minimum of two parent governors and one staff governor.

Academies

Academies are state-funded independent schools. Although not under local authority control, they are directly accountable to the secretary of state, to Companies House, to the Education Funding Agency (EFA), and are required to comply with charities law (though not to register with the Charity Commission). From 2015, newly established academies will be required to demonstrate that they are reconstituting their governing bodies with a view to ensuring the skills and experience governors have to offer (for detailed descriptions of governance arrangements in academies see Paxton-Doggett, 2014).

Academy governors are both governors and directors of the company formed to deliver education on behalf of the academy trust. The foundation trust itself holds ultimate accountability for its performance, but delegates all practical matters to its board of directors, who are also the governing board. As such, they are responsible for every aspect of the school's operation, including the employment of staff, the management and development of premises, and the health and safety of personnel, including the pupils. This raft of responsibilities appeared to be quite intimidating to smaller schools tempted to convert, especially if the overall budget, enhanced as it is with the element that would have been retained by the LA to deliver central support services, is still a comparatively small (and annually uncertain) amount.

For this reason, as well as to enable the support of previously weak or 'failing' schools, there is a confusing variety of formats which enable schools to come together in cooperative or multi-academy trusts, or loose federations (umbrella trusts). Indeed, some of these options of federation are open to maintained schools, and the DfE encourages schools generally to work together under grouped governing boards or boards of trustees.

Single academies are run under a trust set up for a single school. They should usually be at least 'good' or 'outstanding' schools. There is a (usually small) group of members forming the academy trust (a company limited by guarantee), which appoints directors of the company. The members will normally meet no more than once a year to ensure that the board is meeting the terms of its articles of association. The board of directors are also trustees and governors. In addition to the running of the company, they have all the responsibilities laid on school governors. It is not good practice for all the members to be governors, as the board is accountable to the members, and there needs to be some degree of separation between them. Similarly, it is not good practice for the headteacher (or, increasingly, the principal) to be a member of the trust, although they would normally serve as a governor.

Academy chains consist of a number of academies joining together, to gain the benefits of collaboration, such as cooperating together in educational activities and reaping the benefits of scale in their administration and support structures. The partnership arrangements can be as loose or as tight as the member schools decide. There may be some common governors, for instance, and an executive head/principal. The vast majority of academy chains are . . .

Multi-academy trusts, which are the tightest form of academy chain. Here, an overall trust takes responsibility for a number of schools. There will, of course, be only one board of directors, who are the governors of every school in the trust. However, such trusts will normally set up some form of local governance or advisory board. The local governors have no legal accountability to the DfE – that remains the responsibility of the board of directors – but they are expected to discharge the duties of governance to the extent that they are spelled out in the scheme of delegation.

Umbrella trusts are another way in which schools can join together but retain a measure of independence. Here, each school is an individual academy with its own governing body with legal responsibility and accountability, but with an overall body enabling cooperation and, for example, joint employment and conduct of key administrative functions. In this model, different forms of school can come together – most obviously, church schools can work with secular schools without compromising their religious distinctiveness. In an umbrella trust, each school has its own funding agreement with the EFA, and typically, the trust will comprise representatives of each school making decisions for the trust, not for the member schools.

Free schools are essentially the same structures as academies, although their origins lie in a proposer group, usually from the local community. Their governance arrangements and responsibilities are the same as individual academy schools. By the summer of 2014, there were 174 open free schools, with a further 116 approved to open in September.

Two further types of school were created by the 2010 Act, thus more than fulfilling the coalition government's commitment to a diversity of provision. *Studio Schools* and *University Technical Colleges* are mainly small schools set up by local employers and universities to provide a technical education for 14–19-year-olds. Both have academy-type governance structures. There were expected to be around seventy UTCs by the summer of 2015.

Standards

Despite the initial claim by all recent governments that standards, not structures, are the important thing, it is evident that these new schools are subject to constant scrutiny of their achievements. The role of governors in improving standards in schools, whatever their nature, is at the heart of this book.

But the question of establishing whether these new schools are more or less successful than their more conventional counterparts has provided persistent background noise to their development. Every apparently authoritative declaration about the performance of academies and free schools in their inspection and their results made by the government is of course immediately refuted by opponents. This book is not going to get embroiled in these arguments, except to say that a report by the select committee on education published in early 2015 found that academisation appeared to have 'no effect' on the performance of schools:

> Academisation is not always successful nor is it the only proven alternative for a struggling school. Both academies and state maintained schools have a role to play in system–wide improvement by looking outwards and accepting challenge in order to ensure high quality education for all children. Of the 21,500 state-funded schools in England, 17,300 are maintained schools and 4,200 are academies. The Government should spell out its vision for the future of schools in England, including the structures and underpinning principles that will be in place in the next five to ten years. Any future government will have to examine whether the existing dual system of oversight and intervention is beneficial.
>
> (House of Commons Education Committee, 2015)

What governance is for

One interpretation of the significant developments in the importance of school governing bodies between 1988 and the present is that they demonstrated attempts by successive governments to make governance one of the vehicles for continuing school improvement, interpreted in the form of school conduct and 'standards'. The strategies to do this include:

- regular inspection against common criteria, with the frequency of inspection in inverse relationship to the school's 'performance' as judged by pupil attainment and progress;
- publication of school performance against common forms of external assessment, in the form of standardised testing;
- encouraging the autonomy of schools by removing them from the influence of local authorities, which are seen as part of an ineffective public sector with low expectations;
- regular revision of the national curriculum;
- frequent speeches by senior figures, particularly secretaries of state and chief inspectors, criticising teachers, governors and the 'educational establishment', in order to stir up pressure from parents and others to raise 'standards', as interpreted by the DfE and Ofsted;

- the development of more and more responsibilities for, and expectations on, governing bodies to behave more like businesses, so further consolidating pressure on senior staff in schools;
- the offer of substantial amounts of public money to tempt schools into conversion for purely financial reasons.

The move from a stakeholder to a skills-based model of governance has its place in this process. With this last in mind, it is possible – though perhaps a tad idealistic – to see the stakeholder model of the nineties as a quite radical model of public ownership of a service designed to serve the public.

In the conservative, or consumerist, or business, model of society, the public is seen as:

- free from responsibility for the quality of the service, except by complaining when it falls below an acceptable standard, or taking their business elsewhere;
- acting out of self-interest, rather than as a member of a potentially forceful society;
- reactive to services, rather than proactive in formulating them;
- having a one-dimensional, purchaser–provider relationship with services;
- likely to be a member of one or another constituency or interest group;
- unlikely to have his/her relationship with the surrounding world altered by the provision of services.

A *radical* model proposes a more complex provider–client relationship. Here the member of the community is seen as:

- responsible for the direction, content and quality of services;
- committed long-term to the community, and having a complex set of relationships within it;
- acting in the interests of others as well as the self;
- proactive, initiating change;
- likely to develop an understanding of a relationship with the world that allows a measure of control and a capacity for individual growth.

What lay governors contribute

There were many early signs that governing bodies had opportunities to achieve the aims of the radical model. But in order to do so, lay governors need to understand what they have to offer school leadership aside from an obedient implementation of government demands at a local level. What is it that lay governors can contribute in practical terms?

1   Members of the community have a unique understanding of the expectations and aspirations of the community. Professional teachers and

administrators, by their training and experience, bring indispensible skills to school management. However, this very experience means that they see schools as workplaces where those skills are put to use. It is then difficult for them, to put it simply, to see the wood for the trees. They cannot stand back from the school to see it through the eyes of the consumer/client. Lay people from around the community bring an understanding of the unique nature of that community, of what it expects from the organisations and institutions that serve it, its commercial, public and voluntary services. They have a day-to-day status as customer, client, user. They bring intimate knowledge of what it takes to be a successful organisation *in their community*, whether it is a supermarket or corner shop, church or bank, club or garage. Only lay community members can express what parents and others expect from their children's academic, social, personal and cultural education, and what their aspirations are for their children.

2   Schools need the support and understanding of the communities they serve. The community's expectations have to be communicated to the professional staff so that they can be debated, challenged and met. Schools can no longer rely on a reservoir of unquestioned authority and goodwill. The world has changed since the 1944 Act. People are better informed, better educated, less willing to accept authority without question. Social media empower the articulate (and sometimes the less articulate) by broadcasting information and views within minutes of the publication of an Ofsted report or of an unexpected event in the daily life of a school. These consumers expect their voices to be heard and their views taken into account. The alienated can become aggressive if their views are not heeded, or they feel overlooked. Any teacher will prefer to teach children who go home to a family which is supportive of the school, where adults encourage them to do well, complete their homework, go the extra mile. And any child from such a home will learn better because of the alliance between home and school. Lay governors provide the first stage in such an alliance.

3   Lay governors explain and interpret the school to their community. In return, schools must explain their purposes and reasons. Schools sometimes appear to behave arbitrarily, counting the needs of the organisation above those of the individual. While there is a large reservoir of goodwill towards schools, this can soon be drained by isolated incidents, dramatic rumours, negative Facebook postings and poor communications. Lay governors can provide a valuable conduit, passing information and explanations between school and community, checking school procedures and actions for acceptability within the community, and explaining the context of community actions and reactions to the school.

4   A school belongs to its community, not just to its teachers. We have seen how ownership of the education system has been fought over between professionals and local and national politicians. It would not be surprising

if some people see the school as an imposition, a service provided only ostensibly 'for them', but serving the needs of a larger, less determinate but more powerful will. The outcome of the 2010 general election has seen a significant mismatch between what parties promised to do with the public services and what they have actually done. For no period of time more than over the last twenty years has it been clearer that it is the government that decides what shape schools will take, that almost all children will go to school, that there should be such things as schools at all. If we were starting from scratch, would we create schools on the industrial factory model we have today, as the best means of preparing children for the world? Challenging though it is in the face of growing government dictation and standardisation, lay governors provide a channel through which schools can assert their individuality, their response to the community they serve. Governors provide a means through which community ownership of the school can be exercised. Documents supporting the reconstitution of governing bodies in 2014–15 suggest that the DfE believes that the 'consumer perspective' might be met by school-based structures outside governance: 'Meaningful and effective engagement with parents, staff and the wider community is vital. It is not the role of governing bodies to provide this through their membership. They need to assure themselves that specific arrangements are in place for this purpose' (DfE, 2014b). No statement more clearly illustrates the difference between the two models of public participation in the delivery of services offered above. There is an advisory role, of course, for consultation with parents and staff. But this is not a substitute for actual practical participation in, and a share in the responsibility for, effective school leadership.

5   Governors bring skills to school leadership other than those possessed by the professional leadership. As we have seen, governors are particularly valued if they bring professional skills. The coincidence of the implementation of the 1986 Act on the composition of governing bodies with the advent of local management of schools seemed to induce panic in a large number of schools. Even today, schools often feel vulnerable if they don't have certain 'experts' as governors – in accounting, building, human resources, law, for example. Caudrey (1988) reported that

> Many 'ordinary people' fear that they would not be up to the job, and some governing bodies are particularly looking for parents in the professions. There is, of course, a danger that school governors will increasingly be drawn from the articulate, qualified, middle classes.
>
> (Caudrey, 1988)

While this had been more the case one hundred years earlier, how much more likely is it to be true as governors now become company directors and trustees, with all the attendant legal responsibilities.

In many cases, this focus on professional skills may have deflected governing bodies from their primary purpose, the strategic leadership of the school. If one of the aims of the new governing bodies was to make the management of schools accessible to their 'customers', the recruitment of professionals may have undermined this. All over the country, one suspected, bank managers and accountants were giving their own time to produce sets of accounts even more unintelligible to the lay person than those produced by local authority staff. Similarly, human resources staff and small-scale employers were bringing some quite inappropriate experience to the selection of staff, builders and survey-ors were inspecting and sometimes repairing the fabric of decaying buildings, while health and safety inspectors from industry counted fire extinguishers. The way professionals applied their specific skills, albeit with the best of inten-tions, served sometimes to mystify the processes still further, and led governors into quite inappropriate activities. So accountant governors found themselves monitoring expenditure on a weekly or monthly basis, instead of helping to develop long-term financial planning, or exploring ways of producing budget reports and accounts that might be halfway coherent to governors and parents. Governors weren't monitoring and evaluating, because they were too busy doing jobs for and with the staff.

Not only were governing bodies potentially deflected from their strate-gic role by deploying specific expertise, but the display of 'professional' skills undermined the confidence, and so de-skilled, those governors who were not professionals. Candidates for parent governor without the capacity to write in their election address that they are experts on drains or some such might feel inadequate. These governors, who were recruited precisely because they could bring to their schools what governance writer Joan Sallis called 'the precious light of ordinariness', and who were already overawed by the complex world of education, and by the formidable arts involved in being 'at a meeting', were now confronted by another body of knowledge they didn't have.

Of course, the professional/business skills that schools *did* need were generic, not specialist. Specifically, what was needed were the arts of monitoring and evaluating performance, of medium and long-term strategic planning, and of challenging and supporting the school's professional leadership. As we shall see in Chapter 4 it is more difficult to see the understanding of governance in 2015 as a radical reinterpretation of the ownership of schools. Before that, however, in Chapter 3, we need to look at what is expected of school governors – expectations which have grown exponentially since the early days following the 1988 Act.

The strategic governing board

How the governing board brings about school improvement

The expectations of governing

Over the twenty-five years since the 1988 Education Act brought about a seismic change in the way governing bodies operate, there have been numerous attempts to define how governors can best bring about school improvement. The focus has been on ensuring that they are strategic, as opposed to operational, bodies. From the outset, governors were told that they were 'responsible for the general conduct of the school' (DES, 1988). The earlier 1986 Act, pre-dating the National Curriculum, had said that it would be the duty of governors 'to consider . . . what in their opinion, should be the aims of the secular curriculum of the school'. A little later, as governing bodies were bedding in, the Department for Education identified the three main purposes of governing bodies as being 'to provide a strategic view . . . to act as a critical friend . . . to account to parents and the wider community for the school's overall performance' (DfE, 1995).

Until 2010, governing bodies had been supported in doing their job in a regularly updated publication, initially in hard copy, later digital, of a Guide to the Law. However, this was replaced under the coalition government by a Governors' Handbook (DfE, 2015a; updated at least annually). Presumably, the new department was daunted by the prospect of detailing the law applying to every one of the new variety of state-funded school systems described in Chapter 2.

Academy trusts, for example, are governed by their memorandum and articles of association, which are determined largely by the Funding Agreement. Although much of the format is standard, the DfE has the power to make changes pretty well unilaterally. This is what it did in 2014 when it was decided to place restrictions on who might be appointed governors of state-funded schools following the Birmingham 'Trojan Horse' episode (see Chapter 4). Nevertheless, it was stressed that the overall duties of the governing board were fundamentally the same, whatever its legal status, and regardless of the other duties of governors who were also trustees, members of a founding trust body and directors of a company limited by guarantee and with charitable status:

In all types of schools, governing bodies should have a strong focus on three core strategic functions:

a   ensuring clarity of vision, ethos and strategic direction;

b   holding the headteacher to account for the educational performance of the school and its pupils; and

c   overseeing the financial performance of the school and making sure its money is well spent.

(DfE, 2015a)

The language of strategic planning can cause a lot of (mainly time-wasting) argument. Whatever definition we offer for the following terms will be disputed, so these are offered as suggestions – but every governing board needs to agree its own usages.

Ensuring clarity of vision, ethos and strategic direction

The **vision** of an organisation is how we picture it would be like if everything about it is how we want it to be. Here is a vision of a school written by a schools inspector:

> Two things will strike the stranger who pays his first visit to this school. One is the ceaseless activity of the children. The other is the bright and happy look on every face . . . so radiantly bright are the faces of the children that something akin to sunshine seems always to fill the school. . . . The visitor will realise that the brightness of the children is of two kinds – the brightness of energy and intelligence, and the brightness of goodness and joy.

This introduction goes on to describe the children: 'alive, alert, active, full of latent energy, ready to act, to do things, to turn his mind to things, to turn his hand to things, to turn his desire to things, to turn his whole being to things'. These extracts are from a book written more than one hundred years ago, whose sole purpose was to communicate a vision of how all schools might be (Holmes, 1911). Edmond Holmes's nephew, Gerard Holmes, later taught in such a school, which he described in his book *The Idiot Teacher* (Holmes, 1952). So you can read about the vision, then about the reality here.

These are the visions of professional educators, so how might a governing body go about forming and then articulating a vision? Such an exercise requires the commitment of everyone involved. The tools developed by the then National College for School Leadership during the remodelling of the schools workforce during the first decade of this century, such as brainstorming, stakeholder mapping, brownpaper planning, fishbone analysis, five whys and problem-solving/team-building can all play important parts in enabling all governors to participate (Hill, www.mindtools.com). This kind of exercise not only enables the development of a joint shared vision, but can establish an important principle in school governance – that every governor has the right to develop and express a view which contributes to the whole. One technique borrowed from the world of professional coaching is that of the Future Perfect, where the group focuses not on the problems the organisation has in achieving some undefined perfect state, but on what the perfect future would actually look and sound like (Jackson and Mckergow, 2002).

These are the questions we might expect a governing board to address in formulating and revisiting its vision for the school:

In five years' time

- What do we want to school to look like?
- How do we want the school to be governed and led?
- What do we want people to say about it?

  o   Pupils?
  o   Parents?
  o   Community?
  o   Staff?
  o   Governors?

- What do we want pupils to be like when they leave?

  o   Skills?
  o   Qualities?
  o   Knowledge?
  o   Behaviour?

- What would we like them to achieve in life?
- What are the key issues, in the world at large, that are likely to impact on the lives of children and adults connected with the school? (For an exploration of these, see Chapter 10.)

The exercise will be driven, conducted and finally decided by the governors, with senior school leaders, but will also engage the pupils, parents and all the staff.

Out of such an exercise – revisited regularly, say every three or so years – comes a description of the school as we want it to be. It creates an accessible description against which rough judgements can be made by staff, children, parents, visitors and most of all governors themselves on the extent to which the school resembles the agreed vision. It is not necessarily achievable in all its elements, but it is an aspiration.

The keys to formulating and articulating an organisational vision, particularly when it is created by a group rather than one person, are:

- Everyone contributes – pupils, parents, staff, the community – although it is finally in the hands of the governors.
- It describes what the school would look, sound and feel like in its perfect state – this is necessarily negotiated as different people are likely to have different views. But it does have to be something that key stakeholders can live with.
- Once articulated, the final statement needs to be brief and accessible to all the stakeholders, and to create a clear picture against which current practice can be assessed.

Here's an example of a vision statement from the website of a small rural primary school:

Our School

Our school is at the heart of the village. It is safe and welcoming. The school has a caring and supportive atmosphere and upholds Christian values. We celebrate diversity and encourage children to respect and embrace differences. The school promotes children's active role in the community and in respecting their environment. We work collaboratively with other schools and explore opportunities to develop new partnerships to enhance teaching and learning. Our standards are excellent with all pupils achieving their potential. We are an outstanding school (Ofsted rating).

However, as you can see – excellent as this is – it is an ethos statement, not a vision. This is how the school governors actually see the school, not how it might be.

The **ethos** of the school is the totality of its distinctiveness – all the things that make it characteristically what it is and how it works, including the culture and the beliefs that underlie the school: 'the distinctive character, spirit and attitudes' (HarperCollins, 2006). This needs some teasing out sometimes, as it is not always self-evident to the people who work in the school – for many governors, as well as staff, their experience of schools may be limited to no more than two or three in their lifetime, and it is common for them not to know that there are different ways of doing things, different behaviours to value, different aspirations to have. Indeed, as we have seen, the powers that be tend to stress the commonalities of schools in terms of what they are required to achieve, in terms of a common inspection framework and common attainment targets, despite the rhetoric of choice and diversity (it being unclear, and certainly unarticulated, where these diversities among schools might lie). Nevertheless, every school has a distinctive ethos, and it can usually be discerned as soon as, if not before, the visitor steps over the threshold. Defining it is often, however, a tricky task, but it is something that governing bodies have to do and return to again on a regular basis (say, every three to five years).

One way to approach this task is to ask governors to draw their image of the ideal student, staff member, and governors, and to discuss what are the characteristics that they most value. Whereas the vision answers the question 'What would we like our school to be like?' the ethos question is 'What do we value most in our school?'

Here's an ethos statement that really is a proclamation of the school's ethos:

Our ethos can be summarised as follows:

- foster independence, so that our pupils grow up able to look after themselves and make a positive contribution to society;
- encourage children's respect for their environment and a sense of belonging and responsibility towards their local community;
- provide a stimulating environment, making learning fun and exciting;
- give all children equal opportunities, respecting differences in race, gender and ability;
- enable each person within our school to feel special and to develop their skills and talents;
- be good role models, emphasising respect and kindness;
- our school will be known for its academic success, expressive and creative flair, physical endeavours, Christian values, caring family atmosphere and moral ethos.

British values

The 2014 requirement in response to the 'Trojan Horse' episode for governing boards to commit themselves to 'British values' was responded to with various degrees of mystification. One school, Nicol Mere Community Primary School in Wigan, responded thus:

Within the curriculum and our school life we will be raising the profile of 'Britishness' – we will actively promote the fundamental British rules of democracy, rules of law, individual liberty, mutual respect and tolerance of all with different faiths and beliefs.

On their website, this was accompanied by a short blast of the national anthem!

Mission statement: What's the difference between a 'mission statement' and a statement of aims? Not much, except in its length and detail. A mission statement should be a very brief statement of the main purpose of the organisation, without any peripherals – but it should be measurable. A mission statement such as 'Every child should be enabled to reach its potential' is meaningless – partly because, if any school did not want every child to reach its potential, it would not dare to say it. So a mission statement should mean something and not be a statement of the patently obvious. One of the best and most famous mission statements was President Kennedy's commitment in the early 1960s: 'We will land a man on the moon before the end of the decade.' A similar, but possibly inadvertent one, was made by Alf Ramsey, then England's football manager, in 1966, 'We will win the World Cup.' Amazingly this turned out to be as accurate a prediction as Kennedy's, though, perhaps less amazingly, and unlike Kennedy's, it was never to be repeated (to date).

It is difficult to find an effective and useful mission statement for a school. Here's a model one for Church of England Multi-Academy Trusts:

> The Academy aims to serve its community by providing an education of the highest quality within the context of Christian belief and practice. It encourages an understanding of the meaning and significance of faith and promotes Christian values through the experience it offers to all its pupils.

This is an idealistic statement, but it has elements within it that are measurable and so can be put to the test. The question 'Do we achieve this mission?' is not entirely meaningless here.

A **statement of aims**, like a mission statement, should say what the school intends to achieve, so that potential parents and students can make a judgement – do the aims of the school match my aspirations for my child? Here's quite a good one – though perhaps overlong:

- to provide a safe and caring environment based on trust and mutual respect;
- to give students the equal opportunity to develop their academic and applied studies, creative talents and leisure interests;
- to raise aspirations so that everyone strives for success;
- to help establish self-confidence, self-motivation and self-discipline;
- to encourage pleasure and pride in one's own and others' achievements;
- to provide a rich and stimulating learning environment and a curriculum that meets the needs of all our learners;
- to provide teaching to the highest standards;
- to promote a capacity for independent learning and the motivation to use that capacity;
- to identify individual needs and offer the opportunity to succeed to all;
- to provide the highest possible level of care and access to support that is appropriate and effective;
- to offer a wide range of experiences beyond the formal curriculum;
- to celebrate all excellence and achievements;

- to prepare students for the opportunities and responsibilities of adult life and local and global citizenship;
- to promote an active involvement in caring for the environment of the Academy, the local community and the wider world;
- to encourage participation and teamwork;
- to encourage the interest and involvement of parents, Governors, industry, commerce and the community in the life of the Academy and furthering the success of our students.

Each of these statements of aim can be tested, and most are subject to some form of measurement, so each year the governing body could sit down and ask themselves meaningfully, 'Are we nearer to achieving our aims than we were last year?'

Strategic direction

Once a governing body has agreed its overall aims and purpose and articulated them in such a way that they can be shared with others, it has to find a way of achieving them in practical terms. In order to do this, and in order to delegate the task of performing the plan on a day-to-day basis to the staff, it has to decide how it is going to perform its strategic duty:

> Governing bodies are the key strategic decision making body in every school. It is their job to set the school's strategic framework and ensure that it meets all of its statutory duties. This includes ensuring the school has a long-term strategic vision. . . . in the light of this vision, the governing body should agree the strategic priorities, aims and objectives for the school and sign off the policies, plans and targets for how to achieve them.
>
> (DfE, 2013)

Strategic governance has three elements:

PLANNING
Setting the overall mission, the ethos, the aims and targets of the school

MONITORING
Seeing that what is planned is implemented

EVALUATING
Seeing that what is implemented is producing the outcomes
that are wanted

Determining the strategic direction cannot be delegated to the staff. This academy is taking a huge risk including the second sentence in this statement in its annual trustees' report:

> Day-to-day operational management of the Academy is undertaken by the Senior Leadership Team (SLT) of . . . . High School . . . . . . The SLT determines the strategic direction of the School, making policy recommendations to the Governing Body.

Not only is the governing board trying to delegate something that is its own absolute responsibility, but the staff are seeming to take responsibility for something that clearly belongs elsewhere.

Planning

The layout of school strategic plans is not going to be discussed here – there are as many formats, one suspects, as there are schools. However, there must be a plan, and it must contain at least the following:

- areas of the school's operation – e.g. developing the curriculum, maintaining the premises, staff and governor development, and so on;
- specific areas for development, or key priorities – often those areas which have been identified as requiring improvement, either by the staff and governors throughout the year, or by Ofsted through the school's data;
- the actions to be taken;
- the desired output or outcomes, in the form of expected achievement;
- the lead persons responsible for ensuring the actions take place;
- the timescale for the actions to be completed;
- the resources likely to be needed;
- the responsible person or group monitoring the actions.

The DfE has given useful advice about the structure of the plan:

> The board should focus strongly on [the] core functions and avoid its time being consumed with issues of secondary importance. While a range of other issues may at times require the board's attention, this should not be at the expense of its ability to oversee and drive up the overall educational and financial performance of the school . . . Governors need a robust process and framework for setting priorities, creating accountability and monitoring progress. This may be facilitated by a school development plan or equivalent document that sets out strategic targets and key performance indicators (KPIs). The focus should be on significant strategic challenges and opportunities for school improvement in line with the board's core functions.
>
> (DfE, 2014a)

One primary school uses the following headings for its areas of operation:

- Learning and teaching
- Administrative procedures
- Leadership and governance
- Parental and community links
- Learning environment.

How might a school go through the planning process in a way that maximises opportunities to identify areas for development, while simultaneously engaging with its key stakeholder groups? One way is to involve pupils, parents and staff annually in the early stages of the planning process. Two simple questions: 'What have we been doing well?' and 'What might we do better?' can be asked of all groups. One village primary school continues to invite parents to an annual meeting in the autumn term, when the governing body has a chance to talk about what it's done in the previous school year, before asking, in one format or another, these questions. That session forms the first stage in the development planning process. Following that, while senior leaders are identifying internal and external pressures for change, the governing body meets with the staff on the first day of the spring term, set aside for staff training. A rather more focussed discussion takes place here, culminating in the group identifying the new plan's priorities. The senior leadership team then takes all the information gathered and turns it into a draft plan which is presented to governors towards the end of that term, and forms the basis of the following school year's plan.

In this way, the governing board is assured that it is engaged with the school improvement process in an appropriate way for lay people at both the beginning and the end of the plan's formulation. The final approval of the plan then takes the form of a question: 'Does this plan take into account all of the issues that have been raised since the beginning of the consultation?' The leadership of the senior professional team, of course, ensures that all national professional developments and expectations are also included and given proper prioritisation. This process accords with the planning policy described below.

There are two principal ways in which the governing body articulates its priorities and the ways in which it wants the staff to conduct the school, through the policies it establishes and the targets or objectives it sets.

Governing through policy

Policy-making, reviewing and evaluating is a key means by which the governing board exercises its strategic responsibility. The nature and content of the policies reflect the importance that governors lay on the ways in which the staff are expected to conduct the school, and are the vehicle through which the governors hold the headteacher to account for the school's performance. This makes it critical that, since the governing board is where the ownership of the school strategic direction lies, *the governing board must be in at the start and at the end of each process creating or reviewing a policy or a procedure.*

The governing board must lay down the principles which will underlie the finished document. The governors will also determine how the document will be put together: who will be consulted, which groups will contribute, which individual or group of people will do the writing of the draft.

It is also important that the involvement of the governors, whether in full board mode or, more often, in committee, and the breadth and depth of a consultation are proportionate to the importance of the policy.

The process for something as important as a school behaviour policy, for example, might look something like this:

Creating or reviewing a school behaviour policy

1   Governors receive a copy of the existing policy, any legal requirements or constraints, any other documents or procedures in current use.

2   The governing board meets and, through a variety of techniques − discussion, workshop, case-study − agrees the principles which should underlie a behaviour policy for their school.

3   The governing board agrees a process of consultation on the principles: staff workshop day, open meeting with parents; records of discussions with pupils; presentations from the community/neighbourhood, local organisations, youth workers, police, local authority and other advisers.

4   The governing board appoints a small working party with representatives of interested parties, co-opting any non-governors, and agrees its terms of reference, timescale, resources needed, steps to be taken, and a clear written statement of the principles it has agreed. A governor is appointed to monitor the process and report back to the governing board.

5   Following consultations, the working group prepares a draft document that is taken to the governing board for discussion. Does it reflect the principles laid down? Does it match the school's mission statement and ethos? Does it contribute to achieving the school's aims? Will it gain the active consent of pupils, parents, staff, the community? Is a process for monitoring and evaluating the policy on a regular basis included?

(continued)

> *(continued)*
>
> 6   When this is agreed, the governing board formally adopts the policy, and decides which committee or working party will be responsible for monitoring, how frequently it will report back to the governing board, and when the policy is due for review.

This process will vary according to the type of policy or procedure. Most school procedures, as distinct from policies, will be left to staff to determine, and for senior leaders to ensure that they match the overall policy they serve. Creation or review of, say, a school charging policy may be delegated to a committee, with very limited requirements for consultation (although opportunities must be provided for governors and staff at least to express a view at an early stage, rather than just nodding the proposed draft through). Curriculum policies will be very significantly supported and drafted by the staff responsible. Nevertheless, the principle holds true, that each policy or procedure belongs to the governing board, must be supported by the governing board (especially as, in some cases of potential appeal, such as a behaviour policy or a curriculum policy, that support may be tested in a more or less public arena in front of parents), as the body which bears the ultimate authority, while it seeks to gain the widest possible consensus, and therefore ownership, amongst those who have to implement or follow the policy.

The behaviour policy is a good example of this approach, because it is the one area where the law actually lays down the governing body's role:

> The governing body must also make, and periodically review, a written statement of principles to help the headteacher determine the measures that make up the school's behaviour policy. *This duty cannot be delegated.* The governing body must consult the headteacher, other appropriate members of staff, parents and all registered pupils before making or changing this statement of principles.
>
> (DfE, 2013, my italics)

What is a policy?

Is this proposition naive or unwieldy? Can lay people make a genuine contribution to educational policies implemented by professionals? And can a governing board hope to oversee the creation and regular review of those policies.

The first question is probably best answered by the process used by a Dorset First School where the children (aged between 4 and 8) are consulted about the music teaching policy. Collectively, they have useful things to say about what music means to them, and how they best learn from it. The principle here is one of respecting the potential of each individual who plays a part in an organisation, as client, user or governor to make a contribution. We do not expect them to offer advice on the technical processes of teaching, any more than the governor of an NHS Hospital Trust is expected to comment on the procedures of brain surgery. But the lay perspective is not only entitled to be heard but may enable the practitioner to improve their practice by looking at it from another angle.

Is it unwieldy? After all, a school may have up to a hundred policies. How is it possible to cope? But the creation of new policies from scratch is relatively rare. More likely is the need for regular, probably three-yearly, review. On occasions, the DfE may require a new policy. Sometimes, the school may feel that it needs to go back to first principles. For example, a large and highly successful secondary school in the south west was hugely embarrassed, and its staff enraged, when a governors' appeal panel upheld an appeal from parents against their child's exclusion, despite a behaviour policy which clearly required a permanent exclusion for the offence committed. The subsequent fallout threatened the standing of the governors as well as relationships within the governing board and between the governors, the staff and the parents. The school had a comprehensive set of policies, but it had considered neither how it enlisted governor support for them, nor whether governors understood the implications for them in the event of a dispute. In the event, the school had to look again at how it created and reviewed its policies – simple rubber-stamping of documents prepared by staff may be quick and easy, but it can lead to difficulties.

But take a hundred policies – most of them fairly straightforward – some of them, like some employment and health and safety policies largely dictated by statute with only a few potentially contentious ones, then give each GB committee responsibility for those relating to its terms of reference, create a review template which allows a routine three-yearly review period and it is possible to see how this becomes not merely manageable but a potentially effective way in which the governing board conveys to the staff how it wants the school to operate.

Obviously, this depends to a large extent on what a policy should look like. We are not talking here about the detailed strategy for implementation. What we are looking for from the governors is a set of principles. The staff will make decisions about action within the broad parameters laid down by the governing board. If, but only if, the parameters are too broad and allow actions which the governing board don't approve, then narrower parameters need to be laid down. Policies therefore express the collective will of the governing body for what it wants the school to achieve, while staff use their professional expertise to achieve it – bearing in mind, of course, that the lay governors are always accompanied by staff governors, by other staff advisers when needed, and, most of all, by the headteacher/principal acting as chief executive and senior professional adviser to the board.

One local authority offered the following three 'rules' about policy-making:

1   All policies should define:
     WHAT outcome(s) the governing body wants.
     Any limitations on HOW this is to be achieved.
     The governing body's own process (how it will check whether its policies are working);
     Who is accountable for the HOW?

2   The governing body deals with any policy not by addressing every-thing in sight but by addressing the important questions first.

3   The governing body 'stops speaking' when it is satisfied that the policy leads to action which will achieve what it wants.

     When it stops speaking on WHAT and HOW, the headteacher goes the rest of the way.

     Acknowledgements to Jackie Walters and Colin Richardson of the Bradford School Governor Service for their work based on Carver, 1990.

The governors' role in policy-making

At what level, then, should governing body policy operate? How is the line to be drawn between what constitutes the laying down of broad principles, and inappropriate interference in operational matters? Carver draws this distinction helpfully, recognising the impossibility of drawing a definitive line fixed for all circumstances. First, he describes the characteristics of board policy-making (1990: pp. 42–44). Policies must be, he writes:

- explicit (i.e. in written form);
- current (i.e. maintained as up-to-date);
- literal (meaning what they say);
- centrally available (easily accessible);
- bief ('brevity may be the unheralded secret of excellence' p. 43);
- encompassing (resolving larger questions before smaller ones).

This last characteristic leads to Carver's image of the mixing bowl: 'controlling the inside by staying on the outside'. The image is of a stack of mixing bowls nesting inside each other. The governing board deals with the largest first, cre-ating the overall environment and context for each area of the school's work. It then moves to each lower level of policy in turn until 'it reaches a point where a majority of members are willing to accept *any reasonable interpretation* of the policy language' (Carver, 1990: p. 46). For example, in dealing with the curriculum, the board would wish to lay down the broad principles underlying the whole school curriculum: its aims and objectives, its success criteria, and arrangements for monitoring and evaluation. Whether or not it would want to go further – looking at individual subjects, for example – would depend on the extent to which there is agreement that the policy adequately expresses the governing board's view in each subject area. Governors might feel that the policy is clear enough in predominantly technical subjects, but needed more explicit guidance in arts and humanities, and possibly the sciences – in personal, social and health education, religious education, history or geography, biology and physics (for example, in confronting the possibility of the teaching of 'creationism'). In this case, they would move down to the next size of mixing bowl. At whatever point they choose to leave the process – the first, second or third bowl – whatever is left is operational, and the business of management. The mixing bowl approach allows different levels of policy-setting for different areas of the school's jurisdiction. It applies Goethe's definition of genius – knowing when to stop. This has the merit of making *all* delegation to management purposeful and intended, not by default.

The mixing bowl approach can therefore be used as an *interpretation* of the principle that *the governing body is in at the start and at the end of every policy.*

Governing by target-setting

Target-setting became an established part of the education regime in England and Wales in 1997, following Labour's landslide election victory. The new government promised a combination of carrot and stick to raise standards in schools (DfEE, 1997a).

The pressure would involve:

- setting challenging national and local targets;
- having 'tough' negotiations with local authorities on benchmarking categories, on the mandatory targets for schools, and on the optional targets for schools.

The support would comprise:

- quality information on national and local patterns, from the qualifications and Curriculum Authority (QCA) and Ofsted;
- support for school management and leadership;
- requirements for local authorities to produce an Education Development Plan.

(Gann, 1999a)

With the benefit of hindsight, we can now see this document as offering local authorities the last chance to get standards rolling before the wholesale removal of schools from their jurisdiction. Certainly it does demonstrate that the new government saw in governing bodies the capacity to be the agents of significant change. The targets that the DfEE expected governing bodies to set were, of course, hard attainment targets for their pupils, with no scope for prior attainment to be taken into account, although elements of 'value-added' were added later.

Target-setting was supposed:

> to concentrate the minds of the school – mainly the minds of the staff – on *measurable achievement*. As it is presented by the government, it says:
>
> This is what is important –
>
> What is important can be measured –
>
> What is measured can be achieved –
>
> What is achieved can be shown to be achieved.

(Gann, 1999a)

Governing boards are able to set targets across the whole spectrum of school performance – provided they measure what they value, rather valuing only what is measured. So, as Figure 3.1 shows, you can set targets for, and measure, the children as they enter the school for all sorts of skills and qualities (as the 'input'), the activities that they do while they are in the school, the immediate short-term changes and skills they learn, and the long-term gains they make. Currently, however, almost the entire focus of both DfE expectations and Ofsted judgements is on pupil outputs. Why do very few primary schools know how their children perform at A Level, which universities they go to, and what jobs they end up in? Why do secondary schools not know how happy and mentally healthy and resilient their students are three years after they have left? The short-term rewards culture is as evident in judgements about school performance as it is in the shareholder culture in business.

So the way that targets are set can change, and the governing board and staff can broaden their perspective on school performance by considering standards for process, output and outcome. Similarly, they can broaden the achievements they measure, by considering:

- what requirements the school might have of all its students;
- what opportunities it should offer to all students;
- what choices should be offered to students;
- what support should be offered to students.

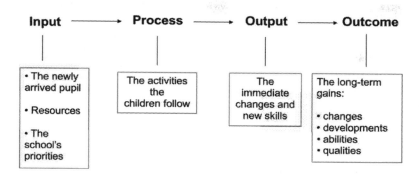

Figure 3.1 The school continuum.

The governing board can go further than this, by treating every area of the school's performance as an arena in which its aspirations for the school can be expressed in the form of targets – the wider curriculum, the environment, the human resources, the school's finances, the school's engagement with parents and, of course, the performance of the governing body (Gann, 1999).

The governing board plans by envisioning the future and developing strategic activities to help the school achieve that future, and it uses three principal tools to help it do that – a rolling plan, its policies, and the targets it sets. As these slot into place, the governors need to monitor the activities of the school to ensure that it is doing what the governing board believes it should be doing.

Monitoring

Monitoring is about ensuring that the school is doing what the governing board has agreed it should be doing in its strategic planning. Governing boards use six principal vehicles to ensure that the school is following the strategic direction it has laid down:

- The headteacher's report *(provided it . . .)*
- Understanding the data *(provided it . . .)*
- Committees *(provided they . . .)*
- Visiting the school *(provided it . . .)*
- Attachment to areas *(provided it . . .)*
- Stakeholder surveys *(provided they . . .)*.

With each vehicle, there is an important proviso.

The headteacher's report to the governing board

Regular reporting from the headteacher is likely to be the single most important source of information for the governing board on the performance of the school. A useful report, probably delivered termly, will address the implementation of the school's development plan and any other plans of the governing body, and deal with a specific set of performance indicators or targets that the governors have decided are most helpful in answering their prime question: 'How is the school doing?' Too often in the past headteachers were given no guidance as to the content and layout of the report, and decided for themselves what to report and how – often on an outmoded model handed down from a predecessor or a standard format recommended by a local authority.

The key is in the title of this agenda item – it is a report to the governors, and therefore it is only of any use if it is presented containing the information that the governing board has agreed it needs, in a format and language that is accessible to them. Fortunately, the DfE now explicitly supports this position:

> It is the headteacher's job (and in maintained schools it is their legal duty) to give governing bodies all the information they need to do their job well. . . . Governing bodies, not headteachers, should determine the scope and format of the headteacher's termly reports. This will mean that they receive the information they need in a format that enables them to stay focused on their core strategic functions and not get distracted or overwhelmed by information of secondary importance.
>
> (DfE, 2013)

So, one of the first jobs a governing board needs to do with a new headteacher is to discuss what information they will need and how it is to be presented. Naturally, in doing so, they will listen to the advice the head has to give them. The conversation might go something like: 'This is what we need to know from you on a twice-termly/termly/yearly basis. What else do you think we might need? What else would you like to tell us?' In multi-academy trusts, where the board will be hearing reports from a number of schools, it is even more vital that the same format of report is used for each school, and the board will need to sort out a process which enables individual school heads to report to their own local governing boards, with key information being passed on to the full board.

A good report is likely to consist largely of data (of which more later). For most schools, this data will need to be put in a historical context, so that the governors can see trends of improvement (or, perhaps, deterioration). Certainly, there should be no assertions without supporting evidence.

The DfE Handbook also goes on to say that 'the headteacher and school should not be the only source of information for the governing body'

(DfE, 2015a). Governors need objective data from other sources. Also, it is probably good practice for the headteacher to enable other staff to report to the governing body.

The governing board should be wary of a headteacher's report which takes up the whole of a meeting (and it should go without saying that it must be circulated to governors well before the meeting so that they have a chance to absorb it and to identify any areas that might need clarification). One governing board in a primary school decided to do without the traditional termly report and asked the head to report to each of the board's committees, focusing on data relating to their areas of responsibility. These were then discussed in committee, and the report and attached minutes were circulated to all governors before the next board meeting, where issues could be raised in front of all governors. Here it could be the committee chair who initially takes the questions rather than the head, so enabling wider governor participation and reflecting governor responsibility. It is vital that the chair controls the discussion to eliminate any unnecessary repetition, but enables those who weren't present at the committee meeting to raise issues that haven't come up before.

The head's report to the governors belongs to the governors and is the CEO's report on progress. It is therefore the core piece of information the board receives on the ongoing performance of the school.

Understanding the data

> To create robust accountability, governors need to ask challenging questions on the basis of robust objective data.
>
> (DfE, 2014a)

The proliferation of school performance data over recent years and the constantly shifting demands of the DfE and Ofsted make it risky to offer advice on the governing board's receipt and understanding of data, other than drawing a few broad principles. Data is becoming more accessible to lay people without professional training, and it may be obvious that not everyone needs to be able to penetrate the most detailed versions other than senior staff and one or two governors. The performance data is not unlike financial data in that respect – all governors need to understand where the school is, but not necessarily how it got there. The DfE Handbook is clear that governors need to be able to interpret the performance data that they are legally entitled to access independently of the school, so that they can 'hold the headteacher to account properly' (DfE, 2013).

The external data available to the school at the time of writing only gives a view of pupil performance and attendance. It is critical, therefore, that the governing board request internally generated data on all other matters that it considers significant. One thing that every governor needs to understand is that data of itself doesn't give any answers about the school's performance. Improved pupil performance in external tests may indeed indicate improved learning. But it may also indicate improved skills in taking external tests without actual sustainable learning taking place. It could also betoken better teaching, or poorer marking, or falling standards (as often argued both in the press and by opportunistic politicians), or higher levels of cheating by staff (reports of which do indeed appear to grow annually). Just as the headteacher's report is only valuable if the headteacher is trustworthy, mainly right, and robustly interrogated by the governing board, so data is only useful if it is correct and contextualised. Let us look at what that might mean.

Suppose that a governing board asks the headteacher for data concerning pupil behaviour, say, the number of formal sanctions imposed on pupils by year, gender, ethnic origin, attainment. Let us suppose that the headteacher presents the view that pupil behaviour is improving year by year, and that the reduction in sanctions imposed throughout the school is evidence that that is the case. But that would also be the case if staff had lost all confidence in the sanction system operated by the school, and had given up using it.

This is precisely where the governing board's monitoring of school performance becomes critical. As we shall see, while the data may of itself prove nothing, it can be verified by applying any of the other monitoring techniques.

Committees

As we have seen, the DfE has expressed a preference for smaller governing boards: 'Smaller governing bodies are likely to be more cohesive and dynamic, and able to act more decisively' (DfE, 2014b). However, the DfE has been unable to offer any robust data to support this view, and research tends to support the opposite view: 'Larger governing bodies, that is, those with 16 or more members, tend to be associated with schools that have higher levels of pupil attainment and better Ofsted grades' (James et al., 2014). Certainly it is more difficult in smaller governing bodies to sustain effective committees, and one of the most frequent responses to the question, 'How could governing be more effective?' tends to be 'Recruit more governors' (James et al., 2014).

The delegation of functions (where allowed) and duties to committees of the governing board is a powerful tool to handle business. However, too often governing bodies delegate by default. Various tools now exist which enable governing bodies to identify clearly which responsibilities are handled at the different levels of full governing body, committee, individual governor, headteacher. In multi-academy trusts, schemes of delegation are critical to the conduct of the respective functions of the board of trustees, the local governing board and its committees; as well, of course, as any division of responsibilities between an executive headteacher/principal and a school head. It is difficult to imagine how a full governing board can take on oversight of the financial performance of the school without some degree of delegation of functions to a committee or an individual.

In most cases, governing boards delegate functions rather than responsibilities, and this is more than a legal quibble. It is still not uncommon to see schools establishing a 'policy and resources' committee or 'First Committee' or some such body, often comprising the chair, vice chair and committee chairs. Devices such as this are guaranteed to create what Joan Sallis aptly labelled 'A and B teams' (Sallis, 1994), partly by investing a body with apparent if not actual executive powers, partly by, by definition, excluding some governors. However benign the process, other governors will always feel excluded.

If the role of the board is properly strategic, focusing on planning, monitoring and evaluating, the role of committees must also be strategic. 'Board committees,' writes Carver (1990: p. 155), 'are *to help get the board's job done, not to help with the staff's job*'. Committees that deal with the school's money and its premises may be particularly prone to this kind of 'helping':

> Committees should work at the board level. With respect to policy-making, the best contribution a committee can make is to prepare truly board-level policy issues for board deliberation. With respect to the non-policy-making aspects of a board's job . . . committees may deal with details, but not in areas that have been delegated to staff.
>
> (Carver, 1990: p. 157)

In the PME (Planning, Monitoring, Evaluating) model, this means that committees may take responsibility for monitoring and evaluating, deciding on appropriate indicators, targets and measures, agreeing appropriate methods for collecting information, reporting the outcomes to the board, and recommending further changes or additions to policy. These committees may also play a role in helping staff to *interpret* board policies, where there is ambiguity. But this is not to give them *carte blanche* to direct or instruct staff, nor to make policies themselves, either in a considered way or 'on the hoof'.

The principal functions of committees, then, are:

1   identifying the need for policies;
2   identifying the issues that need to be addressed when the board prepares a policy;
3   suggesting ways in which the board might go about preparing a policy;
4   proposing and implementing ways of monitoring the implementation of a policy – including monitoring the detail of school performance;
5   agreeing appropriate indicators against which the board can evaluate the policy;
6   ensuring that policies are reviewed, or created from new, at appropriate times.

Committees, then, are effective devices for governing boards to deal with detail (moving down the mixing bowls, using Carver's image), provided they are clear about their purpose, remain strategic and abide by their terms of reference.

Visiting the school

School visits are opportunities for governors to learn about the ways in which the school works. They can also use visits to monitor the implementation of plans, policies and procedures. A visit will allow governors to see the impact of their plans and policies on the day-to-day operation of the school. They must therefore be structured occasions. There are still a number of schools that encourage governors to 'drop in'. This is fine in establishing informal relationships, but it is not part of a governor's role. It is one of those many jobs that governors take on when they are acting as friends of the school, not as governors. Governors often talk about their role including helping out in a number of ways – listening to children read, acting as an unpaid classroom assistant, accompanying school trips, giving interview experience to older students, even carrying out small maintenance jobs. In none of these are governors discharging their governing duties. Any such duties, including visiting, are delegated by the governing body:

> It is the Governing Body which has all the powers in relation to school, not the individual Governor. The individual Governor goes into school to learn, not to judge. Just saying this removes the fear of teachers and makes Governors realise how they should use school visits. A visit can either take place because the Governors have made some decision which makes it necessary (e.g. that they should all look at some special needs provision, or that a different Governor should visit the school once a month) or because the head invites that Governor to come.
>
> (Sallis, 1992: p. 25)

So a visit might focus on a particular department or issue. It might involve formal meetings with staff. It might centre on a 'learning walk' accompanied by a member of staff, or include a lesson observation. It is *always* to learn, not to judge.

Perhaps one of the most dangerous areas of confusion has been around the assumption that governors have the right to attend classes and make judgements about lessons. This has been around since Victorian times (remember that some governors actually 'helped out' by themselves doing a spot of teaching – based on the idea that any educated person could turn themselves overnight into a professional educator).

This issue had certainly been confronted by schools since the reconstitution of 1988, but it took an Ofsted inspection report in 2013 to catch fire.

Ironically, it was a report that graded a new free primary school as 'good' that caused a furore amongst teachers and governors. The report suggested that the school was not yet 'outstanding' because 'governors are beginning to visit lessons but have not had training on what good teaching and learning looks like' (Ofsted 2013).

Could it be that Ofsted was expecting governors to be trained in lesson observation *with a view to them identifying the quality of teaching*?

The existing Ofsted guidance seemed quite clear on its website in April 2013:

While not a statutory requirement, the Department recommends that the governing body draws up a policy on governor visits to the school. This policy should take the following into account that governors do not have any rights of access to the school.

Visits should be undertaken as part of a strategic programme to:

- improve governor knowledge of the school, its staff, needs, priorities, strengths and weaknesses;
- monitor and assess the priorities as outlined in the development plan;
- assist the governing body in fulfilling its statutory duties.

Before visiting the school governors should:

- inform the school of the visit and seek approval of the arrangements;
- ensure that they are familiar with health and safety procedures including what to do in the event of a fire.

After visiting the school the governors should:

- complete a visit report outlining the objectives and results of the visit;
- report back to the committee or governing body as appropriate;
- provide constructive feedback as appropriate.

The purpose of governor visits is not to assess the quality of teaching provision or to pursue issues that relate to the day-to-day management of the school, other than as agreed with the headteacher or senior management team.

Ofsted hurriedly tried to step back, with new guidance published in April, 2013:

Governors are not expected to undertake lesson observations, unless the school has clear protocols for visits so their purposes are understood by school staff and governors alike. However, they hold important strategic responsibilities for the development and improvement of the school.

(Ofsted, 2013b)

But there remained some room for confusion in the apparent possibility that schools might introduce a protocol allowing governors to, effectively, act as inspectors. (At the same time, senior Ofsted officials were suggesting that governors might be professionalised and paid for doing their job – which suggests that there was a worrying organisational confusion about what governors are for.) In the event, the next full revision of the Ofsted Handbook seemed clear that governors should 'contribute to the school's self-evaluation and understand its strengths and weaknesses, including the quality of teaching, and reviewing the impact of their own work' (Ofsted, 2014a). This was all part of a dispute about the extent to which Ofsted should be preferring a particular style or styles of teaching. Eventually, early in 2014, it was decided that they would not promote certain teaching styles and, indeed, that their inspectors would no longer grade lessons observed in the course of an inspection.

Something of a diversion this episode proved to be, but it did have a positive impact by clarifying that governors are expected to know about the quality of learning and teaching in their school, but are not expected to make those judgements themselves – although it is helpful if they know how those judgements are made, so that they can assess how robust they are.

Even so, and with all these caveats, governors will inevitably make judgements about the school as they see it, partly in the light of their own experiences and expectations (and prejudices), as well as in the light of their knowledge of what the governing body wants the school to be doing. It is important for governors to know what to do with these judgements, and it is important that the staff should know what is being done with them. First, they are lay judgements on professional issues, not professional judgements. They are similar in significance to the judgements we all make about the organisations and institutions we meet in everyday life – the supermarket where we do our weekly shop, the garage that services the car, the bank, the internet provider, the mobile phone company. We make them on our perception of the service, of its ease of use, its pleasantness, its efficiency and cost – not on whether it is fulfilling its professional or statutory functions in a way that would satisfy a health and safety inspector or an auditor. Governors need to pass these judgements on to the appropriate person – usually the headteacher – in a spirit of enquiry rather than evaluation. In that same spirit, it is important for the head and other staff to treat such judgements seriously, because they reflect lay considerations, and probably will be shared by some of the parents and children. This is not the same as making a professional evaluation.

There are a lot of tricky issues here, because they touch upon the relationship between governors and staff – a key relationship which will determine at least to some extent the success of governance of the school. Visiting the school can only be an effective vehicle for monitoring if it is covered by clear and agreed policies and protocols. Sample documents are in Appendix 1 and 2.

Attachment to classes, departments, etc.

A close identification with some part of the school allows governors to become familiar with some detail, and to see the impact of governing body policies and decisions over the long term and at close quarters. This enables more effective monitoring. It is not about having an advocate for the department on the governing body to argue for more resources. Attendance at occasional departmental meetings in a secondary school, for example, at in-service training for staff, at tutor group meetings and assemblies, enables the governor to observe the implementation of policy at close hand. This provides a forum where staff can demonstrate and discuss their accountability to the governing body. By observing classes and departmental work in just one department, governors can see how their decisions have an impact at every level of the school's operation. The professional associations were at best sceptical about the expanded role of lay governing bodies in the 1990s. But the large majority of teachers seem to have taken to governors in a big way, welcoming the opportunity to discuss and explain what they do and why they do it. This is despite the fact that very few teachers have received any pre-service or in-service training about the job of governing boards; and newly-appointed headteachers sometimes find themselves attending a governing board meeting for the first time.

Attachments to areas of the school's work are effective vehicles for monitoring provided the purpose of it is understood – to enable better communications and better mutual understanding.

Stakeholder surveys

Schools are becoming increasingly sophisticated at using a range of techniques to maintain a regular flow of information and opinion from users to providers. The Ofsted questionnaire for parents is only one model. Schools:

- use parents' evenings (when parents talk to teachers about their own child's progress) to question parents along a schedule developed by the governing board to raise issues of current concern or importance;
- deliver annual written questionnaires to parents and children;
- have small groups of governors interviewing groups of pupils;

- use regular newsletters with governing board items to raise issues, summarise agendas and minutes;
- maintain an annual parents' meeting that focuses on a dialogue between governors and parents;
- prepare an annual statement of governance for publication to parents, including reports on attendance at board meetings and the impact of board decisions.

Stakeholder surveys can be delivered by interview face-to-face, or on paper, or through small groups. They are part of an ongoing dialogue between the school and its users. The survey process is indispensible *provided* it asks the right questions, analyses and understands the responses, and feeds back the outcomes to the target groups.

Applying the six vehicles for monitoring

Governing boards working with improving schools are likely to use all six of these monitoring techniques. Generally, they can be used in groups of two or three, to test assertions made about the school by governors, staff, parents and pupils, as well as for routine monitoring.

Evaluation

Evaluation is finding out how the school is doing. Most of this comes out of the monitoring process. But it needs now to end up in a series of at least annual judgements on performance.

When Ofsted introduced the requirement of school self-evaluation in 2005, it offered schools a template which it highly recommended should be used. Prior to this, schools had been given a pre-inspection document which they were required to complete, which was mainly background information. The new Self-Evaluation Form (SEF) required schools to make a series of judgements about their own performance, and to produce the evidence to support their claims. In each area of operation, schools had to award themselves one of the Ofsted grades, showing how they had reached their decision.

The Inspection judgement, then, became mainly a process of verifying those school self-evaluations. One of the characteristics of this approach was the very sharp focus on pupil attainment. If performance in external examinations and tests is judged as inadequate, it is effectively impossible for the school to be judged as anything other than inadequate, whatever the starting point of the pupils has been. Quite an industry shot up in training headteachers and preparing materials to help them 'self-evaluate' the school according to the complex criteria developed by Ofsted. However, within two years, the more or less obligatory SEF, which had quickly entered the lexicon of school leadership, became voluntary. While schools were still required to rigorously evaluate their own performance, they did not need to use the Ofsted format to do so. However, the training stuck, and many headteachers held on to the SEF as their preferred format.

In schools, headteachers use different approaches to keep their own SEF up-to-date. Before the 2010 general election, the Every Child Matters (ECM) agenda had been the focus of school self-evaluation. This posited five outcomes to ensure children and young people's well-being (DCSF, 2007a):

- being healthy – enjoying good physical and mental health and living a healthy lifestyle;
- staying safe – being protected from harm and neglect and growing up able to look after themselves;
- enjoying and achieving – getting the most out of life and developing broad skills for adulthood;
- making a positive contribution – to the community and to society and not engaging in anti-social or offending behaviour;
- economic well-being – overcoming socio-economic disadvantages to achieve their full potential.

So the self-evaluation was about the school showing how it addressed these outcomes. This agenda seemed to draw significant support from governors, many of whom were disappointed to see a renewed emphasis on academic achievement from the new coalition government. The language of ECM became much less prominent, but schools still evaluated themselves against the five outcomes as much as against purely academic attainment.

The key element in school self-evaluation is its continuity. This is not a document to be completed once annually by the headteacher, working at home long into the night. Ideally, it is a document to which everyone, but especially the staff, contributes, and which the governing body 'signs off'. It is the collectiveness of the exercise that makes self-evaluation an ongoing exercise, referred to at staff meeting and governing board meetings, with a continual search for evidence.

This means that the process of school self-evaluation has five key requirements (Gann, 2010a):

- the process should be simple and integrated with routine management systems;
- there is an objective evaluation of performance, priorities for improvement, and achievable targets;
- there is 'intelligent accountability' for its judgements;
- it asks: How well are we doing?
- it asks: How can we do better?

Changes to the expectations laid on schools will continue. But these core elements may be seen as having some reasonable life expectancy.

The effectiveness of governing boards

What do we know about the impact of school governance on school performance? First, we should say that the governing board's role in school improvement is only one of its functions. As we have seen, it also has very important parts to play in ensuring the accountability of the school's leadership – a point which is sometimes missed by those few headteachers who still believe that they can do a better job without governors.

We have seen that James et al. have shown a correlation between governing board size and school performance, but there is little definitive evidence that reflects the (hopeful) subtitle of this book.

What we do know, from the now thousands of inspection reports, is that there is a range of performance amongst governing boards, and that there is a clear positive correlation between good schools and good governing bodies. That is, good schools tend to have good governing boards; and good governing boards tend to govern good schools.

James et al. (2012: pp. 3–4) has also shown:

- that 'the lack of a capable governing body . . . is a substantial disadvantage' to a school;
- that 'school governing is important';
- that 'primary school governing and secondary school governing are different. The level of effectiveness of primary school governing is linked clearly and positively to the level of pupil attainment.' But 'the link between secondary school governing body effectiveness and pupil attainment is very weak'.

So what constitutes 'goodness' in a governing board? This will be looked at in detail in Chapter 8. Appendix 5 shows the 2014 guidance to Ofsted inspectors on making the judgement. Since the beginning of 2014, governors have been instructed to require the governing board to commission an external review of governance where inspectors feel it is needed (not necessarily only where governing boards are inadequate or requiring improvement). Certainly, Ofsted has claimed over the years to know what a good governing body looks like and what it does, and we will look further at that in Chapter 6.

One of the most common themes amongst writers and thinkers about school governance is that the single crucial element in the success of governing is the relationship between the governors and the headteacher. We will look at this more closely in Chapter 5. For the moment, it is reasonable to say two things:

1   There is pretty well universal agreement that the single most important task that a governing board undertakes is the selection and appointment of a headteacher.
2   It is likely that the major ongoing task of the governing board is ensuring the continuing competency and effectiveness of the headteacher.

This may have been the case for some one hundred and fifty years, and probably remains so.

The strategic governing body

Being strategic is a state of mind. There is some evidence that governing boards are good at managing money and premises, and at overseeing pupil performance, but actually not very good at strategic planning. Which is a shame because this is the distinctive quality they should be bringing to schools. (Some would add that most headteachers are good at managing and improving pupil performance, too, but also not very good at planning.) We have looked in this chapter at a range of activities that can support the governing board on this focus of 'ensuring clarity, ethos and strategic direction'. But it is the attitude of senior leaders in the school that counts. Governors and staff find themselves fire-fighting and responding to the current mood in education where every week sees a new initiative and a new expectation. Governors wrestle continuously with structures that distract them from the well-being and development of children and young people.

What would our school look like if it was successful in everything we want it to do? is the key strategic question for every governing board. Keeping a strong focus on strategic matters seems as much a political requirement as a social one, but good governing boards of improving schools will keep their eyes on the hills while negotiating the marshy lowlands of regulations and expectations.

Chapter 4

The responsibilities, roles and rights of governors

In which we look at some ideas about governing

What governors are for

Representing the community?

The 1986 reconstitution of governance followed a stakeholder model. This model, containing a balance of parents, the local community, local authority appointments and staff, was meant to ensure that stakeholders felt that they had a representation in the school's leadership. This idea, unremarkable at the time, would later become contentious. Even at the time some denied that staff and parent governors, elected by their peers, were intended to be 'representative'. It is difficult to understand the rationale of those who argued so. There is no dictionary definition of the term used in this sense which does not recognise that election is a system by which electors vote for people to represent them. This does not, of course, mean that elected representatives were required to always discover what their 'constituents' believed or wanted, and to vote accordingly, any more than a member of parliament does. But it does imply a duty on parent, staff and local authority governors broadly to be aware of the feelings of their electors, to reflect those views on the board (though not necessarily to vote that way), to raise any general issues of concern, and to ensure that the actions and decisions of the board are reported back. Nevertheless, it was not uncommon for some governors to tell staff or parent governors that it wasn't their job to 'represent' their electors. What they should have meant, of course, was that representation is not the same as delegation – not a difficult distinction.

What everyone seemed to agree about – though this too was not entirely beyond contention – was that, when the governing board made a decision, whether (rarely) by vote or (much more frequently) by consensus, the governors were required to do so purely in the best interests, as they saw it, of the pupils and the school. Even so, by 2014, the DfE was rowing back on the stakeholder model:

> Once appointed or elected, all governors must operate in the best interest of pupils, not as representatives to lobby on behalf of their constituency.

Their task is to govern the school . . . The membership of the governing board should focus on skills, with stakeholder engagement as an important but distinct activity for which governing bodies will need to assure themselves that appropriate structures and arrangements are in place.

(DfE, 2014b: paras 10–11)

This statutory guidance goes on to try to reconcile the two models – skills-based and stakeholder membership – by suggesting that governing boards should guide electors of parents and staff towards the skills they should be looking for in their 'prospective candidates' when they vote. Clearly 'representatives' is not an acceptable word. But what else can we call them? In addition, the guidance suggests that governing boards should write their own code of conduct in which the commitment to training, though still not compulsory, should figure. This smacks of a government being very unclear about the role of governors – not reassuring at a time when governing boards of all maintained schools were being required to reconstitute.

The other aspect of 'representativeness', of course, is what characteristics are shared between the person elected and their electors – or, at least, the people they represent. There is a general feeling that chambers of elected people – most notably the House of Commons – should have a stab at having a similarly proportionate representation of age, gender, social class, cultural background and educational background, and work experience as the general population. We didn't know, in 1988, how 'representative' in this sense of the communities served by the schools these new governing boards were. Of course, we shouldn't expect all the different social, cultural and interest groups to be mirrored in such a body. But perhaps we should expect to see the major elements of the community reflected in a representative group. As it was, the 1986 Act was unlikely to have a major impact on the social composition of governing boards, except perhaps through the avenue of parent governors.

When we talk about governors 'representing' the community served by the school we might mean several different things. Of course, we mean that the governors *stand in* for the community. Not everyone who has an interest in the school can participate in its leadership, so certain people are selected (by appointment or election) to stand in for all the others. They then have a duty to keep themselves informed about the interests of the community, and to be proactive in keeping the community informed about the governing board's actions and decisions. And they have a duty to report back to the community.

This means that they have a duty to *reflect* the interests of the community as far as they can. Of course they cannot reflect the actual proportions of those people in terms, say, of gender, race, social class, people with disabilities and so on who are members of the community. But they can attempt to address those groups, especially the minorities who are less likely to be represented by reason of experience, availability, self-confidence and so on, and they can remain vigilant about ensuring that their interests are met.

If anyone complains that the people don't really want to know what goes on, let alone participate themselves, in the school's strategic leadership, they should be reminded of Schattschneider's comment in Chapter 2 (p. 34). The fact is that even now, for many years, much of the profession of education has excluded ordinary people from its deliberations. Using a range of techniques, and in all areas of life, the public has been told and shown that it is best to leave matters to the professionals. So it cannot be a surprise that they are reluctant to join in when an offer of participation is made, especially when the offer is half-hearted. Participation in school governance has to be worked at all year round. Genuine interest has to be taken by the school in community views, persistent efforts made to engage people in what the governors do and what decisions they take, and as Lord Nash has suggested, the governing board needs to make sure that people are aware of the impact that it has on the nature and the performance of the school.

'There is no shortage of people wanting to tell you what you *can't* do, and for some reason some may try to play down your representative role. Thus while parents in the supermarket have no doubt that you as an elected parent governor are their spokesperson and are there to put right whatever they see as being wrong with the school, the head teacher and perhaps others will tell you that you don't represent parents at all and are there just in a personal capacity to support the school as a typical parent. Teachers have the same problem when they want to have a little bit of governing body time to report what's worrying the staff this week or how the staff have reacted to the new starting time or registration system . . . Why do people say these things? And who is right? Well, I think that sub-consciously many people in authority feel uneasy about representatives. They see them as one step away from riots and strikes, work-to-rule and demonstrations. You can't dismiss what people say so easily if they speak for many others, whereas it's easy to dismiss someone's personal opinion. As for where the truth lies, as usual it is somewhere between the two extremes.'

(Sallis, 2001: p. 71)

Sadly, we come across too many examples where professionals speak 'for the school' without the real authority to do so. This became particularly apparent during the rush to academisation after 2010 when so many headteachers led their governing boards into independence from the LA in the (often justified) belief that this was power for them, not for the governors. A grant-maintained school headteacher, asked what committees his governing body operated, replied, 'Oh, I did away with the committees last year. They were taking up too much of my time.' This suggests that he saw his governors as a source of support and assistance, not as a group of people whose primary responsibilities were to lead the school strategically and to hold the headteacher accountable for its performance. In a similar vein, a high-profile headteacher from the South West wrote to the *Times Educational Supplement* in September 2010 that 'in the new Coalition world, the headteacher will be king and schools their own masters' (Gann, 2011: p. 383).

Bringing the business model of governance to schools?

And so it came about: governing bodies were first and foremost to emulate the characteristics of the business community. This line was peddled throughout the 1990s, ministers often talking of 'business governors' though no such creature ever existed.

The promotion of the idea of 'business' governors is of a piece with the downplaying of governing boards as representative bodies – it attempts to minimise their democratic function and to focus on their role in the 'market-place' of education. Schools are just like businesses, and they have to be run above all efficiently – they are not a public good whose provision should be mediated by the public for whom they are provided.

Indeed, there is little if any evidence that 'business' governors are any more effective in supporting school improvement than others. This may arise from an early confusion. We have noted above (in Chapter 2) the coincidence of the arrival in schools in 1988 of the new governors alongside the local management of schools – a fairly new concept in many local authorities, though some (notably Hertfordshire and Cambridgeshire) had been experimenting with pilots for some years. Headteachers were in some cases overwhelmed by the demands of self-management and self-governance. The management of budgets, buildings and premises, health and safety, staffing matters and so on, came thick and fast, in the form of brown envelopes containing budgets and demands for policies and processes. Little wonder that headteachers might look to local people with the skills, confidence and experience to handle these matters – accountants, lawyers, builders and so on would prove to be invaluable, as heads felt that the delegated budget was hardly adequate, except in the largest schools, to employ a school business manager – a profession yet to emerge.

The state of Swindon academy, one of seven academies that have received warning letters from Ofsted, suggests that having experts on the governing body is not always a guarantee of success. Sir Michael Wilshaw, the chief inspector, has been complaining that some governors are not up

(continued)

(continued)

to scratch, but Swindon has a line-up other schools might envy. Mary Curnock Cook, the chief executive of UCAS, the university admissions service, has been a governor there for five years. The chair is Sir Anthony Greener, a former chair of the now abolished Qualifications and Curriculum Authority. Fellow governors include Colin Fraser, recently retired deputy head of Marlborough College (£31,000 a year for boarders) and Marlborough's director of science, Nic Allott. From industry, there is Mike Godfrey, who until a couple of months ago was chief engineer at Swindon's Honda plant. He had worked for Honda for 27 years. The blame-hunters might direct their attention at United Learning, the academy sponsor which runs its schools from the centre. United Learning is now run by Jon Coles, a former senior civil servant at the DfE.

(Mansell and Hackett, 2013)

Perhaps some governing bodies shared the view of Lord Rawlinson, one-time chair of London Oratory School, at a time 'when the school underwent an official inspection and was found to be satisfactory in every respect bar one: the governors apparently did not come up to scratch. Rawlinson was furious. The job of a governing body, he argued, was to do as little as possible while the headteacher and his staff were doing a good job – which they manifestly were. Only if and when the school were not being run properly should the governors interfere' (Heald, 2006). Ironically, London Oratory was the school which then PM Tony Blair and his wife chose for their children's education. Rawlinson's view, expressed here in an addendum to his obituary, rather invites the question as to how the governors would know that the school was not 'being run properly'.

The academisation of England's schools, then, offers significant opportunities to business-minded headteachers and to the market [estimated as worth about £2bn per year] . . . Here is Gove in an interview with *The Times* (18 June 2011): 'Gove would welcome school heads taking a lesson from business: "We now have great headteachers who will become educational entrepreneurs. They will build a brand and create chains." He said he would have no "ideological objection to profit-making institutions" in education' (Gann, 2011).

The emphasis on business-like school governance became, twenty-five years on from the 1988 Act, a demand for more 'professional' governing bodies. The DfE adopted a 'more professional standard of school governance' as one of its aims, and this was echoed by senior officers of Ofsted.

Research into board effectiveness

Results from America on research into boards of lay people in the voluntary sector suggest:

- The proportion of business people on boards was either not significantly related to organisational performance, or the relationship was negative.
- There is a positive relationship between involvement in strategic planning and organisation performance.
- Ratings of organisational effectiveness are positively related to the extent to which board members feel informed about their responsibilities and duties.

(Hudson, 1995)

In early 2013, Mike Cladingbowl, Director of Ofsted, appearing before the Education Select Committee Enquiry into governance, called for school governors to be 'increasingly professionalised and work in federations to cater for groups of schools in the future'. He spoke of new 'advanced skills governors' who would help spread best practice between governing bodies; plans to 'look at different structures' and of being 'more creative' with the way in which governance services are delivered. He said such changes could mean that fewer school governors are needed overall.

'You could ensure that expertise in one governing body is deliberately and directly shared with another – a kind of advanced skills governor,' Cladingbowl said. 'You could have a smaller group of governors looking after a larger group of schools, either through a federation of schools or a federation of governors. It is possible to have a small number of governors who know what they're doing. You don't need large numbers, you just need key people' (House of Commons Education Committee, 2013).

All this was of a piece with the drive towards skills-based governing boards. Michael Wilshaw, the Chief Inspector, had been sounding the same or similar notes suggesting, again, smaller more 'professional' governing boards, with some paid governors. Cladingbowl was once head of the most improved school in England, so he knew what he was talking about. But here, perhaps, he misconstrued the way that school governance works.

Governors are not, and never have been, intended to be another professional weapon in the armoury of the DfE and Ofsted in the war that they are waging on schools that do not do their best by our children. If school improvement was solely about best teaching and learning, about data and the interpretation of trends, about behaviour and ethos, it could safely be left to the education profession. No headteacher and leadership team can survive nowadays without a sophisticated understanding of, and ability to analyse, down to its last decimal point, RAISE Online and the myriad other pieces of data-based information that schools have access to. Governing boards need to understand it too, and to absorb its manifold meanings and analyse it and interrogate it to its last jot and tittle of interpretation.

What does a good – even an outstanding – governing board do?

Governors challenge and hold to account the professionals *from the core of the community served by the school*. They contribute robust and rigorous questioning from *outside* the profession. They provide a unique view of schooling from inside the community they serve, with an unrivalled set and network of under-standings and contacts and relationships with that community. They help to provide, and they can help to explain, the complex perceptions of and judge-ments on the school made by local people. They provide a base in which the partnership between teachers and parents which is essential to a child's effective learning can be explored and developed. Where the school really uses gover-nors well, they engage parents in the school improvement process, enabling the parent body to be the first place the governors go to in order to understand what is working well within the school and what can be done better. They are, therefore, the arena for school improvement planning.

What is more, they can make themselves accountable not just to the secre-tary of state and the head of Ofsted. They can and should, and the best ones do, make themselves accountable to the communities and the people the school serves. They do this by being at the school gates in the morning and evening, by publishing their contact details in the school's newsletter, by asking parents and children what governors ought to be discussing, and what they think about the things they are discussing. The outstanding ones still engage parents in accountability exercises like the annual parents' meeting. They run surgeries at parents' evening, conduct questionnaires, talk with and listen to children.

What they are not is also important. They are not in thrall to the education-ists and politicians who make up the education establishment. Although the whole governing board is accountable to the local authority, or to the school trustees, and/or Ofsted, and/or the secretary of state, individual governors are not. And their incomes and their careers are not dependent on what they do. They can, in good schools, afford to challenge without personal risk, to ques-tion without fear of personal reprisal.

They are the face of public service. If they are professionalised in the ways suggested by some, if they are absorbed into the educational community, if they are commodified and turned into just one more piece in the professional jigsaw, something will be lost that many educators have been searching for much of the time since universal compulsory education – a way to engage the whole community in the schooling of its children.

In a way, this conflict – the one between those who believe that the main, if not sole, purpose of education is to serve the needs of the state – needs which are largely economic and wealth-creating – and those who contend that education is principally for the benefit of the community and the individuals within it – is encapsulated in this argument. If this is the case, it is not surprising that, at a time when equality and the fair division of national wealth seems increasingly at risk, people should wonder if the 'business' model of governance is actually serving their communities and their children in a way that will benefit *all* the people.

Stewards or stakeholders?

We have already considered the new forms of governance that may come about through the academisation of schools. Being a governor of a school in an academy grouping is likely to be a different experience to governing a school which is a member of an LA family. Butler (2010), writing at a time when all academies had sponsors, took up the American Charter School model, where governance is regarded as stewardship, as opposed to the stakeholder model, which was established by law in English and Welsh schools in 1986.

Widespread academy conversion might suggest that there will be a significant difference in the way governing boards operate here. So what might these differences be? This question raises fundamental issues about the nature and purpose of school governance.

The American model is built upon a very different tradition of public service. In the UK, voluntary input to state-provided public services has a long history. Its existence threatened by the welfare state in the middle of the last century, it has found a role in providing local governance of state-provided services such as health and education. So the stakeholder model of governance of schools came about, supported by all three major political parties, in the 1980s.

Stakeholders reflect the views of the various groups with an interest in the welfare of the school – the parents, the local community, the local authority, staff, for example. A 'steward' is somebody who manages somebody else's property, finances, or household. The question necessarily arises – who is this 'somebody'? Do steward governors act on behalf of the local authority in a maintained school? On behalf of the sponsors or chain owners in old-style academies? Or, in a converted academy, on behalf of the trustees or the local community? Businesses have boards who act as stewards – no-one expects shareholders to have a significant voice in their management, other than to elect the board.

By contrast, stakeholder governance exists to ensure four functions:

- scrutiny – keeping a close eye on the performance of the school and its management;
- accountability – being answerable for the performance of the school to its stakeholders, i.e. students, parents and potential students and parents, and the wider community served by the school;

- relevance – governors must ensure that the school's services are appropriate to the local community and its particular needs and characteristics;
- non-partisanship – it must remain free from party politics and other factions, and govern purely in the interests of the school and its students.

The membership of a stakeholder governing board must be inclusive, comprehensive, representative and differentiated – it must have a balanced membership which includes people able to reflect the views and needs of all members of the community and able to respond to the unique circumstances of the school. The assumption underlying all this is that every school is different. When the then secretary of state, Michael Gove said, in an interview with the Times newspaper, 'We now have great headteachers who will become educational entrepreneurs. They will build a brand and create chains', and added that he would have no 'ideological objection to profit-making institutions in education', he is not speaking of such a governing board. He is assuming – as some do – that a 'great headteacher' will be effective in any type of school, and that a 'brand' can govern a school in any circumstances (Gann, 2011).

When governing boards appoint a headteacher – and indeed other staff – they do so looking for the right mix for *their* school in *their* community. They identify, in both the person specification and the job description, the particular needs of *their* school at a particular point in its history.

Stakeholder governance establishes equilibrium between, at best, a range of potentially conflicting interests who respect each other's views and provenance. It recognises that good governance, in national and local government and in the provision of public services such as education, health, policing, social services, is a delicate balance of such interests – users, employees, general local interests – which in sum enable the institution to provide the best and most relevant service to the community.

People whose services are provided by a stakeholder model are not having their services looked after on behalf of a, perhaps distant, owner. They have the ability to get involved themselves. They are nurtured by governance, not provided for. Stewardship has the potential to disempower people because it involves doing things *for* people. The stakeholder model empowers – it enables people to do things for themselves – and therefore it impacts on the community as well as the school. People have the capacity to 'catch the vision of their own powers' – surely one of the most important aims of education. If we entirely lose the stakeholder model in school governance, we may threaten the capacity that communities have to regenerate and engage the communities that our schools serve.

Four types of governing board

Of course there are as many types of governing board as there are governing boards. But there have been various attempts to categorise the broad approaches that governors tend to take. Professor Ian Jamieson, formerly of the University of Bath, categorised the four major types of governing body he saw. He suggested in the 1990s that around 80 per cent of governing boards were really supporters' clubs, doing not much more than approving the actions of the headteacher, and cheering on the school from the terraces. If this was the case, some 19,000 school governing boards had, largely by default rather than by design, delegated effective control of the school to the headteacher. This raised a number of concerns. First, what parliament had legislated for was being frustrated; secondly, when problems did arise, there was no effective body of people able to deal with them; thirdly, headteachers had little protection against pressures from outside the school; finally, the large majority of schools were still the exclusive domain of the education profession rather than of the communities they were meant to serve. This total might also include a number of laissez-faire governing boards, who provide neither support not challenge to the professional leadership but, basically, let the headteacher and staff 'get on with it' without any significant interference.

In the third type of governing board, the adversarial model, schools have failed to find a *modus operandi* which allows governors to govern and headteachers to manage. Here the governors provide plenty of challenge to the head, but little support. This might include those governing boards who see themselves largely as 'principal agents' – mechanistic, checking, sanctioning driving forces whose primary duty is to call the head to account. While this may be only a small minority (some 5 per cent, or fewer than two thousand schools), it is these schools that get the publicity when relationships break down.

Only about 15 per cent of governing boards at that time, then, had achieved the status of a critical friend – that is, one who helps to identify what is wrong with a school, and then helps to make it better. For a number of years, the 'critical friend' role was a model much favoured by successive departments for education. Although the term has now fallen out of favour, the essence of it still forms the ideal for many governors. It implies a stewardship role, in that it requires governors to look on their relationship with the head and staff as a partnership, founded on trust and reward, but where the governors remain alert to any changes in performance.

Jamieson's useful categories have been replicated more recently by Professor Mick Waters of the University of Wolverhampton, with three of the types replaced by new terms: Jamieson's supporters' clubs become 'uncritical lovers'; laissez-faire boards become 'sleeping partners'; and adversarial governors become 'hostile witnesses'.

The behaviour of governors

How should governors behave? This may not have been much of an issue when school governance was overseen by local authorities. Now the governing board, as opposed to individual governors, has awesome powers.

It therefore has its own responsibilities, and must be accountable for its actions to those who established the school and who fund it (formerly only the LA but now the DfE, the Education Funding Agency and the trustees); to the inspection process (Ofsted); to parents and pupils; to the community; and to the staff. But there has been no formal monitoring of governing boards themselves except through the inspection process. Local authorities could suspend the delegation of the school budget to governing boards of schools; the secretary of state has powers to remove a governing board of a maintained school, usually on request from an LA, and replace it with an Interim Executive Board appointed by the LA (but with the approval of the DfE). From 2010, this was the standard procedure for dealing with a governing board of a 'failing' school that rejected the DfE's demand for it to begin the process of conversion to sponsored academy process.

Here, an issue became, not so much the behaviour of the governing board, but the behaviour of the 'academy brokers' tasked to persuade the governors to convert. In March 2013, as reported in *The Guardian*, with the then secretary of state: 'due to reappear before the education select committee . . . to answer questions about what he knew about bullying allegations within the Department of Education' an official complaint was made about the intimidating behaviour of one of the DfE's academy brokers by a midlands councillor: 'On each (of three visits to separate schools), [her] behaviour has been intimidating and bullying towards governors, headteachers and local authority staff.' The broker had allegedly provided no agenda or minutes of the meetings and had said on each occasion, 'The minister will make you become an academy, and will intervene both in the school and in the local authority if they do not support this action' (The Guardian, 11th March, 2013).

Fortunately for the DfE a spokesman was able to clear its officials: 'We carried out a thorough investigation and found no basis in the claims'. In 2015 it was revealed that between 2009 and 2014 the DfE had spent £14m on its brokers because 'The Department requires special expertise for the broker role that it cannot find within the civil service. Their expertise needs to be deployed flexibly in different parts of the country' (DfE letter, 5.2.15, in response to a Freedom of Information request).

We will look at some governor behaviour more critically in Chapter 9. For the standard governing board, whether a statutory body or local governing board, a statement of the Nolan principles is a useful starting point:

Selflessness

Holders of public office should take decisions solely in terms of the public interest. They should not do so in order to gain financial or other material benefits for themselves, their family or their friends.

Integrity

Holders of public office should not place themselves under any financial or other obligation to outside individuals or organisations that might influence them in the performance of their official duties.

Objectivity

In carrying out public business, including making public appointments, awarding contracts, or recommending individuals for rewards and benefits, holders of public office should make choices on merit.

Accountability

Holders of public office are accountable for their decisions and actions to the public and must submit themselves to whatever scrutiny is appropriate to their office.

Openness

Holders of public office should be as open as possible about all the decisions and actions that they take. They should give reasons for their decisions and restrict information only when the wider public interest clearly demands this.

Honesty

Holders of public office have a duty to declare any private interests relating to their public duties and to take steps to resolve any conflicts arising in a way that protects the public interest.

Leadership

Holders of public office should promote and support these principles by leadership and example.

(DfEE, 1996)

It is far more common now to find governing boards that adopt their own code of conduct. Originally, in 1995, in response to the concerns of its own members, the National Association of Headteachers produced a draft code, and tried the get the government to endorse it. This resulted in a DfEE publication, 'Guidance on Good Governance' (DfEE, 1996). Much of this was concerned with tracing the boundaries between governance and headship – boundaries which are difficult to define, as we shall see in Chapter 5. Later, the professional associations worked with the National Governors' Association to agree an outline of respective responsibilities (ASCL, NGA and NAHT, 2015).

For an individual governing board, some statement of what it expects from its governors is an important part of inducting new governors and managing their behaviour thereafter (see Appendix 3). Nevertheless, however closely governors adhere to these standards, they may find themselves removed from office for disagreeing with their appointing body or their local authority.

For an individual governing board's interpretation of these standards, a code of conduct such as that in Appendix 3 should avoid the necessity for too many difficult conversations for the chair. Ideally this is constructed by the governors themselves, and reviewed and ratified each year. However well-intentioned governors are, they can fall into traps – like the recently-elected parent governor in a First School who, having a job as a lunchtime assistant in the school, marched into the kitchen and told the staff that they all had to do what she told them from now on as she was a governor now.

The jobs that governors do

Individual roles

For some years, there were individual jobs designated by the DfE that had to be taken on by named individuals, such as SEN governor, literacy and numeracy governors, and so on. Currently, there are no individual roles that must be fulfilled by individual governors. All tasks are given to the governing board as a whole, but it can still be a good idea to distribute leadership on different functions or whole governing board responsibilities to named individuals. Governing boards seem to work best when *each and every* governor, however much of a novice they may be, has at least one specific area of responsibility. This heightens everyone's commitment, allows individual and group development, and makes for a body of people who are genuinely involved in, and responsible for, their actions.

Such areas might be defined by the priorities of the strategic plan, or by key themes in the school, such as reading and writing, numeracy, STEM subjects, personal and social development, additional needs, and IT. They might be extensions of GB roles, such as roles for the committee chairs of resources, premises, human resources, and learning and teaching. The GB could add safeguarding, equal opportunities, parental engagement, special/additional needs, health and safety, governor development and so on.

A formulation which may have been devised originally by Lord Brougham as a definition of a gentleman has been developed by the historian Cicely Veronica Wedgwood as 'An educated man should know something about everything and everything about something'. This could equally apply to governors (of either gender, of course!). An understanding of how well in broad terms the school is doing, including some key factors (such as the list in Appendix 4), plus an area of special interest where that governor knows more than anyone else, provides a good basis for overall governor knowledge and understanding of the school.

Committees

Few governing boards operate without committees, although some manage a system replicating the 'responsible' or 'cabinet' member dependent entirely on individuals. The fact is that a committee, as we saw in Chapter 3, is *both* an effective and inclusive way of doing business *and* a key vehicle for monitoring the school's performance. The size of the governing board, therefore, may need to take into account an effective committee structure. Experience seems to show that most governing boards follow a fairly traditional division of responsibilities for resources (including finance and premises), human resources, and learning and teaching (where detailed study of performance data can take place and information interpreted so that all governors can understand current performance against a historical background). On an average-sized governing board, it is reasonable to expect all governors to serve on one committee. It can be helpful if a vice chair is identified to ensure efficient management of the committees. Committees can play a useful role in keeping policies reviewed and up-to-date, if every school policy is accorded to a committee.

Chairing the board

Since 2010, there has been a new emphasis on the role of the chair.

The chair is the manager of the governing board and its business. By report, few chairs actually seek the post. This underlines the importance of having a strategy for succession planning on the governing board. Useful guidelines might include:

- The usual expectation is that chairs, once elected, will serve a period of, say, four years. This gives sufficient time for the chair to find their feet, but ensures the regular infusion of fresh blood into the post, and avoids over-reliance on one member.
- The governing board will normally elect two vice chairs, one of whom will be regarded as a chair-in-waiting, and undergoing a period of training and preparation; a second vice chair may be an experienced governor able to stand in for the chair on formal and public occasions.
- The chair is expected to undergo continuous training and development, for example, the Leadership Development Programme devised by the National College for Teaching and Leadership.

The job of the chair can be divided into a number of parts, in many of which it will be supported by the clerk, some of which might be delegated to a vice chair or other governors.

Management of the governing board includes:

- ensuring that policies and planning are kept up-to-date;
- communicating with individual governors and committees;
- communicating with the head and the staff;
- ensuring the implementation of good practice (as encapsulated in a code of conduct);
- evaluating the performance of the governing board;
- ensuring that all governors have a role and are performing it;
- ensuring that governors are trained and that they participate fully in meeting and events;
- conducting annual performance reviews of governors.

Doing the business of the governing board includes:

- responding to communications from the DfE, Ofsted, EFA, LA, MAT or other bodies;
- managing and performance reviewing the clerk;
- preparing, with a committee, the plan and calendar of business for the year;
- preparing with a committee the agenda for meetings.

Chairing the meeting includes:

- defining and practising the qualities of a good meeting (see below);
- preparing and planning for meetings;
- inducting new governors;
- sponsoring vulnerable governors (e.g. those who may have difficulty in contributing for one reason or another).

Leading the school includes:

- maintaining close relationships with the head and other staff;
- mediating and listening to problems and complaints;
- representing and speaking for the governing board to staff, pupils, parents, Ofsted and other education authorities, and the wider community;
- attending and leading public and ceremonial and other events.

The job description:

- All individual roles on the governing board, as well as the general role of being a governor, should have their own clear (but brief) written job description against which the role-holder and other judges can make judgements about their performance.

James et al. identify key activities of an effective chair and place it firmly in the arena of community leadership:

The ChGB role was pivotal in five areas:

1   working with the headteacher – ideally in partnership;
2   having a presence in the school as the chair of the body responsible for the school's conduct;
3   organising the governing body;
4   chairing the meetings of the full governing body;
5   being a governor.

Chairing meetings is important. They often need to be shrewdly chaired and it is where other aspects of the role are manifested. However, arguably it is the least important of the roles.

We consider that the role of ChGB in the education system is substantially underplayed and given insufficient status. It is a significant educational and community leadership role.

(James et al., 2012)

The vice chair

The vice chair's post should not be merely to fill in when the chair is away or late, nor is it merely the post for a chair-in-waiting. Once the chair has been elected, the governing board might consider what parts of the joint role description he or she cannot easily fulfil, or what particular skills are required. The vice chair should then encompass these. Vice chairs can also fulfil very valuable roles in meetings, supporting the chair, alerting them to people who want to speak, and so on. They can also help with governing board management, for example, by taking on responsibility for seeing that committees are doing their jobs properly.

The clerk to the governors

Recognition of the central importance of the clerk's role in an effective governing board has come about slowly. In the 1990s it was quite possible for a governor to be nominated to clerk meetings, and it was very common for a school secretary or other employee with little experience in minute-taking to take on the role, often as part of their day-job. The 2013 regulations are quite unequivocal about this:

High quality professional clerking is crucial to the effective functioning of the board. Clerking is not only about good organisation and administration, but also, and more importantly, about helping the board understand its role, functions and legal duties. This is crucial in helping the board exercise its functions expediently and confidently, so that it can stay focused on its core functions.

(DfE, 2014a: regulation 11)

CHAIR OF GOVERNORS
Draft role description

Key tasks

1   Construct and agree the agenda for meetings, together with the clerk and headteacher
2   Plan and keep good order in meetings
3   Ensure governors' participation in, and between, meetings
4   Ensure all decisions are understood and that necessary actions are taken
5   Ensure governors receive relevant information and materials
6   Check that decisions taken by the governing board are enacted
7   Ensure that governors know the rules that keep governing boards democratic are well-known and followed
8   Listen and be a critical friend to the headteacher
9   Report decisions of the governing board to parents, staff and others regularly
10   Coordinate the governing board role in inspection
11   Monitor and review the work of the governing board
12   Represent the school, for example in public meetings and parents' meetings.

VICE CHAIR OF GOVERNORS
Draft role description

Key tasks

1   Support the chair in the conduct of meetings
2   Check that decisions taken by the board are enacted
3   Ensure governors' participation in, and between, meetings
4   Welcome and induct new governors
5   Ensure that committees and working parties of the board are working effectively and to terms of reference
6   Be available to stand in for the chair in his/her absence
7   Coordinate training and development of the governing board and of individual governors
8   Listen and be a critical friend to the chair.

Figure 4.1 Role descriptions.

This commitment has significant implications for the way the clerk is appointed and managed:

> Boards should set demanding standards for the service they expect from their clerk and assure themselves that they are employing a clerk with suitable skills and training. Consequently, they should expect to pay an appropriate amount commensurate to the professional service they expect their clerk to deliver. A model job description has been developed by the National Governors' Association.
>
> (DfE, 2014a: regulation 11)

What does this mean? First, it means that the clerk must be trained and experienced in minute-taking, and in particular, are aware of the need to meet expectations in the meeting minutes. For example, if Ofsted gives little or no notice of inspection, and meets only briefly with the chair, if at all, the governing board minutes may be the only objective indicator of their priorities. It is therefore essential that, for example, the board focus on school improvement is clearly reflected in the minutes. Instances of governors challenging the head and holding her/him to account should be quoted. Records of actions decided on and confirmation that they have been completed should be evident (see Appendix 4 for some of these expectations). The website and blog 'clerk to governors' is clear about what this means in practice:

> A good clerk is more than just a minute taker. A good clerk will be able to advise the governors about their roles, responsibilities and points of law. The majority of the work should be happening at committee level so committees need to be clerked professionally too.
>
> (www.clerktogovernors.co.uk)

This aligns clerks to governors with company secretaries and clerks to boards of directors in business and industry as opposed to the rather cosy arrangements which were adopted (and maybe still are) in many schools.

We should also be clear that the clerk is a direct employee of the board and must be managed (including being appraised annually) by the chair and/or a small group of governors – perhaps by the committee chairs. The employment of a member of the school staff remains too common. Of course, where there is always openness and trust between the governing board and the headteacher, this may work. But it is poor professional practice if it relies entirely on that condition. The clerk's undivided loyalty must be to the governing board, and they must be able to advise the board on actions and decisions without any fear of it impacting on their day-job or their professional relationships within the school.

So, with a job description, an annual appraisal, a set of clear requirements on how minutes should appear, and, most importantly, the capacity to give disinterested professional, legal advice to the board on procedures and DfE requirements, the clerking role is very different from what it was in 1988.

Good governing: some examples of practice

Recruitment and retention

Panic about the proportion of vacancies on governing boards is now a predictable part of our annual calendar. Generally, it seems to run at about 10 per cent which, with a four-year turnover, might be regarded as pretty good in any voluntary organisation. One of the questions most frequently asked by governors is about the recruitment and retention of good governors.

Maintaining an effective governing board is an in-built governing board strategy. It means pulling all the strings of parental and community engagement to deliver the message that the school is a part of the community where its ownership resides. Strategies such as:

- regular newsletters directly from the GB or, at least, a governors' page as part of a regular school newsletter;
- communications to the wider community, such as community/neighbourhood newsletters;
- governing decisions and minutes communicated directly to all parents, with key areas highlighted;
- an annual report to the parents and community showing the impact of governing board decisions on the school;
- an annual (at least) meeting with parents and the community to invite views and comments on the school;
- regular surveys of pupil and parent opinion from the governing board, with results and consequent actions fed back;
- governor attendance at events, such as parents' evenings, celebration assemblies, where governors play a prominent part (doing 'nice' jobs, such as presenting awards);
- governor interviews with pupils and parents, for example, in focus groups, structured to enable discussion of key issues;
- good induction procedures.

Induction

Here's a story of a woman engaged in her local community who, learning of a vacancy through an advert in the local paper (replicated in shop windows and post offices in the catchment area, and in local newsletters) applied to be a member of her local school's governing board. She met with the chair who talked her through the role, and she visited the school. The chair asked her to write a letter telling of her experience and skills and to complete a skills audit. Soon she received a letter through the post. It was a formal offer of a place, informing her that, this vacancy being a direct appointment of the governors rather than subject to election, the board had discussed the candidates and decided she had the most appropriate skill set and qualities to fill the vacancy.

Hardly has she opened and read the letter (which, of course, contains details of the next few meetings) when her phone rings. It is the chair of governors congratulating her and welcoming her. The chair goes on to say that she will be getting a couple more phone calls, but he looks forward to seeing her at the next meeting. Hardly has she put down the phone than it rings again. This time, it is the headteacher. The head welcomes her to the governing board and asks when she can come to visit the school again, this time in the role of governor, for a thorough tour and a rundown of the key issues she, as head, is facing. A date is agreed and the new governor puts down the phone – only for it to ring again. This time, a voice introduces itself as the governor who has been tasked with mentoring her. Can they meet for an informal chat? Can he pick her up before the next meeting so that she won't have to find her way and enter the room by herself? Could they have a chat after the meeting when he could explain what had happened and answer any questions? Could he go through with her the documentation she would be getting soon and point out the most important?

As you can imagine, the new governor is deeply impressed with the professionalisation of this voluntary body. When she arrives at her first meeting, the chair and clerk welcome her and explain that they will go around the table asking governors to introduce themselves. Nameplates are used at all meetings, so there is no need to try to remember names. Perhaps she would say a few words about herself before the business of the meeting begins? The agenda, of course, is clear and all relevant papers attached. Each item has a note attached saying what is expected of the board – receiving a paper, making a decision, hearing a range of views. Impressively, not every item at the meeting is a discussion around the table. With some items, governors are invited to work in small groups, or to discuss things in pairs, so that ideas can be developed before being spoken out loud. (The mentor governor has explained that not all governors are accustomed to attending formal meetings, so some who are less comfortable find it helpful to formulate ideas in such settings.) Everything is explained – including jargon and acronyms – so that non–educationists know what is going on. And everyone participates. Sometimes the chair asks for views from the staff governors, or from the perspective of parent governors, so that the head is not the only person expressing views about the school. Indeed, somewhat to the new governor's surprise (she was once a governor years before, and the head then seemed to run the meeting and spoke more than everyone else put together) the head doesn't say very much at all. Occasionally she answers questions, and summarises a professional viewpoint on something, but it's always prefaced with a rider that this is how it looks from her perspective, but we need to hear other views, too. Sometimes she says, 'I don't know – how can we find out?'

All in all, this looks like it's going to be a very positive, indeed enjoyable, experience. It has been emphasised how hard it will be and how committed the governors are – no pretence here that it's just a couple of meetings a term. This is a governing board that makes a difference to a school, and welcomes the lay view of things.

No problem with recruiting and retaining governors here.

Having a governance framework

An area that appears to be not talked about much in governing schools is the need for every governor to have an overall narrative of their board's engagement with the school. What does it mean *in practice* to be strategic? We have seen in Chapter 3 what processes the governing board needs to engage in, in order to conduct its key activities of planning, monitoring and evaluating. This should presume an annual cycle, as in Figure 4.2.

An annual calendar of governing board focus might involve a self-evaluation exercise in the summer, followed by interrogation of performance data in the autumn and an invitation to stakeholders to evaluate performance, constituting an audit of where the board is. It considers its priorities, addressing key objectives, including overseeing staff performance management, in the early spring. Planning for the key issues to be addressed in the coming year begins in the spring, with plans being finalised and ratified in the early summer.

These issues will dictate the shape and content of the agenda in the, customarily six, meetings of the board in the year, and in the committee meetings. A detailed framework for governance is available from the National Governors' Association (NGA and Wellcome Trust, 2015).

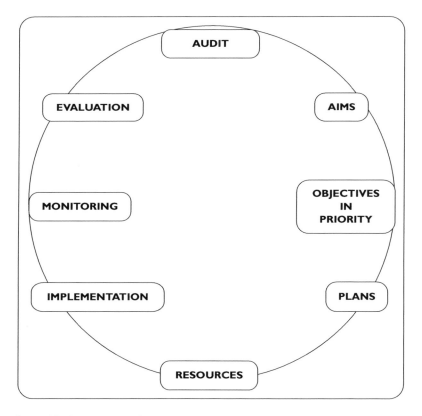

Figure 4.2 A strategic cycle.

Good meetings

Much of the work that governors do takes place in meetings. Actually, some governors think that meetings are the *only* place where governing is done. But this is far from the truth. Lord Nash, minister with responsibility for governors in the DfE in 2013–15, once suggested that the chair should open meetings with the excellent question, 'What have you done as a governor since we last met?'

Meetings are not the be-all and end-all of governing schools. In fact, we may question the extent to which meetings are a reflection of the middle–class and bureaucratised way in which schools are, for the most part, managed. We need to bear in mind that formal meetings are only one way in which groups reach joint decisions, and that, for many people, meetings are not a natural way of life. Limiting the governing role to attending meetings probably means that a significant proportion of governors are not able to make the best contribution that they might. It also hands power to those best able to exploit the meeting environment, probably politicians (and politicians *manqués*) and professional people, and deters many who would otherwise like to play a role in their school's leadership from even thinking about doing so.

Nevertheless, attending and participating in meetings is probably the single most important thing that governors do. In fact, one formal meeting of the governing board comprises all sorts of small meetings, each with a different purpose. It is worthwhile for the chair to spend time preparing for a meeting with this in mind. A chair's meeting guide might look something like Figure 4.3.

Approaching meetings with an emphasis on variety and on enabling everyone – especially those who are not used to speaking formally – to participate, should make decision–making far more meaningful. Sometimes, members find that the structure of meetings and the language used excludes them from effective participation. This leads one to believe that the most effective training for some

AGENDA ITEM	OBJECTIVE	METHOD	TARGET TIME
1 MINUTES	Agreement	Formal proposal	5 min.
4 SCHOOL CLEANING CONTRACT	Decision from options	Committee recommendation/ discussion	30 min.
5 HEAD'S REPORT	Acceptance	Executive summary; Question/ answer/challenge and support	45 min.
9 SCHOOL BEHAVIOUR POLICY	Lay down underlying principles	Small group discussion leading to whole GB draft agreement; followed by appointment of working party	45 min.

Figure 4.3 Chair's meeting guide.

governing boards might be in assertiveness. Appendix 9 offers a range of questions and statements that governors might find helpful.

A good meeting will at least have the characteristics shown in Figure 4.4 recorded by AGIT (Darlington, Hinds and Holt, 1988). The importance of the chair in ensuring that everyone can contribute appropriately is obvious. The chair of a meeting is much like the conductor of an orchestra – varying the pace, ensuring a range of emphasis and significance, introducing humour and allowing, or encouraging, the development of creative tensions. The control element too, is vital. Finally, the governors must be absolutely clear as to what has been decided at a meeting, by means of a definitive summary, and as to what action has been agreed, and who is taking responsibility for it.

The governors might find it helpful to attach a Meetings Charter to the Code of Conduct, so that everyone's commitment is formalised – see Figure 4.5.

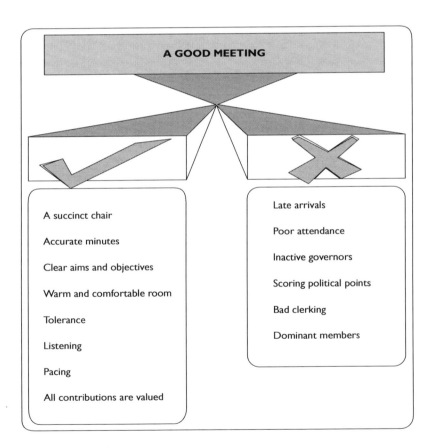

Figure 4.4 A good meeting.

The Meetings Charter aims to remind Governors of good meeting behaviour.

I expect:	Others can expect me:
• a clear agenda and relevant documents and these to reach me before the meeting; • an adequate room and appropriate seating; • a clear understanding of the purpose(s) of the meeting; • people to be punctual; • a chair who is sympathetic, keeps to the agenda, paces the meeting so that time is given to each matter in proportion to its importance, draws on all members for contributions, keeps discussion to the point; • people to tolerate a variety of views and opinions; • my contribution to be heard; • others to contribute to the discussion; • the decision-making process to be quite clear; • members to work together and to want discussions to be fruitful; • members to learn from one another and not be stubbornly partisan; • members to be ready to take collective responsibility for the minuted record of views expressed and decisions reached.	• to have read the agenda, minutes and other papers, and noted the items I want to say something about; • to have the papers and my notes at the meeting; • to be punctual; • to make relevant contributions; • to listen to and consider what others say; • to accept my share of the collective responsibility.

Figure 4.5 A meetings charter.

Schools of a religious nature frequently begin (and some also end) their meetings with brief moments of prayer. The practice of quiet reflection, to put away thoughts of the day and focus on the purpose of the meeting to come, that is, to make the school better for the children, is to be recommended. Similarly, at the end, the chair's question: 'What have we done at this meeting to make things better for the children?', perhaps supplemented by 'What do we mean to do before the next meeting?' can remind us that the meeting itself is not the be-all and end-all of governing. Governing boards are often judged by the quality of their meetings. They are outward and visible signs of the values and effectiveness of the governing board.

Obstacles to effective governance

The following list of seven obstacles to effective groupwork was compiled by the author together with management consultant Paddy O'Brien (see O'Brien

1992 and 1993). We mainly had governing bodies in mind although we were also informed by our work with other teams – multi-agency Sure Start managers, charity and voluntary organisation trustees, parish and parochial church councils, for example.

The meetings culture and the pressure to 'do business'

We come across governing boards whose sole aim, it appears, is to get business done. We can easily be seduced into thinking that our main job is decision-making – there's a lot of pressure from outside to suggest that it is – but maybe that's just the most comfortable part of what we do. We must have time for reflection, and an atmosphere and structure for meetings to encourage it.

Lack of information

Who decides what information governors should get from the head and staff? That needs to be done together, of course. So it is important to build in a regular session where governors and staff agree what's important information to share, and a structure for sharing it between staff, committees and governing board.

People not valuing themselves or others

A lot of governors wonder what they as individuals might have to offer. Governing boards – especially heads and chairs – need to establish by the ways they organise themselves and the ways they behave to each other that every governor counts and that everyone has something worth contributing.

Lack of group skills

Teamwork, assertiveness, questioning and challenging – even how to behave at a formal meeting – are areas we may neglect because we take them for granted. I was much struck when a governor at my own school asked for a rundown of the duties of a committee chair, because 'before I became a governor, I'd never been to a formal meeting'. These skills may need to be worked on together to ensure that everyone is comfortable with them.

Fear of retribution, lack of trust and a sense that whatever people will say, they will be disregarded

It is, regrettably, still the case that some staff governors will not say what they feel for fear of upsetting or angering the head, and who think that any chance of promotion has gone since they joined the governing body. Many parents, too, fear that their children may be victimised if they speak out. Other governors (including the head, sometimes) may worry about being shown up in front of each other. And how many governors go through entire meetings without speaking?

People who are possessive and fearful and who have secret agendas

How often do you wonder what's *actually* going on at a meeting? How do the people really get on? What do they really think of each other? Fear is a great motivator – and makes an even better straitjacket. Very often, meetings are as much about power – what people perceive as being *their* areas of responsibility – as about moving the organisation forward.

People under stress and not managing their energy well

Often meetings take place when members are all at their lowest ebb – at the end of a long day, with their minds on other things. How best can both concentration and dynamic interplay be enabled? There are a lot of techniques around – brain gym, for example – if governors can only learn how to use them.

These seven barriers to best group practice need to be tackled head-on if governing boards are to get best value for time and effort from their members.

The legal responsibilities of governors

All legal governing boards are incorporated bodies. This means that, provided individual governors can demonstrate that they have acted 'honestly and reasonably', they will escape personal liability. For governing boards of academies, including multi-academy trusts, the position is more complex as trustees are governors as well as directors of a company (for detailed dissection of this see Paxton-Doggett, 2014).

Generally speaking, if an LA or VA maintained school governing body follows the advice of its LA or foundation, any liability will lie with the authority. Problems may arise when such advice is not sought, or ignored. LAs will generally not bear the costs, say, of an unfair dismissal, if the governors have acted against the advice of their human resources department. In such a case, the costs would have to be borne by the school budget. However, if the governors have acted recklessly, liability may be a more complex issue.

It is clear that, in selecting staff, governors are under a legal obligation to ensure that the procedure avoids any possibility of illegal processes. Some governors (even chairs) still insist on asking questions or making comments at selection interviews which are potentially or actually discriminatory. Governors should be aware of the potential for the liability of other governors who have sat by, either by design or by default, while this has taken place, or who have continued to delegate appointments to a member who has shown themselves incapable of remaining within the law. This book lays no claim to be a legal tome, so we are raising questions here rather than answering them.

In fact, there are rarely straight and simple answers to the kinds of questions about liability that governors ask. The general answer is that each case will be treated on its merits until there is a substantial body of case law.

This is one of the strongest arguments for adopting a distinctive model of governing through planning, monitoring and evaluating as presented in Chapter 3. The best advice for governing boards is that all their policies are clear and properly implemented, regularly reviewed, and have systems which enable governors to ensure compliance.

So the two primary duties of governors – to know their school, and to lay down broad parameters of action and responsibility through policies and practice – are underlined by their legal responsibilities.

Governors' rights

In return for all these onerous and entirely voluntary responsibilities, and the commitment which threatens any hopes of a normal life, very little is said about the rights that governors have. They should be quite explicit.

Time

When asked about their needs, governors very often say 'more time'. While we may have no effect on the total time available the least we can do is to ensure that the time we do put in is well used. That is why the annual commitments, and the conduct of meetings, are so important.

Governors may need to decide for themselves, or agree among themselves, the priorities – is a school visit more important than another committee meeting? How best to use the one day allowed by my employers? Participating in a school in-service training day will have a range of payoffs beyond learning about the day's themes, including getting to know the staff, and letting them get to know you. There should be frequent cost–benefit exercises in time valuation, with help from experienced governors and staff.

The law is vague about governors' entitlements as employees, but the Governors' Handbook recognises the benefits for employers:

> Serving as a governor helps employees develop board-level skills and experience that they may not otherwise develop until much later in their careers. The learning and development benefits are therefore significant and more than compensate for the flexibility and time off that staff may need to fulfil their governor duties. The CBI has stated clearly that it sees a robust business case for more employers supporting their staff to volunteer as governors.

(CBI, 2013)

By law, employers must give employees who are school governors (currently in maintained schools) 'reasonable time off' to carry out their duties (Section 50 of the Employment Rights Act 1996). The employee and employer must agree on what is reasonable time off. Among the points they should discuss are:

- how much time is needed overall to perform the duties;
- whether the employee is also being given time off from work for other activities;
- the particular circumstances of the employer's business; and
- the likely effect that the employee's absence may have on it.

Employers may give time off with pay but do not have to do so. This is for discussion between the employee and the employer. Guidance on time off for public duties is available (DfE, 2015a: p. 27).

Ironically, it seems that local authorities and other public services are among the least sympathetic to giving governor employees time off. Of course, school staff who are governors should also be allowed time to, for example, visit other parts of the school during the school day, attend governor training and attend any meeting arranged by governors during the school day.

Information

Governors do not complain very often about the shortage of information – rather the opposite. What they may need is to have the masses of documents they are given categorised into vital, important, urgent, 'useful only when it's needed' and irrelevant. Governing schools is a useful field in which to model what is sometimes called 'just in time not just in case' information sharing. The head, chair and clerk are the most likely gatekeepers, and therefore the significant players in this exercise. The DfE has made it absolutely clear that all governors have the right of access to data about their schools, including RAISE online data, and have sponsored the development of 'data dashboards' to ensure that key information about school performance cannot be kept from them.

Resources

Some basic resources are essential: information about the school will include any handbooks, policy lists (with policies where appropriate) and the sort of information discussed in Chapter 3. Most information will be in digital form, but it helps to have a shelf or filing cupboard in the school with books and magazines and other resources to support governance.

Visiting

The importance of opportunities for visiting have been discussed. Governors are entitled to have arrangements in place for regular, purposeful visiting.

This assumes a governors' visiting policy, along with a code of practice (see Appendices 1 and 2).

Training and development

Governors are entitled to access to training, and therefore information about the variety of development opportunities open to them. Governments have to date resisted calls to make training compulsory. Nevertheless, there is continuing pressure on chairs to develop best practice through courses and consultancy provided both face-to-face and online by organisations such as the National College for Teaching and Leadership and the National Governors' Association. It is becoming more common practice, too, for multi-academy trusts to insist on training for local governing boards as well as for trust members.

What is different now from the 1990s is that funding for governor training is no longer ring-fenced in the school budget, so the governors may need to be robust in requiring a portion of the school's CPD budget to be set aside for governors. Where there is resistance to this, it might be worth reminding budget-holders just how dangerous untrained governors can become.

A role description

A simple generic list of what is expected of governors will, as we have seen above, be a useful recruitment and induction instrument, as well as being indispensible in governing body self-evaluation (see Chapter 8).

Self-evaluation

Governors are entitled to know how well they and their governing body are doing – in particular, about the impact they are having on the school's performance. Formats for this will be explored in Chapter 8.

Governing a school is an opportunity for people to contribute to their communities and to one of the most important defining institutions within them. It is a public service of enormous social significance. Governors have an absolute right to be enabled to do it to the best of their ability.

Chapter 5

Governance, leadership and management

Being an investigation of the relationships that governing boards have with their headteacher and staff

Despite all the dramatic structural and political changes that have taken place in English education in the first years of the twenty-first century, two underlying truths about schools remain – that the single most influential individual in the school is the headteacher, and that the single most important relationship that the governing board has is with its headteacher.

The governing board and the headteacher

The position of the headteacher

Both member and servant of the board – and possibly the longest-serving member – often the very visible daytime leader with (at least statutorily) much reduced powers since 1988 and the only senior professional in a sea of 'amateurs'; the person who traditionally holds the final word, with very little visible accountability, in an organisation of up to 2,000 people, whose decisions and practices are not just open to interrogation and challenge but to setting aside, by a group of people, most of whom have had no formal education training. What an imposition a new governing body might be to such a person.

Almost immediately after the setting-up of governing boards with meaningful powers in 1988 the government created escape routes for the truly self-governing head. Grant-maintained status offered the head wishing to be untrammelled by their local authority a neat way out. While some moves towards GM status were taken in a genuine atmosphere of cooperation between a confident head and an innovative governing board, and a very few were led by 'business-minded' governors unafraid of going it alone, most changes of status were led by headteachers who, perhaps, foresaw the weakening and eventual demise of the local authority.

Is the power that heads have wielded a chimera? All research continues to show that the headteacher is the single most influential figure in the success (and, as we have seen increasingly lately, the failure) of a school. Concern about the nature of the role is not a recent phenomenon. As long ago as 1976, the educational philosopher R. S. Peters wrote:

It is an extraordinary thing, really, that a people so proud of their freedom and independence of mind as the British should have for so long taken for granted an institution which is in part a negation of such values, namely that of the head. I say 'in part' because the autonomy of the head in his or her own school has always been respected. But this autonomy has traditionally been exercised in a very authoritarian and paternalistic way at the expense of that of others – pupils, assistant teachers and parents in particular. From the end of the 1960s onwards, however, there has been a growing debate about the role of the head, which is part and parcel of the widespread demand for more participation in decision-making in the community as a whole.

(Peters, 1976: p. 1)

And so the debate rumbles on. Governing boards are increasingly garnering powers, and the authority of the DfE, to challenge and to require the acquiescence of the head. But operationally, in the day-to-day running of the school, few are challenging the absolute right of the headteacher to act as they believe right. More and more, that 'strong leadership of the head' identified by the National Commission on Education (1995) is constrained by centralised diktat on the curriculum and the expectations of Ofsted; more and more are governors encouraged to ensure that policy-making as well as strategic direction is instigated by the governing board. Let us look at the sometimes tortuous relations of headteachers and their governing boards, starting just one hundred years ago, in the year of the beginning of the Great War – although the battle between a headteacher and her governors in an obscure Norfolk village lasted considerably longer.

Burston School: the headteacher vs. the governors

The headship of Burston Village School became vacant in 1911. Annie Higdon had been headteacher of Wood Dalling School, some 40 miles north of Burston, the other side of Norwich. But she and her husband, an assistant teacher, had fallen out with the school managers. Annie Higdon was an awkward, self-opinionated woman but apparently a gifted and popular teacher. The falling-out, almost certainly, arose from Annie's socialist beliefs – something of an anathema among the middle classes who dominated school governance in the villages of Norfolk. So the couple were transferred to Burston, where they quickly came into conflict with the newly appointed vicar who, as was customary in many rural areas, took up the chairmanship of the school's managing body. The Rev. Eland was as stiff-backed as were the Higdons. When Annie insisted using the school's coal allowance to light the fire so as to dry the children's wet clothes on rainy days, the governors instructed her not to, and she duly ignored them. Meanwhile, Tom Higdon was using his spare time to cycle around the lanes of south Norfolk to recruit farm labourers to the Agricultural Labourers' Union.

Things came to a head in the winter of 1913/14, when the Higdons were summarily dismissed for discourtesy to the governors and on a possibly trumped-up charge of caning two girl pupils. On 31st March 1914 the pair left the school, and, the following day, 66 of the 72 children marched around the village and conducted a protest meeting on the village green. An alternative school was opened by the villagers for the Higdons to teach in, first on the village green itself, later in a carpenter's shop. Later still, as the strike continued and became nationally, soon internationally, famous, subscriptions were collected from trade unions, philanthropists, even the new Russian revolutionary government. George Lansbury, the Labour Party leader, chaired the Strike Committee. A new building facing the village green was opened in 1917. The Strike School continued to operate in competition with the official village school until Tom Higdon's death in 1939, shortly followed by Annie Higdon's retirement (Van der Eyken and Turner, 1969: pp. 69–96; May with Berwick, 2014). Thus ended the longest strike in British history, and the only substantial education strike led by children (although there had been a series of children's strikes in more than sixty towns throughout the country during the long hot summer of 1911, which were part of an outbreak of labour unrest that year; see Marson, 1973). Each year, on the first Sunday in September, Burston becomes a mecca for trade unionists and educationalists as the initial village children's march 'around the candlestick' is re-enacted by brass bands and trade unions. The strike school building still stands as a museum and community hall, and some families in the village, divided one hundred years ago by support for or opposition to the strike, still barely speak to each other.

What is strategic and what is operational?

It is unlikely that any modern-day dispute between headteachers and their governing boards would gain such notoriety, or last so long, as the Burston strike. Nevertheless, the arenas of possible conflict between the two remain. As we have seen, the job of the governing board is to be strategic – and never operational (except sometimes). And the job of the headteacher is to be operational, with the day-to-day management of the school as their key task – except sometimes. For example, the headteacher is required, as a governor, or as their chief executive, to work with the governors in identifying the school's vision and ethos. However, some governors, and some directors/trustees of academies, shirk even this responsibility:

> Day-to-day operational management of the Academy is undertaken by the Senior Leadership Team (SLT) of Hipperholme and Lightcliffe High School, membership of which is highlighted in an earlier section of this report. *The SLT determines the strategic direction of the School*, making policy recommendations to the Governing Body.
>
> (HLHS Academy Trust Ltd, 2012, my italics)

Elsewhere, we have examples of headteachers thinking that they 'appoint' governors:

> New governors always start out enthusiastically. *When I appointed one recently*, she offered to remonstrate with parents of persistent latecomers. But scanning the front gate video screen in my office one day, she was astonished to see a parent slip a just-delivered two-litre bottle of staffroom milk under her coat and disappear down the street.
>
> (Mike Kent, *TES* 16th January 2009)

It is this kind of slipperiness that encouraged the professional associations to join with the National Governors' Association to produce a document explaining the respective responsibilities of heads and governors (Appendix 6).

In real life, the boundaries between strategic and operational are difficult to draw. The strategic becomes operational when it begins to become interpreted and implemented in the daily life of the school. Such interpretation is done largely by the head and the senior leadership. The point at which this change happens only exists in people's heads, but it becomes critical when the headteacher has made a decision or taken an action that produces a challenge, from governors, or pupils or parents. A decision to exclude a pupil leads facts and actions to be interpreted, sometimes differently, if the policy or procedure is insufficiently clear. Nevertheless, it is now clear that the DfE, at least, sees the head as responsible for taking any action that is reasonably required by the governors:

> Governing bodies should work to support and strengthen the leadership of the headteacher, and hold them to account for the day-to-day running of the school, including the performance management of teachers. Governing bodies should play a strategic role, and avoid routine involvement in operational matters. It should focus strongly on holding the headteacher to account for exercising his/her professional judgement in these matters and all of their other duties.

However, since the governing body is responsible in law for the school, it may need to intervene in operational matters if a circumstance arises where, because of the actions or inactions of the headteacher, the school may be in breach of a duty if the governing body did not intervene. Having advised the governing body, the headteacher must comply with any reasonable direction given by it (DfE, 2015a).

In what circumstances might the governing board intervene in operational matters? One example revolves around a few packets of crisps. A story told by the then Director of Education of an outer London borough in the early 2000s illustrates how a governing board might stray across the boundary between strategic and operational matters. The headteacher of an infant school became increasingly exercised about the amount of litter which always seemed to be blowing across the school's playgrounds. Most of this appeared to consist of empty crisp packets. One afternoon, fed up with the persistent untidiness of the site, she sat down and wrote a letter to the parents, announcing that the school would no longer allow children to bring crisps and similar snacks to school.

Predictably, all hell broke loose. Parents in the playground the following day asked who this woman thought she was, dictating to them what their children should be eating. Parent governors were approached, who agreed to speak to the chair who, in turn, told the head that he would have to convene a special meeting to get governors' views. The head declared that she would not be attending: the governors had no say in this matter as it was strictly operational. The meeting took place, without the head, and the governing board agreed a resolution to instruct the head to reinstate crisps. The head refused, and the governing board went to the LA and asked for its advice. By this time, the row had reached the headlines of the local paper. The LA referred the matter to its legal department.

This decision of the head's was clearly and unarguably a management decision. Should she not be left to sort out the shambles she had created herself? What children eat at break–times cannot be strategic, can it? Well, through the mishandling of a harmless issue, this initially purely operational issue had been *allowed* to become strategic, and had now fallen into the realm of governing board responsibility, empowering them to make the final decision and to make a now perfectly reasonable direction to the head.

Any operational matter can become strategic if it (a) has strategic implications, or (b) is sufficiently badly handled at operational level to require strategic interference.

At another school, the headteacher wrote to all parents expressing a general concern at the contents of children's packed lunches, with a not dissimilar knee-jerk response from them. In this second school, the head approached the chair with her problem, and the chair offered to 'make it strategic', an offer that, in this case, the head gratefully accepted. The governing board then established a working party of governors, staff and willing parents with a brief to explore the place of food in the school, including the contents of packed lunches and break–time snacks (with reference to the then Healthy Schools initiative), the sale of cakes at PTA events, the bringing into school of birthday cakes or sweets to be distributed by children to their classes – even the rewarding of correct answers by children with sweets, as practised by one teacher.

The working party consulted with parents, both on paper and face-to-face, and came up with a draft school policy, complete with rationale, which was then approved by the full governing board. The chair and head could then write jointly to the parents about the new policy as a *school* policy, fully consulted on and approved by the governors.

Interfacing with the head

One way of looking at the strategic/operational issue is to consider the occasions on which governing boards come together with their headteachers, and observe the level of the discussions taking place. These interfaces are likely to be the main arenas in which governance takes place in a school (see Gann, 2010b):

- governing board and committee meetings: are the topics discussed at a strategic level – how best does the school operate, what is it aiming for, what is the overall policy here?
- inspection: do governors have an overall understanding of school priorities and key performance measures, rather than a detailed knowledge of intricate data?
- self-evaluating the school: is the governing board overseeing the self-evaluation process and responding to it rather than contributing to it on a day-to-day basis? Are they asking about the impact of strategies in terms of pupil performance (including, for example, pupil premium expenditure and performance-related pay)?
- school improvement planning: is the governing board in on the beginning and the end of the process, setting priorities and agreeing monitoring and evaluating, rather than in the middle engaged in detailed preparation?
- monitoring and evaluating school performance: do governors engage in monitoring of the school's performance, rather than of individuals? Do governors monitor and evaluate the implementation of policies rather than procedures?
- engaging with external professional support: do governors receive and interrogate overall judgements of school performance rather than views on individuals?
- setting and agreeing the budget: are governors checking that the budget serves the overall priorities of the school and is achieving best value rather than concerning itself with minutiae?
- recruiting staff: are governors setting parameters for staff appointments, including a recruitment and retention policy, rather than getting involved in appointments at inappropriate levels?
- public occasions: do governors get involved in parents' evenings, open days, award ceremonies at a 'ceremonial' level, rather than getting into detailed discussions and practical activities?

Distinguishing the strategic from the operational

Despite the DfE's key requirement that governing boards are 'the strategic leaders of our schools', there are areas where governors inevitably will be involved with matters that border upon operational, if only in monitoring the school's performance, in overseeing expenditure, and so on, so board minutes and agenda should be explored to ensure that strategic matters dominate:

> The board should focus strongly on these core functions and avoid its time being consumed with issues of secondary importance. While a range of other issues may at times require the board's attention, this should not be at the expense of its ability to oversee and drive up the overall educational and financial performance of the school.
>
> (DfE, 2014a)

So an important occasion should be an annual governor's away day offering opportunities to articulate the vision – what might the school look like in three to five years' time? – to revisit the statement of the school's ethos (what it should feel like and be like to be in the school) or values (what principles and aspirations are expressed through the school's actions and decisions? See, for example, Collins, 2014). More of this in Chapter 10.

Does the head support and develop the governing board?

Two themes on the relationship between headteachers and their governing boards have developed over recent years. First, there is the increasing emphasis on the governing board's overall responsibility for the performance of the school and the head. Second, and perhaps contrarily, is the need for heads to take some responsibility themselves for the performance of the board:

> The governing body runs the school, with the head acting as their principal agent to do so. The head reports to the board. The main role of the governing body is not, in fact, *simply* to support the head. Governors need, in my mind, to be much more demanding of the head.
>
> (Roche, 2014)

Despite this, there are growing indications that some LAs take it into their hands to 'disappear' heads when their schools underperform at inspection, with or without consultation with the governors. This remains legally suspect, as the statutory position is unambiguous: the governing board is responsible in all schools (including multi-academy schools, where the statutory governing board is the board of trustees) for the appointment and dismissal of staff. Indeed, the other growing problem for heads is the way that some academy chains remove them without notice, imposing a new head on an unsuspecting staff and parent body at the beginning of a new term.

While in the past there was understandable concern at how difficult it was to get rid of a headteacher, nowadays the reverse seems to be true, and headteachers are almost as likely as football managers to get unceremoniously dumped when facing relegation to an Ofsted category.

Agnew suggests a number of ways in which heads should be helping to develop their governing boards. It is after all in headteachers' own interests that their governors are well-trained and professional in their behaviour. She identifies two types of failure in the relationship:

> one where the governing body has got this [responsibility] wrong, is aggressive, untrusting or interfering in their relationship with the head-teacher, and the other where the governing body has got it right and is trying to bring legitimate challenge but the headteacher isn't comfortable with it. These situations can be enormously upsetting for governors but, if the situation is not resolvable, as volunteers ultimately they can just walk away. But it can be career-ending for heads.
>
> (Agnew, 2014)

So what should they be doing? Agnew suggests:

- providing high quality, succinct, accessible information;
- providing information in advance;
- ensuring good clerking;
- ensuring a governor training budget;
- encouraging governors to be pro-active;
- encouraging self-evaluation.

But they should also be ensuring that they enable the board – some of whom may still be tentative about challenging a self-confident and asser-tive professional – to take its proper lead in planning, formulating policies, identifying school strengths and areas of development, ensuring all assertions are backed up by evidence, and so on. Appendix 7 offers a format for evalu-ating the head's contribution to the board – if a governing board takes this on, it is helpful if the head has also completed the questionnaire from their own perspective.

Does the governing board support and develop the head?

What duties does the governing board have to the head? We have seen the statutory position, above. In addition to this, perhaps:

- challenging and supporting in an appropriate professional manner (see, for example, Appendix 9 for useful things to say in a board meeting);
- providing effective and supportive performance management;
- ensuring the head gets good quality CPD;
- ensuring the head gets good professional support both internally and externally;
- ensuring and protecting, as far as possible, a good work–life balance;

- ensuring the governing board publicly takes responsibility for its decisions, and making this clear to parents and others when appropriate;
- ensuring staff morale and well-being are protected and developed;
- respecting the head's right to not know everything or have answers to everything;
- agreeing with the head the key performance indicators by which they will evaluate the way the job is done.

This last might, for example, be in the form of the 2004 National Standards for Headteachers (DfES, 2004, later updated). The six standards identified in this document give governors an invaluable platform to look at the head's performance across the range of duties and skills needed, as well as a useful way into performance management.

Does the governing board challenge the head?

Ofsted has suggested that the failure of governors to challenge the head appropriately undermines the running of the school. If governors are not providing sufficient challenge, improvement planning is unlikely to address the real priorities; governors will not understand how to interrogate the head; performance management will be weak as it will not be firmed up by accurate information; governors will be unable to know what impact they are having, if any, on school improvement; they will be unable to identify appropriate professional development for the staff; and the school will find itself on an unstoppable downward spiral.

'Superheads' and 'hero heads'

One of the most valuable things governors can do to support the head is to discount the popular construct of 'super-headship' (popular among politicians and some would-be or self-nominated 'superheads', that is) that developed in the 1990s, supposedly as a means of turning around 'failing' schools.

The new focus on 'education, education, education', aspiring prime minister Tony Blair's three priorities for government post the 1997 general election, brought with it a proliferation of language previously reserved for the shock and awe of Gulf Wars. Some of the chapter headings of a book on inner London Hackney Downs Boys School, for example, are: 'Gathering Clouds'; 'Crisis'; 'The "Race War"'; 'Save our School'; 'To the Rescue'; 'The "Hit Squad"' and 'Picking up the Pieces' – a series of reading adventures that might be more in place in the history of a military campaign. In the final chapter of this sad account, the actual metaphor raised is one of hunting:

Seeking out failing schools had, in the 1990s, become a rewarding pastime for politicians and for the media. A quarry run to ground could be publicly savaged and, if necessary, publicly done to death. The media can compete, as they did over other London schools in other boroughs, and in other parts of the country – notably The Ridings School in Halifax – to discover 'the worst school in Britain'.

(O'Connor et al., 1999: p. 241)

David (later Sir David) Winkley's account of his work at a Birmingham primary school is titled 'Handsworth Revolution: The Odyssey of a School' – two somewhat mutually contradictory metaphors in one short title, but both arousing images of conflict and stress (Winkley, 2002). Wars and conflicts, of course, need heroes. Who better to fill that role than the rescuer of a failing school, the superhead? A similar model was developed by Karpman in the drama triangle he created to illustrate and explain some of the interactions between individuals (or, in this case, organisations) engaged in conflict. Three roles – the persecutor, the victim and the rescuer – perform an endless dance in which they protect or sometimes interchange their parts. One of the characteristics of this process is that people can become trapped in their role because it satisfies a significant psychological need they have. In the case of failing schools, this need belongs as much to the onlooker as to the players.

The scenario plays out something like this: a school appears to be 'failing' to meet standards set by an external judge – parents, the media, Ofsted, the DfE. The school becomes the victim, according to one narrative, or, if the children are seen as the victim, the school becomes the persecutor. In either case, the rescuer is seen as the lone hero who rides in to sort things out. For the media, the narrative is more dramatic if it is a lone hero. For the DfE, the hero was 'business' – one of the non-educational companies brought in, like Tarmac or Harris Carpets, to sort out a problem the educational establishment could not deal with itself. In either case, the needs of the onlookers were met by investing all hope for change, not in the immediate players – the ones who would have to choose change for themselves if things were to improve – but in an incoming agency. For the DfE, in particular, it could be seen itself in a role in which it had never been cast before – a hands–on bit of government prepared to step in and rescue the persecuted. Who in government could resist such a casting?

Peter Clark had come from the experience of heading up a Calderdale school in some difficulties which merged with another to become successful. When the amalgamation of two other local Halifax secondaries into a new school faltered, Clark was called in, as reported on the radio: 'Peter Clark, the trouble–shooting superhead brought in to sort out the Ridings School in Halifax'. Success was registered in 1997 when the Ridings was not named by then Secretary of State David Blunkett as among the 18 worst schools in the country. Clark received a CBE for his work. It perhaps is not Clark's fault that he became a prototype for a model of headship that has been lauded by media and government alike. Most enthusiastic for the superhead model was Michael Gove, Secretary of State for Education in the coalition government between 2010 and 2014. Later models have been damed or knighted, as was the academy chain head praised by Gove: 'If anyone asked me what my ideal education policy would be it would be to clone Rachel 23,000 times' (Grimmer, 2012).

But these heads seem so often to run into trouble. During the coalition years, heads of school after school – mainly academies – were gleefully exposed as, variously, dipping into copious expense accounts, fiddling exam results, hiding poor exam results, giving contracts to friends and partners without governor knowledge, and being given illicit advance notice of Ofsted inspections (see, for example, Gann, 2014). Glittering prizes of dameships and knighthoods, some to be later ignominiously stripped, became common. When the Independent Academies Association met, there was hardly a plain headteacher to be seen among the principals, executive heads, chief executives and operating officers. The oft-expressed desire of politicians for schools to be 'run like businesses' seemed to have come true, with all its ugliness as well as its tinsel (see, for example, Dejevsky, 2013).

As far as governing boards are concerned, they need to return to some of the simple truths. What kind of leadership are they looking for? Amidst all the publicity of poor, sometimes illegal, behaviour, the National College of Teaching and Leadership was developing a model of distributive leadership which would grow new leaders in-house, while ensuring that the old image of the head as 'captain of the ship' would become outdated. None of this seemed to lighten the workload or help to redress what heads themselves often hollowly referred to as their 'work–life balance'.

The fact is that this model was forced on schools by, initially, the 'naming and shaming' of low-performing schools regardless of their intake, introduced in the 1990s. That any element of state provision has reached such a condition that it needs heroes to rescue it is a poor reflection on its overall governance. This kind of high profile, person-centred leadership has the potential to disengage, disempower and de-skill both staff and pupils. An organisation whose principal aim is the personal growth of all its members can hardly be run as an autocracy.

So the superhead or hero model of leadership in schools, though it remained popular in certain sections of the press, and with some of the less self-aware heads themselves, has to be seen as discredited. Other business models of organisational leadership offer a more subtle, complex, and ultimately more helpful model to governors.

'Antihero' headteachers: servant leaders and host leaders

What might an anti-hero headteacher look like – one who rejects 'superness' and seeks to lead in such a way as to enable personal and professional growth throughout the school, and to model such behaviour?

Two models bear looking at. The leader who sees themselves as the servant of the people has a history that dates back to early China and the Christian Bible. It was defined by Robert Greenleaf in his essay 'The Servant as Leader' in 1970:

> The servant-leader is servant first . . . It begins with the natural feeling that one wants to serve, to serve first. Then conscious choice brings one to aspire to lead. That person is sharply different from one who is leader first, perhaps because of the need to assuage an unusual power drive or to acquire material possessions . . . The leader-first and the servant-first are two extreme types. Between them there are shadings and blends that are part of the infinite variety of human nature. . . The difference manifests itself in the care taken by the servant-first to make sure that other people's highest needs are being served. The best test, and difficult to administer, is: Do those served grow as persons? Do they, while being served, become healthier, wiser, freer, more autonomous, more likely themselves to become servants? And, what is the effect on the least privileged in society? Will they benefit or at least not become further deprived?
>
> (Greenleaf, 1977; 1991)

The key behaviours of servant leadership can be summarised as:

- listening;
- empathy – understanding others' feelings and perspectives;
- healing – fostering emotional and spiritual health;
- awareness;
- persuasion;
- conceptualisation – integrating present realities and future possibilities;
- foresight;
- stewardship – holding an organization's resources in trust for the greater good;
- commitment to the growth of people and serving their needs;
- building community.

More recently, Mark McKergow and Helen Bailey have developed the theory of the leader as host (McKergow and Bailey, 2014). The basis of their metaphor is that leadership is not an activity conducted by an individual so much as a relationship between leader and led: 'If heroes step forward and servants step back, then the host does both' (McKergow and Bailey, 2014: p. 23). The host takes on six roles:

- the initiator of action;
- the inviter, who reaches out to people, brings them together and engages them;

- the space creator, who provides the environment;
- the gatekeeper, who sets boundaries and thresholds, and ultimately decides what is acceptable and what isn't;
- the connector, who interprets people's needs and interests and finds opportunities for them to relate productively to each other;
- the co-participator, who joins in with activities.

In preparing this metaphor, the present author worked with McKergow and Bailey to think through a list of ways in which a headteacher might act as a host leader:

- joining in with the staff and pupils;
- standing outside the school in the mornings and welcoming students and staff – creating an event and a ritual around the beginning of the day;
- smiling, nodding and engaging with pupils and staff when you see them in the corridor;
- welcoming visitors when they arrive or phone for an appointment – parents and stakeholders get priority over officers and representatives;
- being at assemblies and other events, even when not running them;
- participating with the governing board, working as a team rather than trying to get ahead; taking a problem along to work through together, rather than having the solution;
- joining in with meals, food and drink breaks;
- joining in with lessons;
- not spending time behind a desk.

'The host', as an old Arabic proverb has it, 'is both the first and the last' (McKergow and Bailey, 2014).

Non-hero heads, working collaboratively with students, staff, governors and parents, might consider the following advice when working with their governors:

- don't always be right – other people wonder why they're there if you can do it all by yourself;
- in fact, don't always know. The words 'I don't know' used by someone in authority open doors for others;
- give two or three alternatives when asked for suggestions with the pros and cons;
- don't always sit in the same place at meetings, to avoid establishing a 'power-place';
- try not to sit *behind* a desk at small meetings;

(continued)

(continued)

- explain things so that everyone can understand them, without being patronising;
- remember that the school doesn't belong to you – long after you're gone, the community will still be there;
- listen in a supportive, not an adversarial, way, and don't always feel you have to defend yourself;
- above all, don't be super! You're not supposed to be doing it all by yourself.

(Gann, 2005a)

Here are two interesting things said by two exceptional headteachers. The first was said by an outstanding primary school head in Dorset. Because he had developed an outstanding senior leadership team also, the local authority had him spend time in other primaries in special measures or otherwise in difficulties. When asked whether this was an unreasonable distraction from his own school, he replied, 'I have never yet worked in another school, however badly it appears to be failing, without finding that there was something they did better than we do, and learning from it'.

The second was said by a secondary headteacher in a large Devon comprehensive. He's talking about the ways in which he supports his staff, and mentions a weekly meeting he has with new staff over tea. Is this so that he can support them and mentor them through their induction? No, he has other staff who do that. He meets with them, he says 'So that they can tell me what's wrong with the place'.

Perhaps doubt is one of the greatest virtues that a headteacher can possess. As one such head wrote in the 1960s:

> [An American visitor] asked me whether I had any criticisms to make of English education, and when I had finished he said I seemed to be the only exception he had met to a complete permanent status quo. No other headmaster had had the slightest trace of an inkling that any British school was at all far from perfection . . . The disease was, and in 1962 I think still is, mainly a consequence of long-standing self-satisfaction.
>
> (Heckstall-Smith, 1962)

As the philosopher Bertrand Russell said, 'The whole problem with the world is that fools and fanatics are always so certain of themselves, and wiser people so full of doubts.' The best leaders know that they don't always know best.

Leading and managing

One of the questions that headteachers face in relation to their governing board is 'who does the leading?' We know from the DfE and Ofsted that the board is jointly responsible for setting the strategic direction of the school – which clearly is a leadership role. But the headteacher is there as day-to-day leader, with or without a leadership team.

Part of the head's role outside school hours is to work with and advise the governors on leadership matters; while in the school they represent and implement the wishes of the board. Meanwhile, they are doing a lot of, but not too much, managing.

Here are some of the differences between leading and managing, according to Warren Bennis, a pioneer of leadership studies (Bennis, 1989):

- The manager administers; the leader innovates.
- The manager is a copy; the leader is an original.
- The manager maintains; the leader develops.
- The manager focuses on systems and structures; the leader focuses on people.
- The manager relies on control; the leader inspires trust.
- The manager has a short-range view; the leader has a long-range perspective.
- The manager asks how; the leader asks what and why.
- The manager has his eye always on the bottom line; the leader has his eye on the horizon.
- The manager imitates; the leader originates.
- The manager accepts the *status quo*; the leader challenges it.
- The manager is the classic good soldier; the leader is his own person.
- The manager does things right; the leader does the right thing.

National standards for headship

One of the most useful documents for governors is the 2004 revision of the National Standards for Headteachers (DfES, 2004). This identifies key areas of the job, providing a list of the knowledge and the professional qualities required for each, together with suggestions for the actions which are needed. This might be seen as an indispensable document for governors who are developing a person specification for a headship vacancy, or who are engaged in the annual appraisal of a head in post. The standards identify six leadership roles:

- Shaping the future
- Leading learning and teaching
- Developing self and working with others
- Managing the organisation

- Securing accountability
- Strengthening community.

Although not as strong as it might be on the head's first accountability – towards the governing board – the document provides a comprehensive view of what the head's leadership role is. If they're doing all of this, and doing it effectively, they're doing the job. These standards were updated, but by no means improved upon, in 2015.

In sum, what we need to see is the headteacher acting as a chief executive, offering professional advice, not dictation; offering alternative courses of action, not single solutions; supporting the board, not purely expecting their support; enabling the organisation to be led by a team in partnership, not by an individual.

The headteacher as chief executive

What worries headteachers about governors?

Unrepresentativeness

Headteachers worry that governors are drawn from very limited sections of the community, and that they cannot reflect all the concerns of the parent body. In 1988, there seemed to be some concern that the new governing bodies would act as a brake on schools, with the stereotype of the parents who believe that their children's education should be as much like their own as possible. However, experience seems to show that parents and teachers are not dissimilar in what they want from schools, and may even see themselves in an alliance against the government's relentless demand for results. No system, however democratic, will ever be truly representative, although we should perhaps expect parent governors to at least reflect the interests and concerns of all the parents. Nevertheless, fears about governing boards being hi-jacked by small cliques are real, recent and seem to have some foundation. Dismissing the views of unrepresentative governing boards is not going to be the most effective method of dealing with the problem; continuing to respond to articulated needs, giving confidence to all parents, and so continually widening the pool from which governors can be recruited is likely to be more rewarding.

Aloofness

Heads seem to worry more about governors who do not get involved than those who might overdo it. The constant appeal from schools is to increase both the quantity and quality of community engagement, while appreciating that governors have lives, and often work, of their own.

Interfering

The corollary of the aloof governor is the one who is constantly and inappropriately interfering. Interference is a more obvious fault, one that can be identified and described to colleagues and the media, so it gets a high profile sometimes. Often, inappropriate behaviour of this type comes about because governors have not grasped what it means to be strategic. Sometimes there is an understandable confusion between the jobs that a governor does *as a governor* and those they might do as a friend of the school, such as listening to children reading, accompanying trips or helping in the classroom as a volunteer.

Prone to division

Governing boards that split along ideological, or sometimes political lines cause headteachers much anxiety. They may feel it is their job to maintain some semblance of private harmony and public unity, and sometimes they will be the only person who can do it. It is one of the reasons why regularly revisiting the school's vision and ethos is so important. The areas of consensus among governors with regards to the work with the students are likely to prove more durable than differences about structures or procedures. Sometimes, when really important issues divide governing boards, such as aims, priorities among children, teaching styles or grouping of children – boards try to duck discussing them so as to avoid rows. In fact, these differences then come out with wearying repetitiveness, manifested in 'trivia' such as endless discussions about uniform, minutiae of children's behaviour and such like. If the ethos statement is clear and comprehensive, the answers to these disputes should be found within it.

Lack of clarity of the role

Headteachers worry that governors do not understand their role. Sometimes, headteachers do not understand what the role is – during the period when the National Professional Qualification for Headship was compulsory, the governance module was only one small and optional module for them. The number of schools without a genuine vision statement which is regularly reviewed by the board suggests they may be right.

What governing boards need for a good relationship with the head

Governing boards need to:

- define and regularly revisit the nature of the partnership – perhaps along the lines of the ASCL/NGA/NAHT document (2015: Appendix 6) but with some specifics relating to the school's particular situation;

- have an agreed code of conduct – perhaps as in Appendix 3;
- have clear decision-making structures in place – with transparent procedures for delegation;
- have an agreed statement of governor's rights – for example of visiting, access to information and so on;
- have a governors' handbook – with all necessary information and advice;
- agree the issues and format of the head's report;
- have a regular programme of training and development – to which all governors, including the head, are committed;
- share the vision of the school regularly;
- follow a clear cycle of activities within a framework of governance.

Appraisal of the headteacher

One of the most effective ways of ensuring that the school stays on tracks laid down by the governing board, says Chris James, Professor of Education at the University of Bath, is good use of the performance management process. James heads the foremost research team into school governance in England, and co-authored a National College document on this subject (Spicer et al., 2014).

The requirement for governors to appraise (at the time, 'performance manage') the head, with the support of an external adviser, and to oversee the head's appraisal of the teaching staff, came in around the turn of the twenty-first century. It was always seen as a way in which the leadership of the school, both lay and professional, could cohere around agreed standards and priorities:

> Performance management provides a real opportunity to unite the governing body and the whole school workforce in their primary task – securing high standards of education for all their pupils. It sets a framework to achieve school improvement and ensure well-trained, well-motivated staff who feel valued and who reflect on their own practice and how it can be developed and improved.
>
> (DfES, 2003)

The avowed intent of the programme was to offer performance management as a right that staff have, to know how the school management evaluates their performance, and at the same time to ensure that staff see continuing professional development (CPD) as a professional duty they have towards their workplace – as opposed to the other way around, perhaps the historical way that staff have looked at appraisal and CPD. The imposition of performance-related pay against, it would appear, the wishes of the large majority of teachers and governors, has soured some of these ideals – arguably by ensuring that the focus shifted from improving performance to justifying it. Nevertheless, appraisal still holds a central position in school improvement.

According to Spicer et al., it also defines effective governance: 'there is a strong case for arguing that the way headteacher performance management is carried out is a leitmotif for governing body effectiveness. Effective head-teacher performance management indicates effective governing; the two are complementary' (Spicer et al., 2014). The features identified as effective performance management are:

- it is integrated within the school development plan;
- there is an annual cycle of objective-setting and review, with interim monitoring;
- there are sound relationships, based on openness, trust and integrity among those involved;
- objectives set for the head are meaningful, challenging but achievable;
- there is an appropriate balance between internal and external accountability, development and reward;
- a wide variety of data is used to inform and underpin decision-making;
- the process is evaluated and adapted as requirements and circumstances change;
- the process matches the stage of development of the school and the head;
- the process is seen as part of a wider process of working with the head and staff to ensure best performance;
- 'effective headteacher performance management is integral to the development of overall governing body capacity to meet the needs of the school' (Spicer et al., 2014).

The conduct of performance management throughout the school is not an additional responsibility laid on governors because there is no other suitable place to put it, but it is one of the tools that governing boards apply to enable them to discharge their fundamental roles of ensuring a coherent strategic direction for the school, and holding the head and staff to account for its performance.

Appointing the headteacher

This is not the place for a detailed guide to headship appointment. However, it would be appropriate to lay down a few markers for governors to take into consideration when doing this most important task.

First, there should as far as possible be full involvement of every governor. While statutory regulations require the appointment of a selection panel, there is no reason why this should not comprise every governor who can make themselves available, including, of course, staff governors. Every governor should understand what is involved in making the appointment of their key employee, and be committed to both the process and the successful candidate.

The observance of standard equal opportunities throughout the process, with advice from a professional as to what that entails, is critical. One of the worst things that can happen in a headship appointment is a challenge to the process from an unsuccessful applicant. A detailed process with thorough and contemporaneous documentation is essential. But the real purpose of equal opportunities procedures, of course, is that you do end up with the best possible candidate – that is, the best possible match for your person specification.

This requires a clear distinction between the familiarisation process, when candidates meet people in the school to find out whether they would like to work there, and the selection process. Blurring these runs the risk of nonsenses like 'social' testing, which is inherently unfair (unless you have written, 'knows how to drink soup silently' into your person spec – which is not recommended unless it is an essential skill for your school). Also, if this distinction is clear to staff, you should avoid staff canvassing for their favourite, or against their least favourite, candidate – an embarrassment all round.

Try also to ensure that every governor who wishes is present, though not necessarily actively involved, in the very final interview followed by the decision-making. This again should avoid later recrimination and the 'well, I never thought we'd chosen the right person anyway' syndrome.

The person specification is the key document. Putting this together, with the involvement of, say, staff, students and parents (but final decision-making by the governing board) is the most important bit of the process. The spec will take into consideration the unique situation and needs of the school at this point in its history, so it can't just be borrowed from somewhere else. It must include the skills, knowledge and experience required, as well as the personal qualities you are looking for to match the school's needs. And there must be an understanding of how those things can be assessed through the selection process. Skills, knowledge and experience are not too difficult to identify – often through the application form and letter – but assessing the personality of the candidates is difficult but critical.

The principal question is: what is a good head – for our school, at this point in time? Some generalities might include: appoint an honest head; appoint a hard-working head; appoint a modest head (one who doesn't claim to have all the answers); appoint a caring head (about people, not just data); appoint a head who shares the governing body's ethos, values and aspirations; appoint a generous head who likes people (even people who work in schools) and children.

And conversely: avoid an arrogant head; avoid a know-all head; avoid a data-driven head; avoid a defensive head; and avoid a head who doesn't show you respect. Above all, find a happy head who enjoys their work. A happy head and a happy governing body have a very good chance of making a happy school.

The governing board and the staff of the school

Governors and the conduct of staff

One of the great educators of the twentieth century was Harry Rée, once professor of education at York University, and later classroom teacher in London, and a great advocate of community education. Tim Brighouse, shortly after Harry Rée's death in 1991, told this story: 'Before he was appointed head of Watford Grammar School, Hertfordshire's famous chief education officer, John Newsom, asked him what he would look for above all when appointing teachers. "An angel must have descended on my shoulders," he confided as he recalled his pause and his one word reply, "generosity".'

As a general rule, governors should not get involved in appointing staff. That is an operational matter, unless it is vacancies in the senior leadership team in question. There may be two exceptions, however.

In small schools founded in their own communities, where applicants for posts such as classroom assistants, supervisors and premises staff are likely to be parents or otherwise connected with the school, it may be helpful if the governing board, rather than the headteacher alone, is seen to be making the appointments. So a committee of head and governors is advisable.

Secondly, governors who are not used to the selection of professional staff need to get some practice for the appointment of a headteacher – as we have seen elsewhere, the single most important job that governing boards do. So some involvement for such governors in teaching appointments may be helpful. But the purpose of the governors' presence should be clear, and should not detract from the overall responsibility of the head as delegated by the governors.

But GBs should lay down the parameters and the procedures for heads to follow. The first imperative here is a code of professional conduct – the need for which is heavily implied by the DfE's teachers' standards:

> A teacher is expected to demonstrate consistently high standards of personal and professional conduct. The following statements define the behaviour and attitudes which set the required standard for conduct throughout a teacher's career.
>
> - Teachers uphold public trust in the profession and maintain high standards of ethics and behaviour, within and outside school, by:
>   - treating pupils with dignity, building relationships rooted in mutual respect, and at all times observing proper boundaries appropriate to a teacher's professional position;
>   - having regard for the need to safeguard pupils' well-being, in accordance with statutory provisions;
>   - showing tolerance of and respect for the rights of others;

     o   not undermining fundamental British values, including democracy, the rule of law, individual liberty and mutual respect, and tolerance of those with different faiths and beliefs;

     o   ensuring that personal beliefs are not expressed in ways which exploit pupils' vulnerability or might lead them to break the law.

- Teachers must have proper and professional regard for the ethos, policies and practices of the school in which they teach, and maintain high standards in their own attendance and punctuality.
- Teachers must have an understanding of, and always act within, the statutory frameworks which set out their professional duties and responsibilities.

(DfE, 2013)

So the first step a governing board should take is to encapsulate these in a clear but brief ethos statement about its expectations of all staff – not, of course, just teachers.

Strangely, this imperative comes about through one of Ofsted's priorities for governing bodies of maintained schools: that they should oversee performance management more rigorously. The conduct of teacher appraisal in schools – apart from the headteacher's own performance management – is the responsibility of the headteacher. But Ofsted is now clear that the governors must make sure that it is happening, and that it is producing results.

Governors must 'provide challenge and hold the headteacher and other senior leaders to account for improving the quality of teaching'; and they must 'use performance management systems to improve teaching' (Ofsted 2014b).

Not that lay governors should be monitoring the teaching themselves, of course. But they now have to ensure that there are robust systems in place, and that it is bringing about consistent improvement in teaching.

How can they do this, without treading on the toes of the professionals? We'll assume that governing bodies already have in place their appraisal policy and their capability policy, and that they are getting formal annual reports from the head on performance management throughout the school. And we'll assume that they conduct the appraisal of the head as rigorously as they can.

The updated Teachers' Standards (DfE, 2013) provide eight benchmarks against which *all* teachers can be assessed, whatever type of school they serve in. These are:

- setting high expectations which inspire, motivate and challenge pupils;
- promoting good progress and outcomes by pupils;
- demonstrating good subject and curriculum knowledge;
- planning and teaching well-structured lessons;
- adapting teaching to respond to the strengths and needs of all pupils;

- making accurate and productive use of assessment;
- managing behaviour effectively to ensure a good and safe learning environment;
- fulfilling wider professional responsibilities, including managing support staff, contributing to the life and ethos of the school and communicating with parents.

Many of these standards can and should be applied to other staff in the school, of course.

Governors need to make sure that their headteacher is reporting to them on the extent to which these standards are being met in the school – not by individuals (except where there are capability issues), but by the staff as a whole.

But the document goes on to specify a 'required standard for conduct throughout a teacher's career'. It is this section which governing bodies should be expanding into a code of conduct for all staff. This should not be overprescriptive. But it should express the governing body's views on the culture and ethos of the school, to which all staff need to sign up.

No governing body would put such a code in place, we hope, without consulting with staff. So this requirement is an opportunity rather than a restraint, and can be met by a period of collective consideration in schools, with *all* staff and governors, students and parents, coming together to decide: 'what sort of school do we want this to be?' And, 'this is how we're going to achieve it'.

This document can then be used to provide a person specification for all jobs in the school.

Other staff responsibilities of the board

The staffing structure

One of the strategic responsibilities of the governing board, perhaps through a Human Resources Committee, is to ensure that there is a document showing the current staffing structure of the school and any ideal structure towards which the school is working. This will be a standard part of the school's development plan. It provides guidance to the senior staff in the vacancies they identify and the appointments they make. Increasingly, the question of the qualifications the governing board expect staff to have is coming into play. More than 400,000 schoolchildren were being taught by unqualified teachers by the turn of 2015. To what extent is this an issue in academies and free schools? Such former certainties as NPQH for headteachers and qualified teacher status for teachers can no longer be taken for granted.

Oversight of staff appraisal

The governing board needs to ensure that staff appraisal is being conducted and that the objectives set for staff reflect the school's priorities as defined by them.

It needs to see the outcomes of the appraisal cycle, and to ensure that the pay policy reflects staff performance. The embedding of performance-related pay in schools continues – although there is precious little evidence for its effectiveness. Nevertheless, at the time of writing, one of the three most common areas for the Ofsted team questioning of governors is about the way that pay reflects performance.

Certainly, the governors need to have an understanding of the *overall* competence and effectiveness of staff, and what measures they need to ensure are in place to develop them – including the support of continuing professional development that the school offers, and the challenge of effective capability procedures. This will form a central part of the head's reports to governors.

Paying the staff

There is some evidence that pay differentials in academies, where there are far greater freedoms currently than in maintained schools, may be as much as three times greater. The perceived and actual fairness of remuneration is critical to staff well-being. And, after all, where there are exceptional rewards (such as inflated salaries and pay in kind, such as private health insurance), the questions have to be asked: 'Who is getting these benefits?' and 'Where would the money be spent if it wasn't going into the pockets of the leadership?'

Knowing about the staff

Staff well-being is not only a clear employer responsibility of the governing board in any school – indeed, in any organisation – but is likely to be a factor in the organisation's performance (as Briner and Dewberry, 2007 have shown). Work–life balance, as research has shown, is probably more difficult to achieve in schools than in almost any other profession. The ever-increasing requirement for continuous assessment of student performance in addition to the planning needs of a constantly changing curriculum leads to long weekly working hours for all teaching staff and constant pressure in school.

Objective evaluations of staff well-being should be carried out annually for the governing board to monitor morale, and to provide support for strategies to address issues raised by the staff.

Knowing the staff

While there is a strong argument for the need for governors in all types and sizes of schools to maintain a professional distance from staff, staff and governors should have some knowledge of each other and what their work is. Governors should visit the school in working hours and meet and talk with staff, and occasionally see them at work – knowing the way the core business of the school is performed is really important. It will enable meaningful decision-making at board level, as well as supplementing the information that governors get from senior leaders. Similarly, staff should have some knowledge about who governors are and what their responsibilities are.

There is certainly a strong case for bringing the whole organisation together at least once a year – perhaps at the beginning of the school year, to evaluate together the school's performance in the year just finished and to establish key priorities for the coming year. The power of putting in one room, if it is physically possible, everyone who works for the school, paid or volunteer, cannot be underestimated.

The shared mission

Developing a shared sense of mission is one of the most important tasks that face governors and senior managers. The key to a successful working relationship with staff is the sense of collegiality, of shared purpose, that the governing board is able to develop. This fails in some schools through ignorance – the governors' ignorance of what staff do, the conditions they work in and the constraints they work under; the staff's ignorance of the governing board's role. First, governors and staff must share an understanding of their respective roles. Secondly, they must develop the confidence in each other to fulfil those roles in partnership, in order to jointly offer to students and the community the best a school can do.

Chapter 6

School governance and school inspection

A consideration of the impact inspection has on school governance

If one of the biggest problems in writing about school governance in England is the rapid changes to which it is subject, how much more is that the case with school inspection? Since the creation of the Office for Standards in Education, Children's Services and Skills (Ofsted) in 1992, there have been at least annual – often more frequent – changes in its conduct and focus. At various times over the years, school governance has been respectively ignored, then had extraordinary detail and focus laid on it, and later, with the advent of no-notice inspection, run the danger of being judged only by its documentation.

Ofsted introduces itself by saying that 'we report directly to Parliament and we are independent and impartial. We inspect and regulate services which care for children and young people, and those providing education and skills for learners of all ages.' However, its independence and impartiality, always questionable, came under intense scrutiny during the coalition government, when there appeared to be increasing tensions between the secretary of state for education, journalist and policy thinktank founder Michael Gove, and the chief of Ofsted, Her Majesty's Chief Inspector and former superhead, Michael Wilshaw.

The birth of Ofsted

Until 1992 school inspection had been a pretty haphazard affair. Her Majesty's Inspectors of Schools (HMI), as we saw in Chapter 1, have been around since the earliest days of state funding. For a period they were actually responsible for testing the children in order to establish how much funding the school (but not the staff) should receive. Matthew Arnold, whom we met earlier, railed against this practice in a (not very) anonymous pamphlet on the introduction of Payment by Results in 1862. Payment by Results, he argued, would lead to

> cutbacks which would 'lower the standard of popular education', at a time when schools were beginning to make progress in their wider aim of compensating for deprived educational backgrounds. By focusing on a narrow

cost–cutting yardstick, the proposal treated a school as 'a mere machine for teaching reading, writing and arithmetic' rather than 'a living whole with complex functions, religious, moral and intellectual'. Arnold wanted to meet 'the strong desire of the lower classes to raise themselves' by giving them the means to acquire a full share in cultural life rather than just a few basic skills.

(Murray, 1997: p. 193)

This probably provides a clue as to where Arnold might have stood on today's methods of judging school performance.

Alfred Graves, a schools inspector between the times of Arnold and Edmond Holmes (see Chapter 3) was also a much-published poet like Arnold, though less remembered today. However, his son, Robert, was the famous First World War poet and author of the 1929 autobiography *Goodbye to All That*. Schools inspection seemed to inspire poets and visionaries in a way that is sadly lacking today.

Throughout the twentieth century, HMI remained a powerful force in education in the UK and Northern Ireland, leading curriculum development, providing advice on best practice in schools, and occasionally inspecting schools – although often a visitation, well signalled in advance, was to look at particular aspects of the curriculum or the conduct of schools, as much for research purposes as for making judgements on the individual school. Much of the onus of judging schools fell on professional educators employed by local authorities. The fact that many of these were titled 'advisers' gives an idea of how they, and their schools, saw themselves, although they increasingly became local inspectors as the government called for more rigour in the oversight of state-funded schools.

Schools might expect an HMI inspection about every ten years. Their reports were confidential to the school and its local authority until 1983. The accountability function of inspection, then, until the early 1980s, remained very much within the education establishment. Schools were not legally obliged to implement the findings of any report, and HMI tended to concentrate on giving good quality advice. Their other duties were to disseminate their overall findings about the education that schools were providing, and to spread good practice. They did this by means of their publications, conferences and in-service teacher training. The annual report of the chief inspector carried enormous weight, especially when, as it often did, it criticised the government for under-resourcing local authorities.

From the inception of Ofsted, inspection became a very different kettle of fish. Most actual inspection was handed out to registered inspectors who, increasingly over the next twenty years, were part of a small, then very small number of private or third sector companies. During 2014, it was announced that all inspections were to be brought back in-house.

After a period when there was a confusing proliferation of documentation for schools (and inspectors) to negotiate, including frameworks, schedules, codes of conduct and subsidiary advice, every part of the inspection process by the end of 2014 was governed by the Ofsted Handbook: 'This handbook now forms the single key resource for the inspection of schools under section 5, except for the additional detailed guidance on safeguarding provided in "inspecting safeguarding in maintained schools and academies"' (Ofsted, 2014b).

The theory behind this is that inspections should be:

- systematic – they follow written procedures;
- uniform – they follow the same procedures;
- consistent – the outcome of inspection should be predictable and repeatable by another team;
- assessed against criteria – all judgements will relate to the areas of the school's work, and against statements of good practice, addressed in the handbook;
- based on evidence – every judgement must be supported by evidence, for example, behaviour observed or documentation seen.

So it should be. But life is not always so simple and human beings, even schools inspectors, are not automata. Different teams do behave differently, and individuals in teams behave differently. As inspection has developed it has, perhaps, become a less attractive prospect for education professionals, including former headteachers. The hours are long and the rewards not necessarily attractive. As handbook has succeeded schedule and framework succeeded guidance, keeping up-to-date with expectations has become onerous in itself. More and more, the nature of the judgement has come to rely on data which are generated from test and exam results. Pupil attainment and, to a lesser degree, achievement (progress) drive the inspection process and determine judgements in other areas. Perhaps this still unfairly disadvantages schools with intakes from challenged neighbourhoods – potentially increasingly so, as we move from a country where the numbers of children growing up in poverty move from one in four to one in three. Perhaps it also unfairly advantages schools where the senior leadership is particularly adept with statistics. The answer for those schools that have had a 'bad year' pre-Ofsted is to produce a raft of internally generated data to combat RAISE online The school that argues successfully against an Ofsted pre-judgement or placement in a category, if it is borderline, may be the school with the best mathematicians amongst its staff, rather than its pupils.

So two suspicions have emerged – first, that inspection is not a process of quality assurance, as it was originally intended to be, but of quality control.

'**Quality control** . . . involves the detection and elimination of components or final products which are not up to standard. It is an after-the-event process concerned with detecting and rejecting defective items. . . . Quality control is usually carried out by quality professionals known as quality controllers or inspectors . . . **Quality assurance** . . . is to prevent faults occurring in the first place. Quality is designed into the process to attempt to ensure that the product is produced to a predetermined specification. Simply, quality assurance is a means of producing defect- and fault-free products.'

(Sallis, 1993: p. 26)

Does the existence of a detailed schedule imply that the process of inspection is actually a check on school compliance with an Ofsted-set standard? Do the ever-changing political imperatives and obsessions mean that schools – and inspectors – are always running to keep up with the latest focus – safeguarding, the advancement of 'British Values', the latest statement on teaching styles or grouping of children? Certainly it would appear that many schools treat inspection as an exercise in compliance. This leads to some uncomfortable moments, as when one of the factors supposedly bringing about an inspection resulting in special measures, was that the governors had not met their statutory obligations in relation to the information that should be published on the school's website. Which report's publication at the beginning of the school year 2014–15 resulted in a flurry of heads spending the early days of the term frantically checking their school websites. Similarly, an inspection around the same time was supposedly generated by a parental complaint about the curriculum information available.

Failure in inspection has since 1992 become something to be avoided at all costs. Not only does it bring public humiliation and local suspicion on the school and its staff, with the consequent lowering of morale. Nowadays, it can bring the end of a career, not just to senior leaders, and an imposed change to the status to the school.

So inspections may be:

- undiscriminating – they do not necessarily make allowances for the individual circumstances of schools and their intake;
- punitive – some schools fail, and the penalty may be dismissal of staff or closure, or enforced change of status;
- unpredictable – it may be difficult to know whether the inspectors' interpretation of data is the same as the school's;
- unreliable – it is not certain that teams can replicate each other's outcomes, and a change in political priorities can result in some surprising *volte-faces*,

as again in the Trojan Horse fiasco, where 'outstanding' schools with excellent results overnight found themselves branded 'inadequate';
- public – success and failure, especially failure, are reported, even headlined in the press;
- stressful – the process, perhaps especially under a no-notice regime, means that schools never know within a term or two when the inspectors may call, and find themselves being ever 'Ofsted-ready'.

At the time of writing, school inspections focus on four areas: pupil achievement; quality of teaching; behaviour and safety of pupils; leadership and management. Each area is graded 1 (outstanding) to 4 (inadequate). Inadequate ratings lead to the placement of a school in category, which leads to further action and monitoring. Both these categories and the frequency of inspection, varying for schools graded as outstanding, good, requiring improvement or inadequate, are regularly subject to revision.

Inspecting governance

Judgements on governance have also changed frequently since 1992, with various approaches to expressing Ofsted's expectations, such as grade descriptors in the 2009 framework.

This set of expectations was issued in autumn 2014:

Inspectors should consider whether governors:

1. carry out their statutory duties, such as safeguarding, and understand the boundaries of their role as governors;
2. ensure that they and the school promote tolerance of and respect for people of all faiths (or those of no faith), cultures and lifestyles; and support and help, through their words, actions and influence within the school and more widely in the community, to prepare children and young people positively for life in modern Britain;
3. ensure clarity of vision, ethos and strategic direction, including long-term planning (for example, succession);
4. contribute to the school's self-evaluation and understand its strengths and weaknesses, including the quality of teaching, and reviewing the impact of their own work;
5. understand and take sufficient account of pupil data, particularly their understanding and use of the school data dashboard;
6. assure themselves of the rigour of the assessment process;
7. are aware of the impact of teaching on learning and progress in different subjects and year groups;
8. provide challenge and hold the headteacher and other senior leaders to account for improving the quality of teaching, pupils' achievement

and pupils' behaviour and safety, including by using the data dash-board, other progress data, examination outcomes and test results; or whether they hinder school improvement by failing to tackle key concerns or developing their own skills;

9   use the pupil premium and other resources to overcome barriers to learning, including reading, writing and mathematics;

10   ensure solvency and probity and that the financial resources made available to the school are managed effectively;

11   are providing support for an effective headteacher;

12   monitor performance management systems and understand how the school makes decisions about teachers' salary progression, including the performance management of the headteacher, to improve teaching, leadership and management;

13   engage with key stakeholders;

14   are transparent and accountable, including in terms of recruitment of staff, governance structures, attendance at meetings, and contact with parents and carers.

(Ofsted 2014b, pp. 47–48, para. 165)

The evidence inspectors use to reach their judgement will be, as well as observation of the school and conversations with senior staff, the school website, the school self-evaluation, the agenda and minutes of governing board meetings, and a conversation with one or more governors.

The governing board should therefore – and this almost certainly holds true for any inspection regime likely in the foreseeable future – ensure that governors should know:

- that governing board documentation will enable inspectors to make positive judgements of its meetings, appropriately reflecting the major strategic concerns of the school and demonstrating a robust and professional relationship with the headteacher – specifically, demonstrating the board's capacity to challenge and support the headteacher and hold them accountable for the performance of the school;

- the key priorities of the school, its strengths and its areas for improvement, and what the school and the board are doing to address them;

- what impact the board has on the school and the evidence it has to support that view;

- what parents and pupils think of the school, and how that impacts on their strategic actions;

- how the school ensures that there is strong financial oversight of the school, and how key elements of its budget are spent, such as the pupil premium, the sports premium (where appropriate), and the staffing budget in relation to the exercise of staff appraisal and performance-related pay;

- what role they play in setting the strategic direction of the school, including the content of the development plan and its monitoring, and the school's self-evaluation.

Appendix 4 is a detailed checklist of the possible expectations of an inspection team, although the details will change from time to time. The key to this approach is, again, that all governors should know something about everything – that is, the headlines of the school's performance and priorities – and everything about something – which enables the inspectors to know that one person has a detailed handle on every significant matter.

From the latter part of 2012, inspectors were quizzing governors – usually, of course, the chair, but these events work better if the chair can be accompanied by, at least, committee chairs and a vice chair – in the following areas (from the Ofsted website):

- performance management and its relationship to performance-related pay (a chair of governors reported in October, 2014, that an inspector had recently probed 'in detail' how governors knew that their pay awards matched the quality of teaching);
- how governors monitor achievement for different groups of pupils – i.e. by gender, ability, ethnic origin, measurements of poverty and so on;
- how governors monitor staff performance;
- governors' use and understanding of performance data;
- governors' monitoring procedures, including visits to the school;
- self-evaluation of the school;
- governors setting targets and checking progress;
- monitoring of the pupil premium;
- arrangements for external reviews of governance.

External reviews of governance

Inspectors were empowered at this time to require schools that were categorised as 'requiring improvement' or worse to commission an external review of governance – although no nationally consistent guidance was given about the content, nature of the outcome and legitimate providers. There also seemed to be no obvious quality control over the product. This practice was extended in 2014 to embrace any school where the inspection team felt that the governing board might benefit from such an exercise.

The governing board and the conduct of the inspection

The role of governors in inspection has been a subject of some contention for many years – should 'volunteers' be subjected to inspection and interrogation about their roles? Why is the headteacher the key contact when the responsible authority is the governing board? Should governors be kept in touch with the draft report? Should governors be present at the inspection team's report back?

Ofsted is clear that it is the head's duty to tell the governors when the inspection is announced, and to arrange for a meeting with the chair, and, where possible, other governors. The inspector should try to get as many governors as possible to attend the feedback meeting, too. The head should share the draft report with the chair and the rest of the board – after all, they are the responsible body. The lead inspector is entitled to see any governing board documentation, including minutes – even confidential minutes. These are important elements. They demonstrate that, for Ofsted purposes, the governing board *is* the school, not a group of enthusiastic amateurs who can be excluded from the serious business.

What inspectors say about governors

The inspectors' judgement on the governance of a school can be critical. Perhaps the most dramatic example of this to come to light was the report on a Cheshire High School in 2013. In the three categories, of 'achievement of pupils', 'quality of teaching' and 'behaviour and safety of pupils', the school is judged to be grade 2 ('good'). The verdict on the school's leadership and management, however, is that it 'requires improvement'. The three reasons given for this are that the governing body:

- does not have an accurate enough view of students' achievement, because it does not have a firm enough understanding of data, especially data relating to how well different groups of students achieve;
- does not have enough knowledge of the school's strengths and weaknesses to provide sufficient challenge and support to senior leaders' successful drive to make the school better;
- is not sufficiently involved in checking how effectively the school deploys its resources.

(Ofsted, 2013c)

These three points lead to the school being graded *overall* as 'requiring improvement' – a category that now carries the assumption of regular monitoring and inspection until it improves, and possible forced conversion to academy status for maintained schools.

There are a couple of conclusions that can be reached from this, both of which are uncomfortable for governors. First, the governing board's actions – or lack of actions – by themselves can bring a school down by a whole grade. Perhaps even more worryingly, it shows that a school may perform perfectly well – in this case – without an effective governing board.

Now it would be a shame if governors spent more time trying to meet Ofsted's expectations than governing the school well. Governance should not be about compliance – or about standardisation and prescription which, as education academic and administrator Michael Barber once said, are simply what gets you from awful to adequate, rather than from good to great. Nevertheless, there is sense in looking at how Ofsted looks at governance – with the caveat that some inspection teams understand governance better than others.

'Outstanding' governance

In outstanding schools, governing boards are fully engaged in giving the school direction. They meet their statutory obligations, especially safeguarding; they visit to look at the school working; they get thorough, clear reports from the head, the format and content of which they have agreed together; they understand what the school does well and what areas need further work; they are robust in holding the head to account for the school's performance, including its financial performance; they contribute to improvement plans, and they see a clear connection between teacher quality and teacher pay. They see how the school performs relative to similar schools, and how groups of pupils perform relative to each other. Currently, governance is not graded separately from leadership and management although, as we saw, it can be judged separately. In secondary schools, 16 per cent of leadership is outstanding, and in primary schools, 10 per cent (figures from Ofsted for 2013).

Here are the team's comments on outstanding governance in a Cheshire primary school:

> Governors have reviewed their membership, roles and responsibilities and taken action to broaden their expertise and ensure good parent representation. Under the leadership of the outstanding Chair, governors are further developing their links into school so that they receive information at first-hand and are able to question, challenge and support staff and pupils exceptionally well. They have a clear view of pupil's achievement and the quality of teaching. They ensure performance management is linked to school improvements and pay progression is appropriately matched to consistently good and outstanding teaching. Governors ensure funding is spent appropriately including the pupil premium and primary sports funding and have taken steps to strengthen the leadership of the work with those receiving the pupil premium. This has resulted in improved achievement of these pupils. Safeguarding is an absolute priority, is managed extremely well and meets requirements.
>
> (Ofsted, 2014d)

Perhaps two qualities sum up this governing board: knowledge and engagement.

'Inadequate' governance

Descriptions of inadequate governance tend to be a list of things that governors *don't* do. In a school that, unusually, declined from 'outstanding' to 'inadequate' in a space of four years, governors were, principally, 'not rigorous enough in holding leaders to account for the school's performance':

> The governing body has not been able to stem the decline in the school's effectiveness.
>
> The school's evaluation of its own performance is extremely over-generous. The reports to governors which leaders provide do not give clear enough information about how the school is doing compared to other schools. Consequently, governors, along with leaders, have an unrealistic picture of the school's effectiveness.
>
> The governing body does not hold the school to account for the progress pupils make. Governors are not aware of the proportions of pupils making good progress in the school and have not ensured that the additional funding for eligible pupils is giving best value.
>
> Governors have not been given a clear analysis of the quality of teaching. Consequently, they do not challenge leaders effectively and ensure that teachers' performance is linked to salary progression.
>
> (Ofsted, 2014e)

This would appear to be a governing board that, presented with an outstanding leadership, took its eye off the ball and was overly complacent about the school:

> Governors are a mixed group. Some governors, particularly the newer ones, know that the work of the school is not currently good enough, and have been appropriately challenging as well as supportive. Others see the school's problems as the fault of the local authority or as a result of the complex students it takes. Overall, this leads to insufficient challenge and too many excuses being made for the school's performance. Governors do not use the information they receive from the school well enough to know how successfully the school is performing or to provide the right level of support and challenge. They do not know enough about how well teachers are performing, the outcomes for students or the impact of the pupil premium funding. Several governors, and particularly the Chair, have worked hard to provide practical support. For example, they were heavily involved in supporting the redundancy process in the recent past.
>
> (Ofsted, 2014f)

This is a school where the governing board has allowed the school's financial position to deteriorate to 'crisis' level, and where its relationship with its local authority appears to be marked by distrust.

Overall judgements on schools

In the autumn of 2014 Ofsted analysed the characteristics of governing boards that were failing to turn schools around with sufficient alacrity and identified four traits:

- chairs in post too long;
- governors not sufficiently strategic or evaluative;
- governors diverted by building projects, falling rolls or academy conversion;
- internal turbulence.

Statistical analysis of inspections in the calendar year 2013 showed the following outcomes of overall grading, together with grading by category:

All secondary schools (percentage – 1990 schools), as shown in Table 6.1.

All primary schools (percentage – 9356 schools), as shown in Table 6.2.

It should be remembered that good and outstanding schools are currently inspected significantly less frequently, so are under-represented in these figures. The other clear feature here is the way that achievement and teaching quality drive the overall judgement.

Since the summer of 2014, judgements on governance increasingly refer to the way the school has responded to the imperative to advance 'British values' (defined, you may remember from Chapter 5, as 'democracy, the rule of law, individual liberty and mutual respect, and tolerance of those with different faiths and beliefs'). Phrases such as 'staff encourage tolerance and respect as they prepare pupils for life in modern Britain' began to appear, and the governors' role in this underlined: 'Governors . . . support senior leaders well in promoting respect and tolerance for all faiths, or no faith, cultures and lifestyles. They use their expertise well to assist the school in preparing pupils positively for life in modern Britain' (DfE, 2013).

Table 6.1 Inspection outcomes 2013: secondary schools.

Category	Outstanding	Good	Requiring Improvement	Inadequate
Overall	11	47	33	8
Achievement	11	48	33	8
Teaching	11	49	33	7
Behaviour	21	58	19	2
Leadership	16	52	26	6

Table 6.2 Inspection outcomes 2013: primary schools.

Category	Outstanding	Good	Requiring Improvement	Inadequate
Overall	7	58	30	5
Achievement	7	58	30	5
Teaching	7	58	30	5
Behaviour	22	66	10	2
Leadership	10	60	26	4

Who is being inspected

While the experience of inspection in academies and free schools is much the same as in maintained schools, there is some confusion about the respective roles of the overall governing board in grouped academies and the local governing or advisory board, as well as in the governance of federated maintained schools. Subsidiary guidance published in April 2014 included a new requirement for inspectors:

> Inspectors will increasingly encounter different models of governance, such as those associated with federated arrangements, free schools and academy chains. Inspectors should ensure that they clearly understand the governance arrangements for a school and that they identify and engage with the right people.

> (Ofsted, 2014b)

This was later clarified: 'Inspectors will always seek to meet with governors, or members of the school's local board, committee or other authority where schools are combined in managed groups, federations or chains, during the course of the inspection.'

The future of inspection

We have seen how it is virtually impossible to pin down the inspection procedure to a moment in time. Pressures from both the leadership of Ofsted itself and the DfE, and the rapid and continuous change in school structures, mean that it is difficult to predict where inspection might be this time next year, let alone in five years' time.

Confusion over Ofsted's right to inspect academy chains seemed to come to an end in early 2015, when the expectation that Ofsted would inspect multi-academy trusts was clarified. Already, Ofsted had identified schools within a MAT for inspection. In just one example, Ofsted inspected 16 of the 34 schools of the E-ACT trust in the space of just 11 days early in 2014. This led to a judgement that 'an overwhelming proportion of pupils attending the E-ACT academies inspected were not receiving a good education'. Further, the inspections found that the chain had been deducting 'a proportion of the pupil premium funding from each academy'. The Ofsted correspondent added that this made it 'unclear how these deducted funds are being used to improve outcomes for disadvantaged pupils' (Fitzjohn, 2014). This followed earlier inspections, as well as the departure of the chief executive after an official warning over financial mismanagement. So Ofsted has the right to inspect chains, to inspect schools over a wide range of performance measures, and to have knowledge of the Education Funding Agency's investigations and concerns.

Close relationships between Ofsted and some chains became an issue in 2014 when it was claimed that the leader of a trust with ten member schools and colleges had been given advance notice of an inspection. This particular 'superhead' had already been lavishly praised in public by the former secretary of state, and happened also to be an associate inspector. Issues of probity had not previously arisen at Ofsted, so this was a particularly harsh blow to an organisation whose future had come into doubt. The predominance of data in determining the outcome of an inspection, the new no-notice inspections, the appointment of the chair of a large chain with a questionable record of achievement as chair of Ofsted, and the possible conflicts of interest of various very senior DfE functionaries who happened to be running chains of schools, all combined to give Ofsted an uncomfortable time. Not to mention the chief inspector's tendency to come out with particularly offensive and self-serving – not to say crass – statements, such as his 2012 declaration to a conference of headteachers that 'if staff morale is at an all-time low, you must be doing something right'. In the summer of 2014, the Birmingham 'Trojan Horse' saga further undermined the HMCI's position, with a number of schools recently judged to be 'outstanding' now being re-inspected and graded as 'inadequate' on the grounds of weaknesses in governance and safeguarding.

For example, Oldknow Academy – a primary school in Small Heath, Birmingham – was judged in January 2013 to be outstanding in all respects, including leadership and management. Re-inspected in April 2014, while achievement and quality of teaching remained outstanding, behaviour and safety of pupils, and leadership and management were now inadequate. An overall judgement so out of line with pupil achievement was almost unprecedented. This was on the grounds that:

- Leadership and management are inadequate. The chair and other governors exert too much control over operational matters in the academy.
- Governors do not meet their statutory responsibilities to safeguard pupils because they have not taken steps to protect them from the risks of radicalisation and extremism.

- A small group of governors is making significant changes to the ethos and culture of the academy without full consultation. They are endeavouring to promote a particular and narrow faith-based ideology in what is a maintained and non-faith academy.
- Many members of staff are afraid to speak out against the changes taking place in the academy.
- Recruitment arrangements are inadequate. There is lack of clarity about how appointments have been made.
- The academy is not adequately ensuring that pupils have opportunities to learn about faith in a way that promotes tolerance and harmony between different cultural and religious traditions.
- Behaviour and safety are inadequate because pupils and staff are not equipped well enough to deal with the risk of extreme or intolerant views.
- Academy leaders and governors have not made sure that pupils are always safe on trips.

One thing we can be sure of – schools will continue to be inspected on a regular basis. And the focus of inspection will continue to be the performance of pupils in externally devised tests and examinations.

International measurements

Governments of all hues still look at schooling as being an activity which is required to be rigorous in its competition with other countries of similar economic development. The PISA league tables shows the performance of children from OECD countries:

> The Programme for International Student Assessment (PISA) is a triennial international survey which aims to evaluate education systems worldwide by testing the skills and knowledge of 15-year-old students. To date, students representing more than 70 economies have participated in the assessment.
>
> (PISA website, 2014)

The tests, in reading, mathematics and science 'are designed to assess to what extent students at the end of compulsory education, can apply their knowledge to real-life situations and be equipped for full participation in society'. Of course, these are very narrowly-based tests, and based on assumptions about how education works that are debatable, at the very least. Nevertheless, they are seen as providing the gold standard for schools in the developed world, and therefore school inspection is designed to assess the extent to which schools are likely to assist the country in measuring up to it. There is no known link between PISA results and children's well-being, or eventual life-satisfaction. Nor is there any measurement of what we might regard as critical elements in children's upbringing, such as their creativity or their ability to make appropriate moral judgements. But this is the system into which we have been locked.

Until the government is itself more creative in the way it wants schools to be judged – perhaps taking into account some of the ways that parents, children, young people and – yes, governors – look at schools, this relentless progression is unlikely to relax. So we have schools that exhaustively and exhaustingly prepare for Ofsted at the expense of real education, finding ways of cheating the system, laying evermore fear and stress on the staff, seeking at any cost that elusive 'outstanding' judgement, and leading to extraordinary anomalies.

In May, 2014, a teacher wrote on the Guardian website of his experience in an 'outstanding' school, where the staff were gathered together one afternoon to be told that inspectors would arrive the following morning. The writer tells of the common signs of stress to which staff were subject – sleeplessness, panic, raised blood pressure, stomach pains, sweating, tearfulness. After three days of the visitation, the staff were again called together. To everyone's relief, the verdict was excellent – once again, the school was 'outstanding'. Then the head dropped the bombshell. This wasn't an Ofsted. The head had called in a team to conduct an inspection just as if it were. No-one knew, not even the senior leadership team. Had he talked to the chair of governors about this tactic? One suspects not. The report was fully published on the school's website, to attract new parents:

> My issue is not simply a sense that the staff were abused by this process, but that we are working in an industry where the very system seems to require this sort of behaviour. The power of Ofsted to make or break a school, the cutting of budgets requiring an ever closer eye to be kept on rolls, the sense that the various data dashboards need constant support all adds up to a profession attacked from all sides.
>
> (Secret Teacher Blog, 2014a)

Not, perhaps, just a profession, but a whole education system whose *raison d'être* is represented by an inspection process that may not carry the whole-hearted support of governors and teachers.

The point of inspection

So, having become slaves to this system, perhaps we should do away with inspection? Well, of course not. What a nonsense it would be if schools weren't inspected by competent professionals to give an objective view of their performance. Even more, if schools were inspected but their governance wasn't.

That would be an insult to governance. After all, it has been said that any problem with an organisation is a problem with its governance.

But does inspection improve schools? You don't fatten a pig by weighing it, but how do you know if the pig is getting heavier unless you do weigh it, with a serviceable pair of scales? For our purposes, can inspection improve school governance? It does set standards, and it does define expectations. It gives us a benchmark against which we can evaluate our performance as governors. It reminds us, too, that we are accountable for how we do the job we have. But just as with schools as a whole, there is a whole lot more about excellent governance which isn't encapsulated by the inspection process.

Chapter 7

Schools, parents and the community

In which we consider the relationships of schools with parents and other local people

Schools and parents: A brief history of a difficult relationship

Schools that are complacent about their relationships with parents tend to say one of two things (sometimes both). They say that parents (those who don't turn up to parents' evenings or PTA meetings) are apathetic: they don't think that their child's education is important. Or they say that parents don't feel the need to come because they are happy with everything the school does. Any governing board that accepts these views is doing its parent body – even if only a small part of it – a grave injustice.

If you read Chapter 1 you will know that parents have not always been welcomed into the world of schools. This is strange, because they, surely, are the clients, customers, consumers, as well as being the first teachers of their children – and indeed the providers of the raw materials to the teachers. Some schools are still very unwelcoming to all outsiders, as some parents have found. Many infant and junior schools, while peddling the rhetoric in their literature, make little or no provision for parents to drop off and collect their children in a civilised manner, meet only the basic statutory requirements in reporting children's progress, and make headteachers and senior staff as inaccessible as they can. Secondary schools can be even more skilled at this game: their buildings are forbidding mazes; sometimes you can't even find the number in the phone book, let alone get on to the premises; the security of the children is used as an excuse to surround the school with impenetrable steel barriers; and parents' evenings are an ordeal, with visitors marshalled from one teacher to another at regular intervals. Parents feel like intruders in many schools and some schools seem happy that this should be the case.

Of course, the advent of published inspection reports, statutory requirements for publication of reports and exam outcomes, the internet and social media have exposed schools far more than in the past. Parents are no longer shamefaced when they make judgements about the school – after all, it's not their judgement any longer, the evidence of performance is, apparently, there for all to see and to interpret.

The lack of parental involvement in their children's schooling has inevitably been deplored by officialdom. The language of these tracts, however, suggests that liaison between home and school is only to be encouraged if it is on the *school*'s terms and as a means of educating the parents in helping to achieve the aims of the school. In the early part of the twentieth century, this sometimes involved undoing the 'harm' that homes had done to the children before they arrived in school:

> Speech training must be undertaken from the outset . . . Teachers of infants sometimes complain that when the children come to school they can scarcely speak at all. They should regard this rather as an advantage . . . It is emphatically the business of the elementary school to teach all its pupils who either speak a definite dialect or whose speech is disfigured by vulgarisms, to speak standard English, and to speak it clearly.
>
> (Ministry of Education, 1921)

When parents *are* to be enlisted, their engagement must, of course, be on the school's terms:

> Most people now recognize how important it is for home and school to work together . . . Parents *should take the trouble* to learn about the school and what it is trying to do for their children; in return the school must take into account how the child lives at home . . . Although such associations are of great value, the best kind of cooperation between home and school springs from the attitude shown in the day-to-day life of the school; *for if a parent feels he is welcome, his confidence is won, and once his confidence is won he will support the teachers in what they are trying to do.*
>
> (Ministry of Education, 1947, my emphases)

No doubt here who are to be the main beneficiaries of home–school liaison.

Teachers and governors can now point to all sorts of acts of parliament and official publications which describe and legitimise their activities and responsibilities, but parents have little statutory backing, except in terms of receiving information, much of it through the school's website. The National Confederation of Parent Teacher Associations (NCPTA) has fought for years for the statutory right to set up parent–teacher associations for schools – and for years successive governments have refused to do even this. Currently, the NCPTA website now appears to be devoted entirely to fundraising rather than in developing the conversation between schools and parents.

The attitude that parents' only significant contributions to a school are the pupil and the money that they bring with them has a long history. The Newsom Report of 1963 (DES), which dealt mainly with pupils in secondary moderns, spoke of the need for the school to be joined to its community by 'a causeway well trodden in both directions' – an image of the school as St Michael's Mount: Most of the time, the school and community will be separated by an intimidating ocean, except for twice a day, when the tides recede, and parents and teachers may tread warily across the treacherous sands.

The Plowden Report (DES, 1967) was an altogether more radical document. Though excoriated by many politicians in the present clime, it was in its time much praised for its recommendations on the constructive involvement of parents in their children's education, even in the classroom. So parents, it suggested, can educate children as well as schools.

But a recurring theme in many authorities was the need for teachers to set the agenda of parent/teacher dialogue. One report, of a home–school workshop which took place in Sheffield in the late 1970s, set the tone. The workshop was an in-service course attended by thirty-one primary teachers, to consider 'the implications of working with colleagues and parents in the development of a home/school programme' (Watson and Johnston, 1979). No non-teaching parents are listed among the participants, and certainly there is no contribution from them to the report. 'It is extremely important', the authors assert, 'that *parents know what the teachers want them to know* about education'. In a section entitled 'What's in it for the teacher?', the answer is: 'A lot of extra work . . . as time passes parents will clearly recognize the vast amount of hard work which a teacher has to put in to a normal day. Experience has shown that parents will not be long in voicing their appreciation and admiration.' Meanwhile, the parent will be rewarded with 'an awareness that they are forming a genuine relationship with their child's teacher' (Watson and Johnston, 1979: p. 29). In order to reassure teachers that parents will retain a sufficiently deferential attitude, we are told that 'Parents will usually rely on the professional expertise of the teachers . . . It is when talking with teachers that most parents will make decisions about what might be the best course of action to take when dealing with the interests or problems of their own child' (Watson and Johnston, 1979: p. 35).

As you might expect by now, the one area where parents are allowed, encouraged, even cajoled to participate in the life of a school is in raising money for it: 'Experience has shown that parents may enjoy the challenge of organizing fund-raising activities. The teachers should clearly make efforts to show interest in what is going on, and quite probably the school will be used to hold some of these events: in which case, staff may wish to come along on the evening and take part in some small way. The teachers' role in any of the fund-raising should be basically supportive, as this is one area where the parents can make a very real contribution and quite often are better equipped to cope. *It may well be that parents can play a significant part in deciding with teachers how the money raised can best be spent*' (Watson and Johnston, 1979: p. 38, my emphasis throughout).

Of course not all teachers are as condescending, nor so protective of their territory, as is suggested by this document. But the fact that this could be published in an authority then highly regarded for the steps it was taking towards meaningful lay involvement in educational decision-making, at the end of the 1970s, betrays how far some members of the profession had to go.

As Regan reported: 'When it comes to running schools, parents have generally been kept firmly at arm's length' (1977: p. 57). Even at the pre-school level where involvement is most natural and expected, there is evidence that parents are frustrated by their powerlessness, and that it must rest with the teacher to take the initiative:

> Parents show considerably greater interest in their children's pre-school experience than the staff in charge of children's groups appear to take into account . . . Open access and shared experience . . . do not necessarily on their own bring about better understanding and greater knowledge . . . parents may need far more explanation and discussion than they are given at present.
>
> (Smith, 1980: p. 77)

As we have seen, the government's answer to this was to offer parents the powers to run schools (DES, 1984), the aim being 'further to increase parental influence at school' (DES, 1985) in terms of *control* rather than *participation*. Indeed, in the run-up to the 1997 general election, the Labour Party committed itself to increasing the number of parent governors so that they would outnumber the LEA nominations. The advent of the free schools programme introduced by the coalition government in 2010 brought about the partial realisation of the dreams of those who wanted to see parents running schools – but the reality, as it turned out, was very far from the dream: 'The free school movement was presented by the government to the public as a way in which parents would be able to set up their own schools. In the event, many more free schools were set up by other organisations' (Gann, 2014).

What was not being addressed in any meaningful way was the question of wiping out 150 years of educational isolationism, of white lines in playgrounds reading 'No parents beyond this point'; the question, that is, of giving parents the confidence to see that their involvement is essential for the children to get the most out of their school, and that this would mean changing the attitudes and values of many teachers. Where, for example, in pre-service and in-service training, do intending and serving teachers learn about communicating with parents, one-to-one and *en masse*? How many schools, LAs, academy trusts and other providers help teachers to understand parents and the community? How many teachers live in their schools' communities and understand where the children, let alone the parents, are, literally, coming from? Do they identify the key issues which are facing parents in a rapidly changing, and increasingly unequal, world? What implications does that have for what goes on in the classroom? And, while schools get much better at reporting what children *have done* in class, how many schools report to parents on what children *are about to do*, so that their participation and involvement might be exploited?

The problems of engagement of parents and schools

The evidence presented here is historical, and you may well be thinking, 'well, it isn't like that in my school anymore'. There is some truth in this. Primary schools, at least, have got much better at involving parents as partners – seeing them as, indeed, the teachers they naturally are. But ever-growing pressure on schools from Ofsted and the DfE to get results may be driving them further away from parents who, much evidence suggests, value other qualities in schools just as much as, if not more than, their latest position in the league tables.

There are historical reasons why parents don't engage with schools in the way that teachers and governors might most like. Is it because:

• for many parents themselves, school was not an entirely positive experience, so visiting them remains an ordeal?
• schools were originally set up by 'the gentry', the clergy and the state, so they 'belong' to the ruling class?
• schools were coercive, through local bye-laws originally, later by national legislation? (the ongoing punishment of parents taking children on school term holidays is a vivid contemporary example of this);
• control of schools was handed over to the politicians and the professionals?
• the history of schooling is the history of bureaucratisation (where systems and procedures are set up for the convenience of managers, not users)?
• local lay people and lay politicians (except for a brief period) had little role?
• the key interests in the formulation of the 1944 Act were headteachers, education officers and the churches?
• the composition of governing bodies, for so long, was left to local government politicians and officers, neither of whom were committed to lay participation?

Eventually, schools were seen as part of a bureaucratic welfare state which, along with other public services – the health service, the railways, housing, social services – was characterised as slow-moving, impersonal, intrusive, unchanging, unresponsive to need or to demand: all in all, as something provided for the good of the people by others, many of whom tended not to use or to need them. Perhaps it was these tensions which led the public to distrust schools, and for schools to distrust parents – not entirely the fault of schools, then, but still their responsibility to do something about it. No-one could accuse the coalition government of 2010–2015 of not trying to do something about that. But has throwing the whole system up in the air to see how it lands actually had an impact on the way communities regard their schools and schools regard their parents?

Just as the historical examples listed above show how the world of education and the public can find themselves at loggerheads, so individual schools can demonstrate a dislike (or fear?) of parents, in ways they don't always intend:

- they accuse parents openly or implicitly of apathy, in mistake for a clash of values;
- they use patronising language in communications and signing;
- they organise public events and meetings to meet their own convenience, using their size and organisational needs to excuse themselves;
- they offer only limited access to people who want to support the school, confining it to fund-raising – support without challenge;
- they react defensively to criticism – being always in the right to the parents, as they are to the children;
- they deny, or limit, access to parents in learning support;
- they allow only participation after the event.

> The head of a school serving a large proportion of children from a minority ethnic group complained that the parents were apathetic – she knew this because they rarely came to parents' evenings. When quizzed about the school's arrangements, she realised that the school chose the very times for their consultations when the wage-earners among the community were at work – in the evenings. A community event planned for an accessible time filled the hall with these 'apathetic' parents, and eventually three of them joined the governing board.

Perhaps those parents who are labelled by schools as 'apathetic' are actually, and actively, rejecting much of what they are being forced to accept. 'The charge of apathy can in some circumstances usefully be rejected in favour of the concept of resistance through withdrawal from, or rejection of, what is provided' (Humphries, 1981: pp 39–40). It is, of course, not in the interests of rulers and managers to interpret apathy as rejection.

> It is entirely characteristic that responsibility for widespread non-participation is attributed wholly to the ignorance, indifference and shiftlessness of the people.
>
> (Schattschneider, 1960)

Apathy is presented as a kind of fatalism, in which people cannot see that they have any control or even influence over events that profoundly affect their lives. It is therefore a product of the system, including the schools' part of the system. 'Fatalism in the guise of docility,' wrote Paulo Freire – a writer who shows signs of coming back into fashion – 'is the fruit of an historical and sociological situation, not an essential characteristic of a people's behaviour' (Freire, 1972).

Perhaps things have moved on a bit, though. Here is an elementary school-girl of the 1920s recalling a memorable episode of her schooling:

> I remember going for a nature walk an' I 'ad a button out of me shoe an' she said 'Who's scuffing?' I used to like going on nature walks too, I liked that. And, of course, me button was out of me shoe an' I was trying to hold on to me shoe as well as I could an' she sent me back to school. So I thought to meself – 'twas only just after half-past two – I thought, 'I'm not going to sit 'ere all afternoon. I can be home'. Mother was in bed with a baby then, so I thought to myself, right, let's go home. So I went out the school an' then she 'ad a prefect come to look an' see if I was at home an' alright . . . An' she caned me next morning in front of the whole class, she really caned me, just for leaving school, because I wasn't going to sit there all afternoon by myself, just because the button come out of me shoe, I could've struggled on . . . I didn't cry. I wouldn't let 'em see me cry. Because she knew my mother was in bed with the baby, she knew my mother couldn't get at 'er'.
>
> (quoted in Humphries, 1981: p. 50)

This is just one small illustration of the general alienation that many children felt from their schools:

> The fundamental cultural contradiction experienced by working-class children was that state schools were essentially middle-class institutions, which embodied official values, and that commitment to schooling required a rejection of the distinctive styles of speech, thought and behaviour characteristic of working-class culture.
>
> (Humphries, 1981: p. 54)

How different it was eighty years later, when an Ofsted inspector joined in a lesson and witnessed, and recorded for posterity, one of those rare moments of 'awe and wonder' that children treasure for the rest of their lives. Once again, a class went on a 'nature walk' – though it wouldn't have been called that in the twenty-first century. Climbing a hill and stopping for a moment to take in the view, one small girl cried, 'Cor, Miss, you can see the whole of the world from here.'

Maybe things have moved on, but who could argue that the first story more nearly reflects some children's experience of school still today. Whatever the reasons, conflict remains in schools today and there are a limited number of responses open to parents in dealing with it. Some of these are similar to those characteristics shown by governors which headteachers particularly dislike – the various manifestations of aloofness and interference. In addition to these, alienated parents indulge in gossip, sometimes of an extreme nature, around the school gates, on Facebook and Twitter, making allegations of sexual and financial improprieties, covert criticism, collusion with the anti-school behaviour of pupils, and aggression towards teachers.

Schools that work with the community

We have seen how some schools can appear hostile to the parents and children who are their clients or customers. The schools which avoid these negative relationships are those that see their parents and children as members. This is, in essence, and whether it is formally labelled as such, a community education approach.

Community education is a series of paradoxes. It implies the de-institutionalisation of education that is still predominantly based on institutions. There are five 'articles of faith' based on a 'belief in mutuality and the strength and virtue of collective endeavour', as identified by Rennie (1990):

- that the seeds of the solutions to a community's problems are contained within that community;
- that education is a lifelong activity;
- that a full and appropriate use of all resources is a matter of common sense;
- that all have a contribution to make;
- that the notion of citizenship remains a basic tenet.

Community education in this country as a formalised concept has its genesis in the work and writings of Henry Morris, chief education officer of Cambridgeshire in the 1920s and 1930s (Ree, 1973).

Morris saw the village college, an institution offering secondary, further and adult education, social and leisure activities, as a way of regenerating rural life at a time of a 'flight to the cities'. This was a religious rather than just an educational vision. Morris saw the college replacing the church as the heart of communal life. It was developed by others, notably Stewart Mason, who brought community schools and colleges at all educational levels to Leicestershire. The concept was reinterpreted in an urban context, notably in Liverpool, by Eric Midwinter, founder of the University of the Third Age, and took root in many of the local authorities in Greater Manchester.

Community education is an approach that any school at any phase can adopt, regardless of designation and resources. Although much provision was threatened by the decentralisation of school budgets in 1988, in other areas enlightened schools found that they actually had more freedom to develop their ideas. What are its characteristics? Community schools regard schools as a service to the community, not a provider of an educated workforce to the nation's government. They regard access to lifelong education and self-improvement as a right. They:

- work with families and the community, recognising adults as learners and as teachers;
- encourage participation, giving decision-making powers to parents and the community;
- identify and attempt to meet needs;
- offer individualised provision;
- are flexible with provision, time and resources;
- regard teachers as servicing need – teachers as 'social prosecutors rather than social defenders', in Midwinter's (1972) phrase.

This vision conflicts with the traditional view of schools working exclusively with children; providing direction and coercion; making uniform provision regardless of need; having time-honoured systems and rituals; and regarding teachers as deliverers of knowledge and sources of power. This has significant implications for a school's relationship with its parents. What can the community education approach offer to all schools in their relationships with parents?

Getting the relationship with parents right

A governing board that knows its duty to, and its role in, the community, will accept that 'Many parents . . . share a number of common expectations. They want:

- the best for their children – in schooling as in everything else. This means for most, a high quality, broad education in a caring, effective institution;
- regular, reliable and accessible information about what the school is up to and how this affects their child(ren);
- information about their children's progress and achievements, about problems and, especially, help in identifying ways in which they themselves can support their children's learning;
- finally, most parents want to be taken seriously – to have a say and be listened to, to contribute to the life and work of the school and to their child's part in it.'

(Bastiani, 1995)

Parents in conversation with teachers

The most meaningful interaction between parents and teachers, for most families, is the regular reporting session when teachers tell them how their children are doing. More and more in some schools this session is an exchange of performance data, often structured in such a way as to give the parent a view of how their child is doing against national, not school or class, performance. At primary and secondary schools, including early years, the parent is regaled with a list of national expectations, dreamed up as much as anything by professionals pressurised by politicians to conform to party policy, and informed how their child appears to be performing against the expectations of children of their age.

In good schools, of course, the parent–teacher dialogue is much more than this. In such a school, the first thing that a teacher might say to a parent could be 'how do you think x is doing at the moment? Are they happy? Do you think they're making progress?' Such an opening reassures the parent that they and their child themselves are at the centre of the review process. Then the conversation is about what the parent needs to know, rather than focusing on what the teacher feels they ought to tell them. Of course there is a place for data in such a conversation, but it is not the most important, let alone the only, element.

A few years ago, in a roomful of around two hundred teachers in their first year after qualification, only one put up her hand when asked what pre-service and in-service support they had been given for talking to parents – although every single teacher agreed that this was one of their most important tasks. That support turned out to have been a one-hour lecture at college.

Stacey gives a checklist for teachers in talking with parents about their child:

- Be honest and specific.
- Be flexible. Seek the parents' opinion so that you can work together on solutions and ideas.
- Observe carefully. Notice how you are feeling and how that is affecting the discussion. Recognise that parents may be feeling inhibited or tense and give time to take in what you are saying and offer their views.
- Listen. Concentrate and show you are listening by adopting an appropriate posture and by seeking clarification, reflecting and summarising.
- Help the parents relax. They are on your territory. Give them a chance to contribute to the conversation.
- Allow silences for thought and reflection. Many of us have been brought up to believe that silences are awkward. Yet talking can be an interruption and disruptive. Silences allow people time to collect their thoughts and continue.
- Be positive about the child. Give examples, not generalities.

- Ask questions which lead the conversation. Avoid putting answers in the parent's mouth. Allow questions which are difficult or challenging for you.
- Answer questions honestly. Avoid justifying or going on the defence. If it is difficult for you to say, express the feeling. If you do not know the answer then admit this. Do not make promises which you know you cannot fulfil or reassure with improbabilities.
- Remember, good relationships take time. Allow the relationship to grow. It is not friendship but a viable working partnership that you are seeking. This does not mean that you have to agree on everything but it means you need to respect and value each other's experience.

(Stacey, 1991: pp. 98–99)

As a governor, ask how much help and support your school's teachers get to do this challenging duty, and ask how sessions are organised to provide the best experience for parents. And don't follow the practice of the secondary school where a child sat in the office throughout parents' evenings, ringing the bell every five minutes to tell parents when to move on. As a governing board, work with the head and staff in setting up protocols for the interfaces between staff and parents.

Parents will also have occasion for relating to the governors, perhaps when they have issues they want the governors to deal with. Appendix 8 offers some guidance to governors to help them act appropriately.

Access

The place where governors need to start considering how their school relates to parents and the wider community is at the gates. Schools need to look regularly and carefully at the arrangements they make for public and parental access. Of course security is a key issue in many schools, but it must not be used as an excuse to develop a fortress mentality. Governors may be particularly well placed to advise on this because they are not in school every day and don't become inured to the surroundings. They can compare the school to all the other organisations, institutions and services that they use in the locality. Figure 7.1 shows some criteria which the governing board may apply.

Governors might devise ways of regularly conducting physical audits of the school and its reception practice, occasionally using people who don't know the school to review it for them.

Some models of parental engagement

Governing boards need to decide what level of parental engagement is appropriate in their school. We will look briefly now at four assumptions behind the engagement of parents in schools and some of the ideas supporting them.

Finding the building
The phone number is easy to locate
The building is easy to find
Signposting and signage is clear and unambiguous
The entry to the premises is obvious and attractive
The doors are easy to find and to open
Reception is easy to find

Welcome
The phone answering is quick and friendly
Someone is always available at – or near – reception
Arrival is welcomed
Security arrangements are simple to follow
Staff are pleased to see parents coming in
Appointments are not always necessary
Parents know when and how staff are available

Physical appearance
The school entrance is clean and tidy
The reception area has attractive, interesting and informative displays
Visible staff are neat and tidy
The school is well decorated
Furniture and fittings are appropriate for adults

What the school sounds like
Appropriate languages are spoken
'Sounds off' are working sounds
'Sounds off' are positive sounds
All people address each other politely
There is a 'friendly formula' for addressing visitors

Figure 7.1 Criteria for ease of parental access.

Involving parents in schools helps children's learning

Charles Desforges (Desforges with Abouchaar, 2003) offers support for the idea that parental involvement in the form of 'at-home good parenting' has the most effective positive impact on children's achievement, particularly in primary school. Other forms of school engagement are less clear-cut in their impact. One of the main thrusts of Desforges' work is that 'Differences between parents in their level of involvement are associated with social class, poverty, health, and also with parental perception of their role and their levels of confidence in fulfilling it. Some parents are put off by feeling put down by parents and teachers' (Desforges, 2003: p. 5). This may arouse particular concern at a period when more than a quarter of children in the UK are living in poverty, and there is an ever-increasing emphasis on academic attainment in schools at all levels.

Bastiani supports this position, suggesting that evidence of parental contribution to pupil progress is more convincing when there is a lot of it and it is 'spontaneous' rather than solicited, specific and detailed rather than bland or general, and perceived and valued in the same ways by teachers and parents (Bastiani, 2000). Janis-Norton (2005) suggests a range of ways of developing parental support for pupil learning, focusing very much on parents constructing home life in such a way that the child can continue learning at school. Here, the parent as substitute teacher has a guide to behaviour, though little evidence is presented that this systematic approach has a measurable impact. Hallgarten, though, provides a wider approach to parental involvement in schools, considering actions at national, local and school level (Hallgarten, 2000). Other models of parental participation through, for example, supplementary schooling (mostly seen as an approach confined to confronting the disadvantages faced by some minority ethnic groups) are advocated, but the key actions are those taken by schools themselves. So the 2004 Headteachers' National Standards included the expectation that the head 'creates and maintains an effective partnership with parents and carers to support and improve pupils' achievement and personal development' (DfES, 2004). Somewhat regressively, though, any reference to parents other than as observers of a headteacher's 'personal behaviour, positive relationships and attitudes' has disappeared by the time the DfE came to redraft the standards in 2015 (DfE, 2015b).

Schools and parents in partnership help children learn

An approach developed initially in Italy after the Second World War works on the belief that parents are 'the first teachers', the second teachers are classroom teachers, and the third teacher is the environment. The Reggio Emilia approach is an educational philosophy that privileges the natural development of the child and his or her relationship with the outside environment. The involvement of parents and communities is at the very core of the philosophy. This presents a picture of a far more dense partnership than is envisaged in the previous model. It could be argued that it requires a new mindset alongside a systemic reconstruction of the school, as offered by Page and Millar (2009):

Ten ways to build effective school–parent partnerships:

- appoint dedicated link staff members to liaise between parents and the school;
- improve communications in both directions: listen to parents and they will listen to you;
- develop one-to-one relationships between parents and staff: talk more, write less;
- help parents understand more about what their child does at school;
- involve more parents more often in decision-making;

- develop and encourage parent support groups, social events and holiday schemes;
- celebrate success: tell parents about the good things as well the bad;
- help parents to build their own confidence and skills;
- take advantage of the skills and experience parents can offer;
- have a clear complaints policy in place and treat complaints positively.

(Page and Millar, 2009)

At a practical level, it means simple communications between school and parents *before* the event, such as that practised by a small primary school in Somerset:

Dear Parent,

Thank you to all of you who have continued to support and encourage your children with their weekly homework and spellings. Your involvement is much appreciated. We would be grateful if you would make the daily 15-minute home reading session a priority, whenever possible. There are still a few children who are not yet reading fluently, and at this stage in their learning it is vital that they receive every possible help and support.

This term at school, your child will be studying the following curriculum topics.

English: Adventure and mystery stories, letter writing, humorous poetry, discussion texts, non-fiction books used for research.

Maths: Number calculations, money and real-life problems, measuring, fractions and decimals, data handling, shapes and angles.

Science: Insulation, solids and liquids.

ICT: Creating patterns using a design package, databases.

Geography: Studying and improving the local environment.

Music: Texture – combining different sounds, orchestral instruments, two-part singing.

PE: Striking and fielding games, athletics, swimming.

RE: Our Church, questions and mysteries.

Art: Textiles.

Design and technology: Sandwich snacks.

Yours sincerely,

(Reproduced by kind permission of Norton-sub-Hamdon
Church of England Primary School, Somerset)

Accompanied by an invitation to participate on a range of levels, and weekly updates of specific topics with suggestions for simple home activities, this is about opening doors to parental engagement, not dictating or reporting.

A governing board might set out a range of targets to be met by the school, as illustrated here:

EXAMPLES OF TARGETS FOR SCHOOLS IN THEIR RELATIONSHIP WITH PARENTS AND THE COMMUNITY

Input targets

- *A satisfaction questionnaire will be delivered to all parents once a year, covering areas such as learning outcomes, social aspects of the school, health, safety, confidence, enjoyment, values.*
- *Coopted governors will reflect the life of the local community.*
- *There will be a published complaints procedure which parents will be encouraged to use when appropriate.*
- *The governing body will exceed statutory requirements in the information it makes available to parents.*
- *The information given to parents will be appropriate, and presented in an appropriate format and language.*
- *There will be a clear published procedure for parents to gain quick access to staff.*

Process targets

- *Where possible and appropriate, governing body planning and policy-making will take account of consultation with representative groups of parents.*
- *The Parent Teacher Association will meet x times each term.*
- *There will be x curriculum workshops for parents for each year group each year.*
- *Where appropriate, parents and other members of the community will be invited to participate in school activities, for example, parent/pupil reading schemes, classroom work, school trips.*

Output targets

- *Requests for admissions and transfers from other schools will hold at between x and y per year. This figure will be reviewed annually in the light of changing circumstances in the community.*
- *Attendance at the Annual Parents Meeting will reach x by the year . . .*
- *Attendance at parents' evenings will be between x and y per cent of pupils.*
- *The Parent Teacher Association will have an active membership of between x and y.*

Outcome targets

- *Parents will feel a sense of ownership over the school.*
- *The community will protect the school.*
- *The use of school buildings will reflect the needs of the local community.*

(Gann, 1999a: pp. 84–85)

A community-based framework for education improves schools and communities

While proponents of community education had been arguing for years for governments and local authorities to recognise the benefits of an educational provision from 'womb to tomb', the Labour government of 1997–2010 introduced an unprecedented national strategy that would at least confront the issues facing the 0–18 age range. Entitled 'Every Child Matters', the initiative was first presented as a response to the tragic death of a vulnerable child which gained enormous publicity because of the perceived failings of a very unjoined-up set of social and educational provision in local authorities. As we saw in Chapter 3 it formed the core of school self-evaluation for some years.

Every Child Matters attempted to address the piecemeal nature of child care and schooling with a coordinated strategy relying on the cooperation of education, social services, health, policing and so on. After a wide consultation led by the then Chief Secretary to the Treasury, the publication identified the five life outcomes which seemed to matter most to children and young people – being healthy, staying safe, enjoying and achieving, making a positive contribution, and economic well-being (House of Commons, 2003). The strategy was implemented in most local authorities by the merging of educational and social provision into a single department for children's services, and the post of director of education was replaced by a single director of children's services. The relatively newly-founded National College for School Leadership (now the National College for Teaching and Leadership) took the lead in developing training for professionals. Changing the branding for children's services did not automatically lead to a single unitary approach to young people, but enormous strides were made in broadening expectations of national provision. The original recipe included a massive expansion in Sure Start children's centres in deprived areas, the provision of extended services in *all* schools, increased investment in child and adolescent mental health services (CAMHS), improved speech and language therapy services, development of out-of-school activities and tackling family homelessness.

This enormously ambitious plan did come to dominate education and social services in local authorities throughout the first decade of the twenty-first century. The holistic model was reflected in the Department for Education's rebranding as the Department for Children, Schools and Families, and the report in 2007 enabled the government to claim that the number of registered childcare places had more than doubled since 1997, standards in schools continued to rise, the number of children in relative poverty had fallen by 600,000, and teenage pregnancy rates were at their lowest level for twenty years (DCSF, 2007a). Achieving the five outcomes came to dominate social service and educational providers, including governing bodies, and was grafted onto the inspection framework for schools.

Certainly the massive investment pointed to a genuine commitment by the government to address the persistent image of services for children as a set of fragmented provisions by professionals who failed to understand or sympathise with each other's often conflicting priorities. It drew attention particularly to the dearth of provision in areas already disadvantaged by poverty before the 2008 crash. Some of the project's ideals have survived the onset of austerity, although the overall vision of unity of provision of services and training has disappeared along with many of the Sure Start Centres and other integrated family support provision.

Governing boards now, perhaps, feel that they can legitimately consider and address the barriers to learning that there are for some children in all schools, perhaps particularly in those in disadvantaged areas.

School improvement is dependent on the engagement of the community

This idea is at the root of the Every Child Matters movement. In fact, in 2006, an Ipsos Mori poll showed that two-thirds of parents wanted to be more involved in their children's education, so schools working on this are pushing at an open door (Ipsos Mori, 2006). In periods of economic austerity, of course, there are opposing forces. Parents may be less available to their children or their children's schools when they need to be working longer hours, although others may find themselves more available than they willingly would be. Most parents claimed to attend parents' evenings and to help with homework, but a significant minority also attended school meetings and took part in school surveys, fundraising activities and tutoring out of school hours. People in deprived areas are less likely to become engaged in community activities, for a variety of reasons, often as much to do with self-confidence and self-esteem as anything else. Certainly, parents in deprived areas seem less likely to get involved with the formal aspects of the management of the school such as governance.

The most common myths about parents and schools seem difficult to shift, despite hard evidence and experience. The Labour and Conservative parties both seemed convinced for many years that parents wanted two things – the power to choose their child's school, and the power to control it.

In fact, what parents say they want is a good local school, and the opportunity to influence, not to run it.

There do seem to be significant barriers to the involvement in the lay leadership of schools of certain groups – identified in 2003 as being: 'people from black and other minority ethnic groups, young people, disabled people, lone parents, people with low incomes and people who are unemployed, and business people' (Ellis, 2003). This seems to be connected with difficulties in defining what we encourage parental and other community participation *for*. Are we clear why we want to engage people in governance, especially in disadvantaged areas?

The problems and possibilities of school governance cannot be divorced from a wider set of issues around governance in disadvantaged areas.

These centre on the perceived disengagement of large numbers of people from traditional political processes and the quest for new forms of democratic participation. In principle, governing bodies offer a promising vehicle for such participation. However, the challenges they face in such areas are exacerbated by the lack of any clear and consensual rationale for their existence. Different potential rationales can be identified in terms of the managerial, localising and democratising contribution that governors might make, but each of these assumes different characteristics on the part of governors, different forms of legitimacy and different definitions of serviced quality.

(Dean et al., 2007)

The 2010 coalition government's preference for non-geographically-orientated academy chains over local authorities, and the 2014–15 shift towards skills-based over stakeholder governing boards clearly moves the current emphasis towards expectations on the managerial, rather than localising or democratising contributions of lay governors.

School and community: taking the community and the parents with you

Whatever the neighbourhood, whoever its components are, the vision of community cohesion – still an element that schools are expected to be advancing – is a potentially powerful one:

Working towards a society in which there is a common vision and sense of belonging by all communities in which the diversity of people's backgrounds and circumstances is appreciated and valued, a society in which similar life opportunities are available to all, and a society in which strong and positive relationships exist and continue to be developed.

(DCSF, 2007b)

A governing board that articulates such a vision, and builds its strategic direction around it, is most likely to engage successfully with both the parent body and the community at large.

Chapter 8

Evaluating governance

How do we know how well we are governing the school?

We have already seen how important the induction and training of governors is, in ensuring the effectiveness of governance. But how does the governing board know that it is doing its job well, so as to have a real impact on the performance of the school?

Models of governing board self-evaluation

Self-evaluation models have proliferated over the years, ever since governing boards began to be inspected. Shortly after the establishment of the coalition government in 2010, a Member of Parliament with a strong interest in school governance recommended the creation of an All Party Parliamentary Group (APPG) on Educational Governance and Leadership, which he himself chaired. Earlier, Neil Carmichael had recommended ten questions that governors should ask themselves, from the government's early white paper.

The Education White Paper 'The Importance of Teaching' suggests 10 key questions for governors to ask which we regard as highlighting the essence of the responsibilities of governors:

1 What are the school's values? Are they reflected in our long-term development plans?
2 How are we going to raise standards for all children, including the most and least able, those with Special Educational Needs, boys and girls, and any who are currently underachieving?
3 Have we got the right staff and the right development and reward arrangements?
4 Do we have a sound financial strategy, get good value for money and have robust procurement and financial systems?
5 Do we keep our buildings and other assets in good condition and are they well used?

6 How well does the curriculum provide for and stretch all pupils?
7 How well do we keep parents informed and take account of their views?
8 Do we keep children safe and meet the statutory health and safety requirements?
9 How is pupil behaviour? Do we tackle the root causes of poor behaviour?
10 Do we offer a wide range of extra-curricular activities which engage all pupils?

(Carmichael and Wild, 2011: p. 31)

In the summer of 2012, the APPG published a set of twenty questions that governing boards should be asking themselves in the cause of self-evaluation (see Appendix 10). As Ofsted became more rigorous in its inspection of governing boards, it produced a series of grade descriptors specifically on the school's governance. Later, these were subsumed into the section of the report on leadership and management, and at the time of writing (though subject to frequent amendment) the document from July 2014, in Appendix 5, is the one used by Ofsted inspectors.

The National Governors' Association, developing its own consultancy service in addition to the advisory and support services it provides to its members, identified eight characteristics of good governance:

1 the right people round the table;
2 understanding role and responsibilities;
3 professional clerking;
4 good chairing;
5 good relationships based on trust;
6 knowing the school – the data, the staff, the parents, the children, the community;
7 committed to asking challenging questions;
8 confident to have courageous conversations in the interests of the children and young people.

NGA consultants use this list as the core of the review process they provide in response to, or in anticipation of, inspection. Now that Ofsted inspectors can require governing boards to commission an external review of their governance, the NGA and other organisations provide this service to varying degrees of scrutiny.

From these characteristics, the NGA has developed a framework for governance (NGA, 2015) offering a structure within which the governing board can discharge its key strategic role. This describes a cycle involving three elements:

agreeing governing principles against which governing boards can evaluate their practice; setting a strategy – a shared vision and long-term strategy for the school, from which annual school development plans can be derived; monitoring the strategy – agreeing key performance indicators against which progress towards the school's vision can be charted, including examples of the evidence that can be used to monitor and review the school's performance.

The aim here is to set the governing board's work firmly within the strategic mode, and to ensure that it does not become distracted by operational matters.

Accountabilities

In evaluating its work, school governors have to take into account the multiple accountabilities they have. Governing boards are variously accountable, for one or more of its areas of operation, but overall for the performance of the school, to the Department for Education and to Ofsted. Maintained schools will be accountable to their local authority, and voluntary aided and controlled schools, additionally, to their diocese or other foundation. Academies will be accountable to their academy trust, while local governing boards, depending on the scope of their scheme of delegation, to their board of trustees. It is to be hoped that all schools will feel themselves accountable to their pupil and parent bodies, and to the communities they serve.

In turn, governing boards of all schools, regardless of type, will hold the school's professional leadership responsible for the day-to-day running of the school(s).

Governor development

Twenty years ago, the world of governor training was relatively simple. Every local authority employed a governor services department which offered centralised topic-based training and whole governing body sessions. This allowed governors from different schools to meet each other and explore the different ways in which good governing practice could be disseminated. Annual local authority conferences would provide opportunities to hear speakers of national status.

Inevitably, the quality of these services varied between LAs. Some took the responsibilities very seriously. Others, however, and especially as the large LEAs of the past were broken up into smaller unitary authorities, offered only the most rudimentary of provision. Some training was led by very under-qualified trainers, often experts in their own field but with no experience in adult education. Some appeared to think that governor development need only be a sort of watered-down teacher education, and that there wasn't such a thing as a governor curriculum of its own. The list of obstacles also suggests that some of the most valuable training for governors would be in developing personal skills and qualities necessary in the governance of any institution, such as assertiveness, debate and strategic planning.

The picture is now very different, with local authorities finding it increasingly difficult to maintain specialist departments, and often buying in skills on a piecemeal basis from whichever experts happen to be in the locality. It is not clear whether this has changed the overall practice or not. Most academy chains of any size seem to employ their own governance organisers, some at least of whom have experience in the field. The former local authority conferences have, in many cases, been taken over and are now managed by the LAs' governor associations. With the National Governors' Association, the All Party Parliamentary Group on Governance, the National Coordinators of Governors' Services (a body of professionals in governor development support), the National College's National Leaders of Governance, the Governor Charter Mark, the awards of excellence in governance and clerking offered by the National Teaching Awards and the NGA, we have a proliferation of professional and volunteer bodies engaged in furthering the work of school governors.

One big question remains – should governors be required to be trained, as are volunteers in most other statutory roles, such as magistrates, are? Currently, there is a fine balance between those who support compulsory training and those who don't. There does seem to be a majority developing that believes that chairs of governors may soon be required to receive some basic training in the role.

Characteristics of the best governing boards

Throughout this book, I hope it has been clear that the best governing boards set themselves high standards in the qualities that matter. These might be summarised as follows (see Gann, 1999a):

1 efficiency – that is, competence in planning, monitoring and evaluating; and in conducting the executive functions they are responsible for; and in communicating with staff, pupils, parents and the wider community;
2 effectiveness – that is, doing the business well so as to enable leaders to lead best, teachers to teach best, staff to work to their best, and pupils to learn best;
3 democratic accountability – that is, managing itself fairly and equitably, and encouraging stakeholders to hold it accountable for its actions and the performance of the school;
4 openness – that is, sharing difficult issues with staff, pupils and parents, opening itself to scrutiny, enabling challenge and communicating in accessible ways;
5 challenging – asking difficult questions of the school's leadership, always seeking new ways of enhancing the pupils' learning and experiences.

The story is told of a houseguest visiting the great cellist, Pablo Casals. When leaving for the day, the guest walked past Casals' rehearsal room, and paused to listen to him going over and over a particular phrase. Returning some hours later, the guest was astonished to hear the same phrase being repeated, almost imperceptibly differently, over and over. At dinner that night, the guest asked Casals: 'Tell me, Casals, that phrase sounded perfect to me when I left this morning, yet hours later you were still going over and over it. How can that be?' Casal's reply was one we should take to heart: 'Ah,' he said, 'I'm still searching.'

The best governing boards, like the best headteachers, keep searching.

Chapter 9

Schools in uncertain times

What the present looks like and what
the future might hold; the state of
the nation and its schooling

Predicting the unpredictable

At no time in the past fifty years or so has the future of schooling in England
seemed less predictable. Even so, we're going to have a go at it. This chapter
is going to consider what has happened to Britain, to England's schools, and to
their governance over the last twenty years or so. The purpose of this is to try
to provide a context into which we can put the possible priorities for action for
governing bodies in the immediate future.

What should governors focus on? What aims might we lay down for our
schools, and what actions might we take to provide a medium- and a long-
term strategic picture? This will lay down the parameters for an exercise in
'future-proofing' to be conducted in Chapter 10.

First we will look at long-term trends over recent years. How has the way
Britain has been governed changed? How has this affected education, especially in England? How has this impacted on schools? How has governing
schools changed? These trends may continue, or accelerate, or decelerate, or
be reversed. Whichever, identifying them may give us some clues about the
future we have to be ready for.

What's happened in Britain

The dominant trend of British governments since 1979, whether Conservative,
Labour or coalition, has been the growth of neoliberal ideas. By this, I mean
an economic philosophy which promulgates a strongly capitalist approach
promoting a market economy under a strong centralised state. The key features at national level are the privatisation of state-owned utilities, the centralisation of decision-making, and deregulation leading to an open market.
It has been defined by American scholar and co-editor of the socialist magazine Monthly Review, Robert McChesney as 'capitalism with the gloves off'
(McChesney, 1999).

'I shall try to put into a few words the neo–liberal view of humanity, to sketch the mirrors that surround us:

People are competitive beings focused on their own profit. This benefits society as a whole because competition entails everyone doing their best to come out on top. As a result, we get better and cheaper products and more efficient services within a single free market, unhampered by government intervention. This is ethically right because success or failure in that competition depends entirely on individual effort. So everyone is responsible for their own success or failure. Hence the importance of education, because we live in a rapidly evolving knowledge economy that requires highly trained individuals with flexible competencies. A single higher–education qualification is good, two is better, and lifelong learning a must. Everyone must continue to grow because competition is fierce. That's what lies behind the current compulsion for performance interviews and constant evaluations, all steered by an invisible hand from central management.

This is a brief summary of the grand narrative that controls our culture today and that consequently forms our identity.'

(Verhaeghe, 2012: pp. 112–113)

Three key elements of neoliberalism in the state

Privatisation

In the Britain of 1979:

Much of the economy, and almost all its infrastructure, was in state hands. [. . .] How much of the economy? A third of all homes were rented from the state. The health service, most schools, the armed forces, prisons, roads, bridges and streets, water, sewers, the National Grid, power stations, the phone and postal system, gas supply, coal mines, the railways, refuse collection, the airports, many of the ports, local and long-distance buses, freight lorries, nuclear fuel reprocessing, air traffic control, much of the car-, ship- and aircraft-building industry, most of the steel factories, British Airways, oil companies, Cable & Wireless, the aircraft engine makers Rolls-Royce, the arms makers Royal Ordnance, the ferry company Sealink, the Trustee Savings Bank, Girobank, technology companies Ferranti and Inmos, medical technology firm Amersham International and many others. In the past thirty-five years, this commonly owned economy, this people's portion of the island, has to a greater or lesser degree become private.

(Meek, 2014: pp. 8–9)

This policy is now extended to state-funded schools.

Centralisation of state-controlled activities

More than half of all state-funded secondary schools, and a growing number of primary schools, are now run by independent trusts accountable directly to the secretary of state. Before 1988, secretaries of state for education famously had only three powers of direction over schools: removing air-raid shelters from playgrounds; organising teacher training; and approving the opening and closing of schools. Now, the secretary of state has over 2,000 powers of direction over schools, with maintained schools having 30,000 regulations and academies 6,000 regulations.

Deregulation of the private sector

The process of deregulation of private sector activities runs parallel to that of the centralisation of state-funded provision. The ideology of neoliberalism, suggests Owen Jones (2014: p. 6)

> is based around a belief in so-called 'free markets': in transferring public assets to profit-driven businesses as far as possible; in a degree of opposition – if not hostility – to a formal role for the state in the economy; in support for reducing the tax burden on private interests; and in the driving back of any form of collective organization that might challenge the status quo. This ideology is often rationalized as 'freedom' – particularly 'economic freedom' – and wraps itself in the language of individualism.

Jones goes on to point out, ironically, that such freedoms are actually over-reliant on the support, including the financial support, of the state. When a business pays its staff the bare minimum wage, or employs them on zero hours contracts, the state is left to subsidise low incomes with housing and other welfare benefits; when bankers' speculation oversteps the mark and brings about global financial collapse, the state bails them out; when private landlords, buying out council-built properties, raise rents beyond the reach of essential public sector workers such as nurses, firefighters and teachers, it is the state that steps in to provide emergency housing for them. There is increasing evidence that tax cuts for the wealthiest in society are paid for by cuts in benefits for the poorest (MacInnes et al., 2014).

Neoliberalism at work

Individualism is at the heart of neoliberalism, and manifests itself in a number of ways. The concept of universal perfectibility is essential to a neo-liberal outlook. Anyone, in theory, can achieve perfection: the ideal body, male or female; untold (preferably untaxed) wealth; 12 A*s at GCSE. If perfectibility can be sold to us, it is through the market, owned by those who have already achieved perfection. The market creates the model, sets it up and invites everyone to follow it. No-one, so the rhetoric goes, need be below average. Indeed, secretaries of state have been known to express the aspiration that every school should perform above average. We can all be better than average, if we work hard enough and spend hard enough. Success is open and available to all in a meritocracy, so selection of the fittest, even at eleven, is a useful tool. Michael Young, who introduced the concept of meritocracy, coined it as a description of a dystopia, but instead, somewhat ironically, it has become a rallying cry of the neoliberal. Who, indeed, can argue against the mantra that 'rewards should come to the talented and hard-working'? Individualism, therefore, glorifies the strong leader, the hero, the superhead, the rescuer. So the authorities will hold up certain individuals who appear to meet the superhead criteria as models for the rest of us. When secretary of state Michael Gove met Dame Rachel de Souza, he is reported to have said: 'If anyone asked me what my ideal education policy would be, it would be to clone Rachel 23,000 times' (*The Observer*, 17th August 2014).

This individualistic view of education is also inclined to lead to increasing disparities in pay. Under the standard teacher's pay and conditions of 2010, a headteacher might earn, at most, five times as much as the lowest paid schoolteacher; some academy chains now pay their heads as much as twenty times as the new teacher.

Results-focused and target-setting management

Political rhetoric, inspection methods and media focus on education over the last few years have all concentrated on the outputs of schools – the results that children attain in standardised tests. Requirements and demands on schools come from a centralised source, the Department for Education, and are imposed through Ofsted. This top-down definition of effectiveness and description of quality leads to an inspection process that makes summative judgements, as opposed to providing advice and support. Mediators between the centre and local institutions, such as academics and local government, may be removed, disempowered or disregarded.

Target-setting, with failure to achieve the targets punished by sanctions or dismissal, is the dominant mode of management in a neoliberal setting. Thus while the political parties were setting out their proposals for post-election policies in early 2015, the prime minister suggested that after a Conservative victory, the government would require *all* children to know their times tables by the age of eleven, and the headteachers of primary schools failing to ensure 100 per cent success would be removed from their post.

Because qualitative evaluation is tricky, it may be largely disregarded, and quantitative measurement is promoted as the true picture of an institution – promoted to global significance through the application of PISA league tables, where the nation's positioning is carefully scrutinised each year, although PISA actually seems to compare relatively small (though indisputably important) elements in the schooling process, between nations whose schooling differences are so great that they might make statistical comparison meaningless.

Target-setting also encourages people to concentrate on behaviour which achieves the desired objectives regardless of its impact on the wider picture. In the United States, setting police forces, and individual officers, arrest targets, has the impact of criminalising whole neighbourhoods, while focusing on the 'low-hanging fruit' of young black men living in ghettoes (Goffman). In Britain's schools, concentration on pupil performance targets for higher level GCSE passes, for instance, has for a long time tempted some schools to focus on getting students from grade D to grade C, while comparatively neglecting those students on borderline grades above or below the significant threshold.

Competition

Although there is pretty well universal recognition that the key to school improvement is collaboration between schools, the current system may tempt schools to compete – lauding schools that do well in official league tables and Ofsted outcomes, and providing incentives to grow pupil numbers. Competition is a very public game, and provides an element of exposure which came very new to the education sector. In January 2015, a press release from Ark Academies Trust printed its own GCSE results in 2013 and 2014, alongside the other nine largest academy networks, which happened to show that Ark was 'the only one of the top ten largest academy networks to see GCSE results improve in 2014'. Competition has brought some benefits in terms of accountability. But the free market in pay, while leading to much popular vilification, nevertheless provides a ready way for people to measure their own and others' 'success'. Much of the neoliberal rhetoric, then, is about the value of competition, how it sorts out the wheat from the chaff, and rewards the naturally talented and 'hardworking'. When resources are scarce, this rhetoric seems to strengthen, and anger may be disproportionately targeted against the small numbers of people who seem to take from the support systems, often the sick, old and disabled or temporarily disadvantaged.

Shifting expectations

If you keep changing the demands on them, people and organisations are kept on their toes and in a constant state of anxiety. So it was that a media scare in the summer of 2014 led to a rewriting of Ofsted's expectations on schools to promote 'British values' and the consequent regrading of some schools from 'outstanding' to 'inadequate' overnight. A little later in the year, it became apparent that Ofsted was identifying schools for early inspection if their websites did not meet statutory requirements – in particular, schools which did not explain their curriculum on the website would be visited as a matter of priority. Again, the introduction of 'short notice', to be quickly followed by 'no notice', inspections ensured that schools would not relax if they were anything but 'outstanding'. This meant that many schools would spend all their time in a constant state of readiness. So the content and the manner of inspection continued to engender uncertainty and, often, fear.

> One consequence of neoliberal organisation (an example drawn from the Dutch health system) is 'the inevitable proliferation of rules and regulations it creates, along with an unseen monitoring system and a heavy burden of administration . . . non-stop changes, ranging from continual structural alterations to the installation of the latest computer software, new partnerships with other hospitals, or the umpteenth merger between services . . . the "Big Brother" feeling. It is not the changes themselves, but the staff who are being constantly evaluated, through performance interviews, audits and suchlike. This does nothing for the working atmosphere, and in many departments you'd be hard put to find any team spirit. Here, too, measuring and counting goes on, and here, too, it has a perverse effect. In no time, staff at all levels adapt their behaviour, ceasing to do things that 'don't count'. . . . less and less focus on the work itself and more on administration, management and monitoring.'
>
> (Verhaeghe, 2014: pp. 134–135)

The diminution of the worth of the public sector

The explosion of private sector salaries in, for example, banking and the media, may be at least partially responsible for the diminution in regard for the public sector. Since the 1980s, the public sector has been increasingly vilified in the media and by prominent politicians of both major parties. Paradoxically, while polls regularly seem to show that teachers and health workers are more highly respected, valued and trusted by the general population than most other professions – and notably more so than politicians, bankers and the media – nevertheless, much of the media is highly critical when public sector workers complain about pay or working conditions.

The diminution of social capital

Social capital is the strength and breadth and depth of networks of social reciprocity within a community to which people have access.

> Social capital – that is, social networks and the associated norms of reciprocity – comes in many different shapes and sizes with many different uses. Your extended family represents a form of social capital, as do your

Sunday school class, the regulars who play poker on your commuter train, your college roommates, the civic organizations to which you belong, the Internet chat group in which you participate, and the network of professional acquaintances recorded in your address book.

(Putnam, 2000: p. 21)

Social capital is, according to Putnam, both a 'private good' and a 'public good'. But it is undermined in a recession. The first targets of cuts will be those activities which promote social capital, as opposed to those which address emergency social and health needs. Libraries, youth clubs, arts and culture activities; children's centres and Sure Start provision; day care and the provision of home care number among those services which are top of the list, threatening reciprocity, mutual trust and honesty, altruism and volunteering, and well-being.

Probity at risk

It is difficult to conclude whether or not the behaviour of workers in both public and private sectors has deteriorated over recent years as neoliberalism has become entrenched. There is greater public scrutiny and accountability, in a proliferation of traditional and social media. In education, there is some evidence that the new arrangements for schools have offered opportunities in education for key players to further their own interests. We see excessive rewards available to senior staff, governors and trustees benefitting from 'associated activities', and profit-making from the provision of publicly funded schooling. We also see varieties of financial malpractice and the furthering of political or religious agendas by state-funded schools (see Gann, 2014).

The impact on schools

How do these changes translate to the nation's schooling? There is, of course, a direct and very personal link to the most extreme applications of neoliberal principles.

Inevitably, while international companies such as Murdoch's NewsCorp identified a growing market in state-funded education, British companies were not slow to follow. One private company, run by a former chair of Ofsted, told its investors in 2011 that the expansion of academies and the creation of free schools would 'create increased opportunities for private sector companies to manage and run state-funded schools at all levels', having 'identified significant savings' in existing state schools' financial models. Of course, the free school movement was presented by the government to the public as a way in which parents would be able to set up their own schools. In the event, many more free schools were set up by other organisations. Claims were made at the end of 2013 that the DfE had spent more than three times the allocated budget on such schools, and their performance in Ofsted inspections appeared to be about three times worse than other schools.

In March 2014, the TUC published a detailed research report (Johnson and Mansell, 2014) which levelled a series of concerns at the academy and free school programme. The major issues were:

- the use of private consultants in providing 'additional' services to schools (calculated at over £75m);
- poor value for money (with many free schools remaining under-subscribed);
- conflicts of interest of major players;
- the payment of taxpayer-provided funds into private companies (termed 'value extraction' by the report). The increasingly corporate ownership of state-funded schools (contrary to the government's stated purpose of parent-run schools, 'between 2011 and 2013 applications [to run free schools] shot up from 8 to 25 per cent' while 'applications from teacher-led groups plummeted from 24 to 6 per cent and applications from parent and community groups fell by a third').

In sum, state-funded education had been identified as a major source of profit in a variety of ways to the corporate world. Indeed, the TUC Research report suggests that 'education is the world's second largest traded service'. For more than one hundred years, local government's participation in and provision of all state-funded schools had provided a significant control on this, ensuring that the bulk of taxpayer-provided funds remained devoted to the staffing and resourcing of schools, with profit-margins for private suppliers of services and resources remaining at acceptable levels. Indeed, in most schools, somewhere between 85 and 90 per cent of the funding was given over to staffing, with salary differentiation based on professional responsibilities and held in check by the statutory annual Schoolteachers' Pay and Conditions Document.

It began with the provision of building maintenance, starting with the Private Finance Initiatives increasingly demanded of new-build schools by the Labour Government of 1997–2010, and has led to the now extensive engagement of the private business sector in the actual provision of education, buildings and all support services. The involvement of private companies in state-funded schooling can be seen as a rapid process of the commodification of public education (see Gann, 2014).

What's happened in schools?

As we enter a new phase in education following a general election, it would be useful to review what the dominant trends have been in schools. We have seen above how neoliberal policies have significantly affected the way schools operate:

Where does this leave us? If what we are experiencing is a deliberate application of 'disruption innovation' – an application that spreads into a number of areas of coalition government policy – then it is likely that we are in for more of the same. Disruption enables organisations to dismantle all past practices, effective or not, in order to establish a new set of protocols, aims and values. Despite the increasing popularity of disruptive practice, initially in the US, more frequently seen here, there is little evidence for its claims of long-term success.

(Gann, 2014)

The claim that 'the government's flagship policies for improving schools . . . have had little or no effect' couldn't be more wrong. Unfortunately, the effects have been almost entirely malign.

Government education policy since 2010, written in haste to grab tomorrow's headlines, has resulted in millions (if not billions) of pounds in public money being wasted on free-school and academy vanity projects. Children's educations and teachers' careers have been damaged and disrupted as their flagship schools are found to be unfit for purpose and closed. Communities have been divided by bitter, forced-academisation interventions. In the absence of strategic planning to meet the educational needs of all local children, thousands of primary age pupils have no school places.

The list of the victims of this Tory experiment in disruption theory is long. However, it may be that all the chaos and confusion have simply provided an effective smokescreen for the primary purpose of the piecemeal privatisation of state education in our country. Since May 2010, on a scale not seen since the Enclosure Acts of the 18th and 19th centuries, billions of pounds' worth of publicly owned land and assets have quietly been transferred to a bewildering number of trusts, boards and companies whose members are accountable only to the secretary of state for education, while billions of pounds of public money sits in the deposit accounts of free schools and academies.

Government policies have not improved our children's schools but they have been extremely effective in transferring public money and assets to private pockets.

(Cathy Wood, letter to *The Guardian*, 4th February 2015)

Pegging back?

Are there any indications of a pegging back in the breadth and speed of reform? It is a characteristic of disruption innovation that the biggest innovations happen in the early stages. After that, there is a period of settling and seeing what is left, and how it can be tidied up in such a way as to benefit those who have survived. Millar (2014) suggests that two of the 'fundamental pillars of this particular reform movement' might now be in question. The belief that market forces would increase parental choice and improve schools has, it seems, run its course. The free school movement, as we saw, has added little to the availability of good schools for ordinary people. The narrowing of the curriculum continues with its focus on knowledge above skills, but may be soon subject to the pendulum of British education which, for some 150 years, has swung periodically from the Gradgrind approach to the 'informal progressive'. The last quarter of a century has been relentlessly Gradgrindian, so it's probably time for a change. This may, as Millar predicts, mean a switch from the narrow view of education to the broader, and from the competitive to the collaborative.

Hardening of attitudes?

A contrary view is that attitudes among key decision-makers in education continue to harden. 'England's children are being taught in an "unforgiving system" with no real second chances', the president of the Girls' Schools Association was quoted as saying by BBC News in November 2014. Alice Phillips went on to talk about a 'lack of wriggle room' and 'an intensity of expectation' that is 'greater than ever' on students in the newly introduced GCSE grade structure.

Staff morale, especially among teachers, seemed lower than ever, as shown up by the DfE's own survey in the autumn of 2014. Some teachers found themselves subjected to harassment when they took time off for sickness, and to inquisition when they returned. Teachers 'are hounded about why they failed to complete data entry for the last assessment window (despite the fact they were absent for it), why they haven't answered parents' emails and how they plan to ensure absence isn't repeated' (Secret Teacher Blog, 2014b). Workload continued to increase, as Ofsted's demands for a constant flow of data filtered down through the system.

The impact of a poor, or even mediocre, Ofsted report on schools became ever more toxic. Parents were bewildered to find that a happy, apparently successful and certainly over-subscribed school could overnight turn into one that 'required improvement'.

> Over the two years following the inspection report teachers have become demoralised and left the school in droves as the pressure to meet Ofsted's criteria was piled upon them. No new teachers want to join what now looks like a sink school. It has gone from being oversubscribed to the school that will take pupils from anywhere.
>
> (Hirschkorn, 2014)

And the outcome of a poor Ofsted seemed to become ever more inevitable. As the 2015 general election approached, the Conservative party declared that, were it returned with a majority, it would insist that all schools 'requiring improvement' would be forced to convert to academy status, and the head-teachers of primary schools where fewer than 100 per cent of all children could recite their times table would find themselves out of a job.

Simultaneously, and inevitably, reports of increasing cheating and manipulation of data in some schools also grew. If the valuation of numerical data outweighs any other consideration, it is inevitable that some people will feel forced into using any means to produce the desired data.

So the continuing narrative of the right, that the country is covered in 'graffiti-daubed disaster schools' needing to be rescued by superheads 'fearlessly transforming them into centres of academic achievement' (Fryer, 2014) often and ironically swamps the government's legend that schools are on a continuing rising arc of improvement. The inbuilt contradiction of these messages escapes the average parent. But the need for redemption by heroes – heroes who would never stoop to such underhand educational methods as 'niceness' – remains untouched: 'misplaced niceness is the enemy of goodness: If you are too nice to children, and keep letting them off, they never improve' (ibid.).

Changes in academisation

As the numbers of academies, stand-alone, sponsored and federated, and free schools, progressed, it became obvious that the DfE could not manage their establishment and supervision by itself. In September of 2014, a team of eight Regional Schools Commissioners (RSCs) was appointed to cover the regions of England. The RSC job description includes monitoring the performance of academies and free schools and helping them to improve, deciding on academy conversions and sponsors and advising the DfE on free schools. In each region, a headteachers' board (HTB), its members elected from and by academy and free school heads, shares responsibility for approving new academy projects.

This structure might be seen as the first much-predicted step in the eventual replacement of local authorities. Three characteristics mark it out as significantly different from LAs. It is, of course, undemocratic, with neither the general public nor the wider educational world having any say in the personnel responsible for running it. Neither does it acknowledge the ownership and governance of the trusts which are responsible for academies and free schools. Thirdly, it is accountable only to the secretary of state for its performance.

By early November, one of the RSCs was telling school governors gathered in a conference that the DfE 'doesn't talk about forced academisation any more'. In reality, the pace of forced academisation was growing. At around the same time, the RSC for the east Midlands and Humber was vetoing the LAs choice of sponsor for a new primary academy, and giving it instead to a neighbouring 'outstanding' school. Indeed, there seemed to be a shift towards getting both brand new academies and forced converters to be sponsored by other schools in preference to one of the national or local chains that had previously been favoured. This must have been at least partly due to the growing numbers of chains that were disqualified from taking on more schools owing to their continuing under-performance. In response to a Freedom of Information request, the DfE revealed that some £14m had been spent between 2009 and 2014 on the academy brokers responsible for recommending and overseeing academy conversions – because

> The Department requires special expertise for the broker role that it cannot find within the civil service. Their expertise needs to be deployed flexibly in different parts of the country. These and other needs are best secured through a contracted service. This type of engagement also achieves value for money for the taxpayer; it would be far more expensive to employ brokers on permanent terms.
>
> (DfE letter, 5th February 2015)

There was clearly growing concern about the performance of chains. The National Audit Office published a report at the end of October 2014 (NAO, 2014) which revealed that, of 129 underperforming maintained schools where formal interventions had taken place since 2010, only 62 had improved by their next inspection, with the remainder staying the same or getting worse. At the same time, more than half the schools that did not receive any such intervention improved anyway. Meanwhile, the DfE allowed the opening of a free school in south London with just 17 students at a cost of £18m, while the borough of Lambeth actually had a surplus of 200 Year 7 places.

This all suggested a worryingly incoherent, and sometimes mutually contradictory, set of strategies being employed by the department. The outcomes of this rebounded on local authorities, who discovered, at a time of almost unprecedented austerity for local government, that between 2011 and 2014 they themselves had had to spend at least £22.4m on converting maintained schools into academies. The performance of the biggest trusts was increasingly under scrutiny, as it became clear that improvement to underperforming schools was by no means guaranteed by conversion (House of Commons Education Committee, 2015).

Changes in inspection

It is difficult to see the relationship between the DfE and Ofsted continuing as it has been over the last few years. With strong figures heading up both, during 2010 to 2014, there appeared to be a constant struggle over who was setting educational policy. Ofsted became increasingly problem-oriented, rather than solutions-focused, defining what was generically wrong in England's schools, and, increasingly, what should be done about it at a national level, while not addressing the issues in individual schools. This led to it becoming, in the eyes of many in schools, ever more divorced from the daily reality of the classroom and school improvement, and increasingly interested in dictating national policy on, for example, selection in secondary education, and strategies for moral and cultural education. Simultaneously, the DfE developed policies for the curriculum that Ofsted couldn't measure, while Ofsted declared expectations for schools that the DfE hadn't endorsed. To those teachers, parents and politicians who were anyway suspicious of the results-focused agenda, Ofsted represented, by the end of 2014, the key vehicle in the imposition of everything they abhorred: 'The state of Ofsted is a reflection of the state of a system that is vastly overfocused on exams, has lost local democratic accountability, and has left teachers overworked, disempowered and increasingly demoralised' (Natalie Bennett [Leader of the Green Party], letter to *The Guardian*, 29th October, 2014).

Education is a national issue

No-one can argue that, contrary to the immediate post-war years, education is no longer a political issue. From Callaghan's 1976 Ruskin College speech, through Blair's identification of 'education, education, education' as the three big issues of the 1997 election campaign, to Cameron's eye-catching promises leading up to the 2015 election, education – especially schooling – is a big issue. It is blogged about and tweeted about by educationalists, politicians and ordinary consumers as much as any other national issue. It is variously cited as the fifth or sixth most important issue in the election, even at a time of austerity and European discord. We all now care about education. This can only be a good thing.

Schools are (much) better than they were

Schools and GBs are unrecognisable from 25 years ago. Pupil performance, in literacy and numeracy at KS2, in GCSE passes, in behaviour, in physical resource provision, in the quality of professional leadership, is almost immeasurably stronger. Bad schools are rare. Governing boards are stronger, better equipped with skills, more confident in their relationships, more competent and self-assured. They are certainly more aware of the responsibilities that come with the role, which continues to broaden. The government continues to support the unquestioned leadership of schools by a team of predominantly lay governors elected or appointed by the community. Headteachers accept this in a way that might have been unimaginable in the 1990s.

Local authorities, whose performance remains notoriously variable, no longer pretend that they can manage schools from county halls, and headteachers have professional support and development of a high order in a national context. We have a far greater understanding of what constitutes good school leadership, and many competencies have been imported from other sectors to strengthen the headteacher's role.

Free schools and academies have the potential to conduct radical experiments in schooling that would have been very rare, perhaps impossible, in publicly funded schools in the twentieth century. The capacity of on the ground research and development in schooling patterns is unprecedented, and likely to produce genuine advances in the thinking about learning.

There is a much deeper understanding of parental rights and roles. The amount of information about schools and the duty to publish it is now firmly embedded. This may, for some at least, have provided parents with a degree of informed choice impossible before the advent of the worldwide web and the social media.

Teachers and classroom assistants have a clear focus on children's learning, and the creation of new accredited roles in schools for higher level teaching assistants and school business managers has made even the smallest school a formidably professional workplace.

Perhaps – this is a speculation – communities feel more attached to their schools through the localisation of governance and the effective or actual disappearance of local government from the scene. Perhaps governing boards are more obviously accessible to their parents than the local authorities of old. Perhaps governors have a much greater focus on a wider range of school performance measures than before.

What might happen next?

If the current neoliberal agenda for schools continues, there are some trends that are clear. Local government's role in educational provision will continue to wither, with the likelihood being that, by 2020, all remaining schools will have academy status, with a growing regional support structure and likely federated status with other schools, especially in the primary sector. Should the central budget for schools continue to shrink, it will bite in the form of the closure of small schools, especially in rural areas (the major obstacle to such closures hitherto being the understanding by local councillors that this would always be one of their biggest vote-losers). Local government would be left with the provision of a mere rump of transactional services, such as school transport, ensuring school placements and general admissions.

We might well see the expansion of existing grammar schools, and possibly the creation of new areas of the country with selection for secondary schools at eleven or fourteen. A growing number of, initially 'outstanding' and 'good' schools at secondary level would be encouraged to admit a percentage of students by ability. We may even see a time when 'over-subscribed secondary schools would be allowed to make places available for those who can pay top-up fees' (Gann, 2011).

There also looms the likelihood of further, and potentially extremely damaging, cuts to school budgets. There is quite possibly a tacit political agenda, likely to be cross-party, to bring about the closure of small, especially rural, village schools. It has been noised for some years that the smallest viable primary school is likely to have no fewer than 210 pupils. This would cut swathes across counties such as Somerset, Devon and Cornwall in the southwest, Herefordshire and Shropshire in the midlands, Norfolk and Suffolk in the east and Northumberland and Cumbria in the north.

Teacher recruitment is another growing problem. Warnings from experts at the end of 2014 suggest that there will be 27,000 fewer teachers than will be needed in 2017. The country is estimated to need more than 52,000 teachers to enter the profession each year between 2014 and 2017, while it appears that only 44,107 teachers entered in 2011–12. This would lead to larger class sizes, and real crisis in, again, small primary schools, being unable to recruit both teachers and leaders.

Pressure appears to continue on schools to confront terrorism and other extremist thought. At universities, this is already a significant issue, with police engagement against student protest. The Trojan Horse episode in Birmingham may be repeated in other cities across the country, especially those where the authorities suspect that black and minority ethnic groups see school governance as an opportunity to further their own religious and political agenda.

Continuing exclusive focus on examination and test results in schools is likely to see a proliferation of cases of data-fixing in schools. In the autumn of 2014, a primary academy school in north London saw its executive head (awarded a CBE in 2011 for services to developing academies), its head and the director of the school's trust (who happened to be the husband of the executive head) suspended for alleged gross misconduct in this area of the school's operations. Similarly, the number of academy trusts being issued with financial notices to improve from the Education Funding Agency continued to grow. Sometimes these were concerned with accumulating deficits, others with weaknesses in financial management and governance.

At the end of 2014, HMCI Michael Wilshaw, in his annual report, held both school leaders and teachers to blame for the observed slowing down of progress in improving secondary schools. These examples of leaders blaming the troops for poor performance demonstrate a growing trend in any organisation where results are paramount and where leaders see their own personal reputation at stake. It seems in dramatic contrast to the more widespread and understandable issues about the work-life balance of teachers and other school staff which were beginning to be confronted in schools with more emotionally intelligent leadership.

Pressure, competition and accountability to the centre are characteristics of the English schooling system at present. As Pasi Sahlberg, Finland's leading education policy expert told the annual conference of the Specialist Schools and Academies Trust in 2014:

> Competition, choice, test-based accountability and school-based teacher preparation have become common tactics in recent education policies in England. . . . there is an alternative way to improve the nation's educational performance. It is the way of inclusion and equity, teacher and leader professionalism, collaborative practice, and trust-based responsibility that has been the way of Finnish education policies since the 1970s. There are both visible and hidden lessons from Finland for those seeking to transform education systems and enhance overall performance. . . . there is much that England can learn from successful education systems. One key lesson is that equity of outcomes seems to be a common feature behind successful reformers and strong performers.

Chapter 10

The future of governing schools
Future proofing the school

Governing schools from 2015: key issues

School governance may be in crisis. The democratic model is under threat
from the structure of many multi-academic trusts and chains. The probity of
some prominent school leaders, both governors and headteachers, is in question. Measures for school performance are narrowing. While collaboration
between schools is recognised as essential for improvement, competition is
becoming more common. The representativeness of governors, and their relationship with the community, is threatened by the demand for 'skills', if skills
are defined in a limited way. Few governing boards demonstrate a broad and
creative approach to strategic thinking. Governing boards may be becoming
less answerable to the communities served by their schools.

School improvement

Within the limited parameters by which schools are judged, there is plenty of
evidence for continuous improvement since the new structure of governing
was introduced in 1988. Advocates of effective governance would point to this
as at least a possible outcome of better governing among many other elements,
such as the national curriculum, improved leadership and teacher training, and
regular school inspection. However, improvement has not been (and probably
never will be) sufficient to quieten the advocates of current schooling structures, let alone its critics. Most recently, we seem to be experiencing a period
of sustained improvement in primary schools (only some 13 per cent now
being academies) and of a stalling in the improvement of secondary schools.
Here, neither academisation nor the intervention of inspection seem to be
positively affecting results (Ofsted 2014c): Results in external exams are not
improving nationally, school leadership is 'not good enough', there are not
enough good teachers, and the gap between the performance of advantaged
and disadvantaged children is not closing fast enough. The outcome seems to
be C+ : could do better.

Cooperation and collaboration

There is a general consensus that the most reliable way to improve schools is through cooperation and collaboration, ranging from hard federation and academy chain membership to soft federation and curriculum collaboration. The task of governing groups and federations of schools, as a task with different characteristics to the governing of an individual school, is beginning to attract attention:

> The relationship between . . . federations and improved student out-comes . . . indicate the potential for locally generated solutions that impact on schools in challenging circumstances. This is a welcome sign in a system that has been preoccupied with mandated, top–down driven change.
>
> (Chapman, 2013: p. 13)

Academy chains were seen in 2012 to contribute to this: 'Academy chains are a positive development within the English education system. They are bring-ing innovation and systematic improvement and helping to raise attainment in some of the most deprived parts of the country' (Hill et al., 2012: p. 102) However:

> Sponsored chains have challenges to address as they expand. They need to reflect on what it means to be a chain and be clear about their teaching and learning and operating model. They are having to adapt their leadership, governance and management structures and practices. The performance of weaker chains needs addressing.
>
> (Hill et al., 2012: p. 102)

As time went on, the benefits of academy chains became less clear. And the fact remains that, for many schools, especially those in the secondary sector, and for many such free schools, the dominant mode remains competition with other schools in the locality. But how indeed could it be otherwise in the ethos that dominates in much of the schooling world? Of course, competition and choice require spare capacity, which can only be found in the per pupil funding intended for expenditure on educational provision. Continuing competition is unsustainable, except where it diverts funding from its intended purpose.

Governance as social capital

Good local school governance represents a form of social capital, offering com-munity engagement in the delivery of a public service which is seen by pretty well everyone as a public good. At its best, it enables communities to develop a sense of ownership over their local school, providing accountability of the service and requiring professionals to be responsive to local need.

However, constant demands over 25 years that schools be more 'business-like' and learn skills from business models are now being formalised. The SGOSS (School Governors' One-Stop Shop) initiative 'Make Schools Your Business' launched in the autumn of 2014 has the potential to overplay the contribution that business-related skills can play on a local school governing board. One aspect of the impact of the business model in school governance can be readily seen in the behaviour of some of the academy chains we looked at in Chapter 9. Expertise without probity, skills without appropriate values, may undermine the local accountability and ownership of schools and turn them into another local business, judged primarily by its capacity to meet standards imposed by a centralised state.

It is estimated that there are some 15 million volunteers in Britain; 350,000 or more of these are governors. What might our gross domestic product look like if this contribution to schools were recognised in financial terms? Taking a modest average of 60 hours a year contributed by the 'average' governor, on minimum wage rates, would offer something like £150m a year provided to state-funded education by volunteers. In reality, and in actual value, it would be much more than this. Pricing and paying the value added to a school by its governing board might be rather too business-like for any government to consider. Meanwhile, Jones (2014), among others, suggests that growing inequality and relative poverty tend to reduce volunteering.

Protection of the social capital offered by democratically accountable school governance needs to be a priority at both national and local levels, with governors rejecting the opportunities offered by the current structures to become a self-perpetuating clique.

Probity

Probity and disinterestedness in the leadership of schools appear to be more of an issue in an increasingly privatised state-funded schooling system than in the former more unified system. Chris James, national expert in school governing and Professor of Education at Bath University has said, 'every governor has to behave in such a way that the governing board has legitimacy'. That is, just as one bit of inappropriate behaviour can bring a whole process into question – like appointing a member of staff, for instance – so one piece of wrongdoing can undermine the board's moral right to lead the school. We have seen over the last fifteen years how immoral, and sometimes illegal behaviour can damage the reputation and legitimacy of the House of Commons, of the press, of the police, of the banking industry. Volunteers normally hold the moral high ground, but if they act venally or stupidly, the whole movement can find itself at risk.

Thinking strategically

The requirement for governing boards to set the strategic direction of the school places it firmly in the higher level of leadership. But is it possible for the governors of an organisation who have no say in the definition of quality or effectiveness to take on that strategic leadership role? Governors of organisations in the private and voluntary sectors determine the purpose of an organisation, and lay down the parameters of success and failure; they then monitor the extent to which the organisation is meeting those demands; and are able to respond to changes in circumstance or environment. None of these lies in the purview of a state-funded school governing board. Ofsted defines the standards to which a school must conform, the DfE determines the desirable outcomes of schooling. All that actually remains to the governors, with the headteacher, is to lay down the route by which they should meet these requirements.

Perhaps it is this that explains why so few governing boards have a clearly defined strategy, and why their stated values and ethos are likely to be so unoriginal and platitudinous. All the investment and exhortation to governors to provide the strategic leadership of a school or a chain of schools will find it difficult to overcome the plain fact that governors have no power to decide what makes a school good.

Democratic accountability

In 2014, the then chair of the parliamentary select committee on education told a conference of governors and academics that he was 'less interested in democratic accountability than in quality'. This apparently throwaway comment, however, betrays a commitment to centralised thinking and planning that undermines the whole accountability process of school governance. Quality in schools, as we see, is effectively defined outside the democratic process. There was no public commitment in 2010 by either of the coalition parties to a policy about the widespread academisation of the schooling system. No-one – neither lay, professional nor academic – was invited to express views about this and, indeed, those opposed to it were characterised as 'the Blob' and as 'enemies of promise'.

Governance of schools *appears* to hold both democratic and professional accountability, by the process of election to the board by stakeholders, and by accountability for the performance of the school, upwards to the secretary of state, and downwards to the headteacher. But much of this accountability is spurious. Academy chains and stand-alone academies have largely internally appointed and potentially self-perpetuating trustees and boards of governors, and Ofsted, the DfE and, for maintained schools, local authorities have the powers to remove governors, to remove schools from trustees, and to remove headteachers from schools. How sustainable is this model?

As Wilkins (2014) suggests, perhaps: 'The definition of good governance should be expanded to take account of the different mechanisms by which schools aim to enhance local accountability through greater stakeholder engagement and the creation of student-, teacher- and parent-led feedback systems, including councils, forums and Friends' Associations' (though we might want to expand 'teacher-led' to 'staff-led').

What might it be like?

What might a more democratically accountable *and* educationally robust structure for the piecemeal system we have now look like? At local level, we could seek a partial restoration of the local coordination of educational provision. The challenges faced by educational establishments should be addressed by the creation of Local Education Boards to cover all areas of England, coterminous with local authority boundaries. These would replace both existing local authorities' responsibility for schools and the regional schools commissioners with their headteacher boards.

The Boards would be partly directly elected by the public and partly elected by governors of existing educational establishments. Boards would be responsible for:

- the oversight of the efficiency and effectiveness of all educational provision from early years to further education (re-establishing local input to colleges of further education), including all independent and private providers;
- ensuring universal access to high quality comprehensive provision and public accountability;
- enabling cooperation between educational providers from all sectors;
- ensuring fair admission arrangements and equality of access (including the provision of transport);
- ensuring provision of appropriate education for children regardless of need;
- disseminating best practice amongst all providers;
- enabling innovation in educational practice;
- providing information to the public and an appeals process in the event of unresolved complaints.

Boards would be responsible directly to parliament for their performance, and subject to inspection against agreed criteria, including achievement levels across the locality.

Boards would also take responsibility for ensuring multi-agency approaches to children's social care, working with local authorities while current arrangements obtain. The Boards would provide oversight and some level of standardisation, while enabling and encouraging innovation and experimentation within a controlled environment. No extra costs need be caused by this structure, as they would replace many of the functions currently carried out by local authorities (see Gann in House of Commons Education Committee, 2013).

At school level, the status of all schools currently academies or free schools would be required to reflect their position as community-based charities – whether as stand-alone academies or as members of a chain or multi-academy trust. They would be required to be membership charities, with membership including:

- any parent or carer of any child enrolled in the school (or 16+s who are enrolled), would automatically take up membership.

Other individuals could apply for membership, for example:

- any member of the community served by the school who would like to be a member;
- any individual with a connection to the school who would like to be a member;
- any person with a skill or quality that the school would find helpful, and would like to be a member.

Membership duties and responsibilities would include annual election of a third or a quarter of the board with local responsibility for the school (in chains and MATs, this would be a step in the election of the overall collective trust board). Members would receive an annual report from the board on the school's performance across a wide range of measures agreed by the membership, at an annual general meeting. In order to involve staff and to observe rules on employee engagement with charity governance, employee membership might offer a distinctive category of membership, either non-voting, or voting for a limited form of board membership.

All grouped academies would be limited geographically and to an optimum size around two dozen, and would have overall governance developed on these lines.

This membership, above all, would be empowered to hold the board to account on an agreed set of performance standards and, ultimately, under extreme circumstances (where the board's probity or effectiveness is seriously compromised) to remove it altogether. It allows any member of the community, and encourages parents, to become 'social shareholders' in the school. They will have already made a financial investment in the school through paying taxes and council charges. By investing their time and interest, care and responsibility in the school, their returns include a successful and energising school, a vibrant community and a generation of young people with the skills and qualities to lead that community into the future.

Strategic directions

So now let us look at the things that should be on the strategic checklist of every school governing board, whatever type of school it is, whatever its internal arrangements are. These matters will apply also to governing boards and bodies in other countries where they exist, in our increasingly global school culture. Consultation with groups of headteachers suggest that the following are medium and long-term strategic issues on which governing boards should have a view:

- poverty, hardship and inequality;
- accountability;
- staffing and staff well-being;
- the character of the school;
- collaboration and governing groups of schools;
- performance;
- managing in austerity;
- population change;
- children's well-being and experience of the world.

Does your governing board have a strategic take on these issues?

Poverty, hardship and inequality

Currently, it is estimated that about 1 in 4 children are living in poverty in the United Kingdom. Despite previous governments' pledges to end child poverty by 2020, it is, according to many commentators, most likely that by that date 1 in 3 children will be affected. At the time of writing it is estimated that 5 million people are living on poverty wages and 90,000 children were believed to be homeless on Christmas Day, 2014. We have seen increasing incidents of teachers and schools supporting children in poverty, sometimes feeding them from their own pockets, and certainly dealing with the consequences of homelessness, emergency accommodation and other family crises. It is beyond question that this is the most serious issue likely to affect the conduct of schools in the UK, whether in already challenged areas or in 'leafy suburbs'. Governing boards need to have systems for monitoring and tackling the actual and relative deprivation brought about by poverty. It will impact on every aspect of the school – attainment, both relative and actual; progress; behaviour; ethos, staffing and engagement with governance.

In addition, of course, state schooling brings its own costs. A Children's Commission on Poverty Inquiry in the autumn of 2014 suggested that parents faced significant annual bills on basics such as dinners, uniforms, course materials and trips:

> For many families, education-related costs make up a large portion of the family budget. Parents told us that, on average, they spend £800 per child each year on school costs. It is clear from the inquiry that many families are burdened by these costs:
>
> - More than two-thirds (70 per cent of parents say they have struggled with the cost of school. This rises to 95 per cent of parents who live in families that are 'not well off at all'.
> - Half (51 per cent) of parents said they had cut back on clothing, food or heating to afford school costs.

- A quarter (25 per cent) of parents (and more than half of those in families which were 'not well off at all') said they had borrowed money in order to afford the cost of school.

The inquiry heard that many children are acutely aware that their parents struggle with the cost of school:

- More than half of children have avoided asking their parents or guardian for something school related because they thought they would struggle to afford it.
- Nearly two–thirds (63 per cent) of children in families who are 'not well off at all' said they had been embarrassed because they could not afford a cost of school.
- More than a quarter (27 per cent) said they had been bullied as a result.
  (Children's Commission on Poverty, 2014: pp. 4–5)

The Report's twelve recommendations for schools are:

- simple affordable uniforms with sew–on logos;
- cashless systems for meals;
- expansion of free school meal eligibility;
- roll–over of unspent free school meal money from day-to-day;
- 'poverty-proofing' of all school activities;
- voluntary activities not to exclude children for inability to pay;
- no non–returnable deposits for activities, and options to pay by instalment;
- itemised costs available to parents when signing up for activities;
- communications from school to be direct to parents, not through children;
- transparency in spending of pupil premium money;
- training of staff to improve understanding of poverty;
- Ofsted inspections to consider support of poorest pupils and school's performance in lessening the impact of poverty.

(ibid., p.11)

It is not just poverty, whether real or relative, that has an impact on schools. Increasing inequality, both global and national, will inevitably play a role in relationships, and will impact on schools' capacity to manage.

Of course, poverty and the growing problem of low pay leading to working poverty also affects the composition of governing boards. It is likely to become increasingly difficult to get a comprehensive social mix on a board if more and more people have to work longer and more 'flexible' hours at work, or can't afford child care. The minds of governors might at the same time give consideration to how well they reflect both the social and the cultural diversity of the neighbourhoods they serve.

There is a sense in which every other strategic issue that governors will face in the foreseeable future will be both dwarfed and fed by poverty.

Accountability

Accountability is at the heart of the democracy which is vaunted as perhaps the first and most important of our 'British values'.

How do governing boards enable the local community – pupils, parents and the wider community – to hold governors accountable for their conduct of the school? State-funded schools – whether maintained or independent – need to build systems which will give people the confidence to challenge them, just as governors need strategies to challenge the professional conduct of the school.

Similarly, how do governing boards demonstrate to their communities – the school community and the neighbourhood served by the school – that they are spending taxpayers' money wisely and in the way that is most likely to benefit most children? From the figure available on the remaining maintained schools (around 18,500 at present, a number that shrinks each year as schools convert to academy status and whose finances are calculated differently), it appears that some £30bn were spent in the financial year 2013–14. The average reserve per school was estimated at a whopping £422,000. This is money intended for current pupils and not being spent – for a variety of reasons (DfE, 2014d). It seems likely that the overall figure for all state-funded schools in England is in excess of £4bn.

Schools, by dint of their educational role, should be in the forefront of constructing systems which will actively empower the population to develop the skills, the confidence and the language to hold public services, starting with the school, to account.

In 2013, the minister with responsibility for school governance suggested that governing boards should report to parents annually on the performance of the school. A report might include:

- numbers of meetings and main topics;
- membership of the board and attendance at meetings;
- training undertaken by governors and its impact;
- simplified financial report showing annual accounts totals and reserves, with key areas of expenditure;
- impact of the board's actions and decisions on school improvement;
- plans and priorities for the coming year/three years.

Ultimately, governing boards of all types of school should be asking themselves the five questions about power proposed by Tony Benn:

1   What power have you got?
2   Where did you get it from?
3   In whose interest do you exercise it?
4   To whom are you accountable?
5   How can we get rid of you?

Staffing and staff well-being

After the Second World War a whole raft of people, many privately educated, saw a vocation in the not particularly well-paid public services that were changing and expanding rapidly under a radical Labour government. This attitude lasted for at least a generation, so that there was still a genuine idealism among people going to work in state education in the 1970s.

Whether or not that is the case, the respect in which teachers, nurses, doctors, council officers might have been held by government ministers and other politicians, national and local, no longer seems evident. Teachers and other school staff are variously excoriated for idleness and general lack of moral fibre. This change happened throughout the 1980s and '90s, and was all part of the political aim of 'shrinking the state'.

This leaves us with two immediately observable problems – staff supply and staff well-being.

Numerous reports have shown increasing problems in recruiting both head-teachers and other senior school leaders. Serving headteachers seem to be leaving the profession well before retirement. A survey of heads in the summer of 2014 found, of those who responded, 67 per cent were considering leaving the profession before retirement age ('Head teacher recruitment "increasingly difficult" warning', www.bbc.co.uk, 21st June 2014). This seems to be an outcome of the increasing pressure on heads to produce continuous sustainable improvement in results, while managing evermore complex demands from Ofsted coupled with dismissive comments from the chief inspector of schools. No surprise, as we saw earlier, that headship is no longer the attractive career target it used to be.

Applications for teacher preparation courses starting in September 2015 saw a drop of more than 3,500 applicants compared with the previous year, suggesting that teacher supply, senior teacher supply, headteacher supply are all in retreat while pupil numbers continue to grow. In nursery and primary schools, numbers are projected to be 18 per cent higher by 2021 compared with 2010, reaching levels last seen in the 1970s. Meanwhile, teacher and other staff morale appears to be ebbing fast, driving even the DfE to conduct its own survey on work–life balance in schools. DfE figures showed that almost fifty thousand teachers left the profession in the 12 months to November 2013, an increase of 25 per cent over four years.

So retaining good staff, recruiting new staff at all levels, and managing staff morale are three priorities for all governing boards. It seems unlikely that the DfE's plans for performance-related pay are, by themselves, likely to address these problems. Indeed, some staff say that they exacerbate the issue, by promoting competition rather than cooperation between individuals.

While staff in schools generally report high levels of job satisfaction, they consistently also report very high, often unmanageable, workloads and often poor communications. The extent and frequency of change, usually imposed from above, cause high levels of stress. While workload levels are unlikely to change, schools that address the issue by consulting staff and introducing strategies to support them in their work management seem to do better for both pupils and staff (Briner and Dewberry, 2007).

Here are some questions which governors should ask themselves:

1   What do we do to make the school an attractive place to work for newcomers and serving staff?
2   How do we ensure that the school is a learning organisation, and that all staff leave better off than when they arrived?
3   How do we give staff opportunities to develop skills?
4   How do we acknowledge that staff with rich personal lives are likely to make more inspiring models for children?
5   What does the school do to manage change, and help staff to manage workload?
6   What does the governing board do to ensure that staff are working under the best possible conditions to enable their pupils to learn?
7   How do we engage all staff in the continuous improvement of the school?
8   How do we ensure that staff careers flourish?

The character of the school: tough or tender?

The branding of a school is critical to its ability to achieve its strategic aims. All schools have an image, but not all schools determine their own image, and many allow it to be determined by events that brand it in the eyes of the public. Often, the school is branded by an image determined, not by the governing board, but by actions of the headteacher or other leadership.

It is unclear, in the case of the Ryde school where the headteacher condemned 'niceness' ('misplaced niceness is the enemy of goodness: if you are too nice to children, and keep letting them off, they never improve'), as we saw in Chapter 9, whether the governing board had previously approved, or even supported after the event, the actions of the head in excluding large numbers of pupils for wearing the wrong trousers. At the other polar extreme, the letter sent by a primary school head to children clearly labelled the school as a primarily caring institution, where children's performance in external tests was seen as secondary to their confidence and self-esteem (Letter to *The Guardian*, 22nd December 2014).

Dear . . . .

Please find enclosed your end of KS2 test results. We are very proud of you as you demonstrated huge amounts of commitment and tried very hard during this tricky week.

However, we are concerned that these tests do not always assess all of what it is that makes each of you special and unique. The people who create these tests and score them do not know each of you the way your teachers do, the way I hope to, and certainly not the way your families do. They do not know that many of you speak two languages. They do not know that you can play a musical instrument or that you can dance or paint a picture. They do not know that your friends count on you to be there for them or that your laughter can brighten the dreariest day. They do not know that you write poetry or songs, play or participate in sports, wonder about the future, or that sometimes you take care of your little brother or sister after school. They do not know that you have travelled to a really neat place or that you know how to tell a great story or that you really love spending time with special family members and friends. They do not know that you can be trustworthy, kind or thoughtful, and that you try, every day, to be your very best . . . the scores you get will tell you something but they will not tell you everything. . .

(Barrowford Primary School, Nelson, Lancashire)

These two schools represent the extremes of only one scale, but a very important scale to its pupils and parents and staff, by which it is characterised. Others might include: arts or sciences; more or less able; egalitarian or elitist; formal or informal. It is one of the governing board's most important jobs to determine what their school will be known for, and how it will be reported.

Collaboration and governing groups of schools

There appears to be widespread agreement that inter-school cooperation is as sure a route to continuing improvement as any other strategy. The academy chain model would seem to provide that. But it may not be the case. A school that is out on a geographical limb in a large and perhaps faceless chain can be as isolated as any small village school, and chain membership can sometimes act as a bar to cooperation with local schools. Certainly we have seen, in Chapter 9, that where schools compete for pupils, cooperation may be a mere facade. The coming of further cuts will only intensify that competitiveness.

Governing groups of schools offers substantial challenges – what should central governing boards know about individual schools under their control? What formats should schools share? What procedures and policies should federated schools share or hold individually? What should the strength of the collective 'brand' be in the face of the character of individual schools? (The All Party Parliamentary Group document, 2015, helps to focus on some of these issues.)

It is possible for schools in small groups or on an individual basis to begin to confront this issue. The academy model, as Professor Ron Glatter points out, 'is essentially based on the governance structure of private schools. It is a top-down model and allows for minimal engagement on the part of key stakeholders' (Glatter, 2013). Glatter proposes models

> that avoid the two extremes of the present set-up: an exaggerated focus on autonomy and competition on the one hand and alienating and unsustainable centralisation on the other. They should surely be models in which:
>
> - power and control are dispersed rather than concentrated;
> - co-operation is placed above competition;
> - there is a strong focus on communities; and
> - local stakeholders including staff can have a sense of belonging – if not of ownership, then at least of membership.
>
> (Glatter, 2013)

The model proposed above, in the 'what might it be like' section, sets out to meet these criteria.

Performance

Most research – most recently, Baker et al.'s for the DfE published in 2014 – continues to show high levels of pupil and parental satisfaction with their schools. As many as nine out of ten parents of children in Year 9 described their child's school as good or very good, though this decreased in areas of deprivation. They were 'overwhelmingly' satisfied with the schools' discipline, children's behaviour, the curriculum. The young people themselves reported that they generally enjoyed school and that they worked as hard as they could. This view contrasts with the official view held by the DfE and Ofsted. For them, one third of England's secondary schools are failing, with 170,000 pupils in 'inadequate' institutions. Somewhere, different criteria are being applied.

First, there is now sufficient evidence around to say that the structure of a school is irrelevant to its performance. Whether maintained, voluntary aided or controlled, academy or free school; whether stand-alone or member of a chain or a federation, there appears to be no discernible difference in performance according to Ofsted's performance criteria. These criteria are, of course, largely about the outputs of schools measured by test and examination results. But a characteristic of recent governments is to suggest that other countries do better – though the fashion of which countries those are changes regularly. Once, everything that was done in the USA had to be done here. Sweden has had its time in the spotlight. More recently, the Far East has become the model – despite there being some evidence that the PISA results reported by the Chinese are highly selective and not to be trusted. In fact, generally, PISA's validity and reliability are questioned, along with 'the way it has been elevated into a measure of the performance not just of samples of 15-year-olds in limited aspects of their learning, which it is, but of entire education systems' (Alexander, 2014: p. 360). Always in schools there must be, it seems, problems to be solved, rather than successes to be celebrated. Indeed, for many, Ofsted itself is one of the problems.

The lesson here for governors is to ensure that they are using more than one measure, and more than one view of their school, to reach judgements about its performance.

What questions does this raise?

- What measures does the governing board use to determine the school's success?
- How many different perceptions and needs does the school try to satisfy?
- Does the governing board celebrate success while helping to sustain improvement?
- What does the governing board know about what happens to the pupils after they leave the school?

Managing in austerity

One thing we do appear to be able to guarantee about the short-term future in schools is that they will not be generously funded. At the time of writing, both major political parties are committed to continuing reductions on spending. In the year 2013–14, the UK government spent about £27bn on primary schooling and £36bn on secondary schooling. One suggestion by their coalition partners is that a Conservative government elected in 2015 would cut around £13.3bn a year from the education budget by 2020. Their commitment to lowering income tax would be almost certain to make further inroads into public services. Governing boards will certainly need to plan for lower annual budgets and further financial uncertainty.

This goes also for the supply of school places overall. Local authorities are responsible for ensuring school places, but have few powers to provide them. The Local Government Association reported in early 2015 that the shortage of school places had reached crisis point, with classrooms already overcrowded and the DfE predicting that 900,000 extra places would be needed in the next decade.

Population change

Austerity has also brought about shortages in the supply of school places, particularly in towns and cities, while there is some evidence of a 'flight from the countryside', making some rural schools less viable than ever. Changes in population trends are discernible some years in advance, and governing boards need to be aware of these and planning for them. This might sometimes involve consideration of admission arrangements and of age ranges.

Increasingly for many schools, the nature of the school population is changing. With freer movement of European nationals throughout the community, children arrive in schools in all parts of the country from all parts of Europe, sometimes with little grasp of the English language. An issue that tended to be confined to the larger urban areas is now likely to affect schools in every part of the country. The school needs a strategy to embrace not just the children, but also families in often fragile conditions.

Children's well-being, mental health and experience of the world

The rapid changes in information availability and communication, including developments in social media, progressively make the experience of each generation of children more different from its predecessors. Is the world better for today's children than it was for us, or worse? And in what ways? Governors and schoolworkers should not make assumptions about this, and the children's experience of the world should be at the forefront in consideration of curriculum and structural school changes.

There is evidence that children's well-being, too, is progressively more at risk, and governing boards need to be conscious of this and ensure that the school has ways of actively promoting it within the whole school experience. (See, for example, Child Poverty Action Group, 2009; Savage, 2010.)

Being strategic

As we have seen, 'being strategic' is probably one of the least developed of skills in many governing boards. For some twenty-five years, there have been continuing attempts to help governors focus on the strategic rather than the operational. We know that some governors shy away from the difficult tasks of predicting and planning.

An Ofsted analysis reported in the autumn of 2014 suggested that governing boards that were failing to improve their schools sufficiently quickly showed four traits: the chairs had been in post too long; the governors were not being properly strategic and evaluative; the governors were being diverted by building projects, falling rolls or academy conversion; or there was 'internal turbulence'.

One issue here is that, for the governors to know how to act as a board, the headteacher needs to know how to act as a chief executive. Governance, much to the frustration of many governors and of those who work with them, has never played a prominent, or even a required, part of the National Professional Qualification for Headship. Now that the qualification itself is optional, it is possible for headteachers to take up their post without any practical experience, let alone formal training, in serving a board. Governing boards can only make a difference to a school when they do a different job from the senior leadership – not just ratifying or checking, but planning and initiating. The school is a public service agency, and it should be unthinkable that such an organisation might be run by a group of people, not one of whom need have received any formal training in their role.

Conclusion

This book has been written in the face of considerable political and economic uncertainty, nationally and globally. It may turn out that that could be said of anything published in the foreseeable future. I have therefore tried to avoid making predictions, or assuming that anything that is happening now, or is required of schools and their governors, will still be so, even by the time this is published.

Does this picture we have drawn in the last few chapters suggest that school governors are living up to the big write-up they got in the introduction to this book? Probably not. But the seeds of a genuinely democratic process in the oversight of schools are there, even if they have lain dormant for longer than one might wish. It would, perhaps, take not very much to establish a system of school governance that is accountable, responsive, strategic and genuinely responsible.

Just imagine. Suppose the governing board of a maintained school, or of an academy, in a town, were to demand better support and provision for children's mental health and well-being in the area. Or to play an active role in the area's planning for new housing? To agree to work with social services in setting up support networks for migrant workers and their families? What about a school governing board which brought a neighbourhood or a collection of rural villages together to combat poverty? Or an urban group of schools of all types met to decide how best to confront rising demand in a time of frozen budgets? Suppose all the governing boards of all the schools in a town or a region were to get together. What influence such a child-centred lobby would have! How their networks would spread into all sorts of different organisations and agencies! What power would they have? Then, truly, a community might be said to have 'caught the vision of its own powers'.

In the end, governance cannot ignore the big questions, however hard it tries and whatever the circumstances: what is school for? How do we want it to be in three or five or ten years time? What do we want children to learn? How do we want children to be? These are the strategic challenges that we now, excitingly, face.

As I suggested in the introduction to this book, school governance is not a straight line or a series of straight lines. Some agencies would seem to like the process of governing a school to be a set of compliances – tick these boxes and it will be good; tick a few more and it will be outstanding. Some would like nothing more than that governance keeps a school 'in line'. Give a straight strategic direction; keep the headteacher in line; ensure the bottom line of the school's finances.

But the best governance is more than one-dimensional. It is full and rounded, like the life of the school, like the lives of the children in the school. Like the girl in the story of the class nature walk in Chapter 7, the very best governance allows the school to say to its pupils, its students, its staff, its parents and its community: 'Look! You can see the whole of the world from here.'

Reading list

This is a select list of reading that school governors and staff may find helpful. It consists of books that may be *useful* to them in performing their tasks, that offer something more *interesting* to liven up the way they do their job, or that they may find *inspiring*; that is, they may be of no immediate practical use, but will help them to develop a vision of what schools can be like.

At the end, there is a list of blogs and tweeters that you might find helpful, too: the governance twitterati comprise an eclectic community sharing information, discussions and sometimes bizarre views.

Useful

Adamson, S. (ed.) (2014) *The School Governors' Yearbook 2015*, Norwich: Adamson Publishing Ltd.

Allcroft, G. and Knights, E. (2014) *The Chair's Handbook*, Birmingham: National Governors' Association.

ASCL, LGA, NAHT and NGA (2015) *What Governing Boards Should Expect from School Leaders and What School Leaders Should Expect from Governing Boards* (3rd ed.), Association of School and College Leaders, Local Government Association and National Governors' Association.

Children's Commission on Poverty (2014) *Through Young Eyes: At What Cost? Exposing the Impact of Poverty on School Life*, London: The Children's Society.

Department for Education (DfE) (2015) *Governors' Handbook: For Governors in Maintained Schools, Academies and Free Schools*, London: Department for Education.

Forum (Journal for promoting 3–19 comprehensive education, published by Symposium Books).

House of Commons Education Committee (2013) *The Role of School Governing Bodies: Second Report of Session 2013–14*, London: The Stationery Office.

House of Commons Education Committee (2015) *Academies and Free Schools, Fourth Report of the Session 2014–15*, London: The Stationery Office.

James, C., Goodall, J., Howarth, E. and Knights, E. (2014) *The State of School Governing in England 2014*, Bath: University of Bath/National Governors' Association.

Johnson, M. and Mansell, W. (2014) *Education Not for Sale: A TUC Research Report*, London: Trades Union Congress.

McInerney, L. (2011) *The Six Predictable Failures of Free Schools . . . and How to Avoid Them*, Cambridge: LKM Consulting.

National Audit Office (2014) *Academies and Maintained Schools: Oversight and Intervention*, London: NAO.

National Governors' Association and Wellcome Trust (2015) *A Framework for Governance: A Flexible Guide to Strategic Planning*, London: Wellcome Trust.

O'Brien, P. (1993) *Taking the Macho Out of Management*, London: Sheldon Books.

Ofsted (2014b) *School Inspection Handbook, September 2014*, London: Ofsted.

Paxton-Doggett, K. (2014) *How to Run an Academy School*, London: ICSA Publishing.

Sallis, J. (1977) *School Managers and Governors: Taylor and After*, London: Ward Lock.

Sallis, J. (1993) *Basics for School Governors*, Stafford: Network Educational Press.

Sallis, J. (1994) *Heads and Governors: Building the Partnership*, Coventry: Action for Governors' Information and Training.

Sallis, J. (2001) *Effective School Governors: A Practical Guide*, Harlow: Pearson Education.

Spicer, D., Crawford, M., Earley, P., James, C., Bubb, S., Furniss, R., Jones, J., Nelson, R. and Wood, E. (2014) *Effectively Managing Headteacher Performance: Research Report*, Nottingham: NCTL.

Interesting

Benn, M. (2011) *School Wars: The Battle for Britain's Education*, London: Verso.

Chitty, C. (2014) *Education Policy in Britain* (3rd ed.), Basingstoke: Palgrave MacMillan.

Hallgarten, J. (2000) *Parents Exist, OK!?: Issues and Visions for Parent–School Relationships*, London: Institute for Public Policy Research.

Heckstall-Smith, H. (1962) *Doubtful Schoolmaster*, London: Peter Davies.

Jones, O. (2014) *The Establishment: And How They Get Away With It*, London: Allen Lane.

McKergow, M. and Bailey, H. (2014) *Host: Six New Roles of Engagement for Teams, Organisations, Communities and Movements*, London: Solutions Books.

May, A. with Berwick, D. (2014) *The School of Freedom: The School Strike, Burston, Norfolk (1914–1939) and its Legacy*, Norwich: David A Berwick.

Meek, J. (2014) *Private Island: Why Britain Now Belongs to Someone Else*, London: Verso.

Putnam, R. (2000) *Bowling Alone: The Collapse and Revival of American Community*, New York: Simon and Schuster.

Verhaeghe, P. (trans. J. Hedley-Prôle) (2014) *What About Me? The Struggle for Identity in a Market-Based Society*, London: Scribe Publications.

Wilkinson, R. and Pickett, K. (2010) *The Spirit Level: Why Equality is Better for Everyone*, London: Penguin.

Inspiring

Berg, L. (1968) *Risinghill, Death of a Comprehensive School*, London: Penguin.

Carver, J. (1990) *Boards That Make a Difference*, San Francisco: Jossey-Bass.

Freire, P. (1972) *Pedagogy of the Oppressed*, London: Penguin.

Holmes, E. (1911) *What is and What Might Be: A Study of Education in General and Elementary Education in Particular*, London: Constable.

Holmes, G. (1952) *The Idiot Teacher: A Book About Prestolee School and its Headmaster E. F. O'Neill*, London: Faber and Faber.

Ree, H. (1973) *Educator Extraordinary: The Life and Achievement of Henry Morris 1889–1961*, London: Longman.

Robinson, K. and Aronica, L. (2015) *Creative Schools: Revolutionizing Education from the Ground Up*, London: Allen Lane.

Sandel, M. (2012) *What Money Can't Buy: The Moral Limits of the Markets*, London: Penguin.

Stacey, M. (1991) *Parents and Teachers Together*, Milton Keynes: Open University Press.

Van der Eyken, W. and Turner, B. (1969) *Adventures in Education*, London: Allen Lane.

Blogs, websites and Twitter

Department for Education: https://www.gov.uk/government/organisations/department-for-education

National Governors' Association: http://www.nga.org.uk/Home.aspx

National College for Teaching and Leadership: https://www.gov.uk/government/organisations/national-college-for-teaching-and-leadership

Ofsted: https://www.gov.uk/government/organisations/ofsted

An information website for clerks and all governors: http://www.clerktogovernors.co.uk

A website for all who work in schools: http://www.workinginschool.net

Information and support for governors: http://www.governornet.co.uk

Information about schools regularly updated: schoolsimprovement.net

Twitter

If you tweet, you'll find you get almost all of your up-to-date information about schools and governance by following a few of the following:

@clerktogovernor; @SchoolsWeek; @andewilkins; @GuardianTeach; @GuardianEdu; @GovernorHub; @jackieschneider; @warwickmansell; @miss_mcinerney; @TeacherROAR; @katiecpd; @5N_Afzal; @Schools_News; @rmagovernance; @ClerktoGovernor; @UKGovChat; @SchoolsImprove; @rrunsworth; @schooltruth; @Robt_Hill; @Samfr; @NGAMedia; @localschools_uk; @WorkinginSchool; @hamdoneducation; @SchoolGovNet

Bibliography

Adams, J. and Punter, A. (2008) 'Finding (and Keeping) School Governors: The Work of the School Governors' One-Stop-Shop', *Management in Education*, 22(4): 14–17.

Adamson, S. (ed.) (2014) *The School Governors' Yearbook 2015*, Norwich: Adamson Publishing Ltd.

Adonis, A. (2012) *Education, Education, Education: Reforming England's Schools*, London: Biteback Publishing Ltd.

Agnew, R. (2014) 'How Can Headteachers Support Good Governance and Why Should They?', http://www.rmagovernance.com/2014/04/09/how-can-headteachers-support-good-governance-and-why-should-they (accessed May 2015).

Alexander, R. (2014) 'Evidence, Policy and the Reform of Primary Education: A Cautionary Tale', *Forum*, 56(3): 349–376.

Allcroft, G. and Knights, E. (2014) *The Chair's Handbook*, Birmingham: National Governors' Association.

Ambrose, P. (1974) *The Quiet Revolution: Social Change in a Sussex Village 1871–1971*, Sussex University Press: Chatto and Windus.

ASCL, LGA, NAHT and NGA (2015) *What Governing Boards Should Expect from School Leaders and What School Leaders Should Expect from Governing Boards* (3rd ed.), Association of School and College Leaders, Local Government Association, National Association of Headteachers and National Governors' Association.

Auld, R. (1976) *William Tyndale Junior and Infants Schools Public Inquiry: A Report to the Inner London Education Authority*, London: ILEA.

Bacon, W. (1978) *Public Accountability and the Schooling System: A Sociology of School Board Democracy*, London: Harper and Row.

Baginsky, M., Baker, L. and Cleave, S. (1991) *Towards Effective Partnerships in School Governance*, Slough: NFER.

Baker, C., Dawson, D., Thair, T. and Youngs, R. (2014) *Longitudinal Study of Young People in England: Cohort 2, Wave 1: Research Report*, London: DfE.

Balarin, M., Brammer, S., James, C. R. and McCormack, M. (2008) *The School Governance Study*, London: Business in the Community.

Baron, G. and Howell, D. (1974) *The Government and Management of Schools*, London: Athlone Press.

Bastiani, J. (1995) *Taking a Few Risks: Learning from Each Other – Teachers, Parents and Pupils*, London: Royal Society of Arts.

Bastiani, J. (2000) 'I Know it Works! . . . Actually Proving it is the Problem', in S. Wolfendale and J. Bastiani (eds), *The Contribution of Parents to School Effectiveness*, London: David Fulton.

Benn, M. (2011) *School Wars: The Battle for Britain's Education*, London: Verso.

Bennis, W. (1989) *On Becoming a Leader*, Philadelphia: Basic Books.

Berg, L. (1968) *Risinghill, Death of a Comprehensive School*, London: Penguin.

Brent, L. B. (2009) *Sunday's Child? A Memoir*, London: Bank House Books.

Briner, R. and Dewberry, C. (2007) *Staff Wellbeing is the Key to School Success*, London: Birkbeck College, University of London.

Brundrett, M. (ed.) (1999) *Principles of School Leadership*, Norfolk: Peter Francis.

Brown, A. (2014) *The Myth of the Strong Leader*, London: Random House.

Burgess, T. and Sofer, A. (1978) *The School Governors' and Managers' Handbook and Training Guide*, London: Kogan Page.

Butler, M. (2010) 'Governance at Academies', *Matters Arising*, Birmingham: National Governors' Association.

Carmichael, N. and Wild, E. (2011) *Who Governs the Governors? School Governance in the Twenty-First Century*, London: Wild Search.

Carver, J. (1990) *Boards That Make a Difference*, San Francisco: Jossey-Bass.

Caudrey, A. (1988) 'Analysis: Can Governors Run Schools?', *New Society*, 18th March.

Chapman, C. (2013) *From One School to Many: Reflections on the Impact and Nature of School Federations and Chains in England*, London: Sage Publications for BELMAS.

Child Poverty Action Group (2009) *Child Wellbeing and Child Poverty: Where the UK Stands in the European Table*, London: CPAG.

Children's Commission on Poverty (2014) *Through Young Eyes: At What Cost? Exposing the Impact of Poverty on School Life*, London: The Children's Society.

Chitty, C. (1999) *The Education System Transformed*, Tisbury: Baseline Book Company.

Chitty, C. (ed.) (2011) *Forum*, 53(3), Oxford: Symposium Books.

Chitty, C. (2014a) *Education Policy in Britain* (3rd ed.), Basingstoke: Palgrave MacMillan.

Chitty, C. (ed.) (2014b) *Forum*, 56(3), Oxford: Symposium Books.

Clark, P. (1998) *Back from the Brink: Transforming the Ridings School – and Our Children's Education*, London: Metro Books.

Collins, C. (2014) 'Clarity of Vision', *Governance Matters*, September/October.

Commission for Local Government in England (1980) *Investigation 314/5/79: Complaint Against the London Borough of Haringey*, London: Commission for Local Government in England.

Committee on Standards in Public Life (The Nolan Committee) (1996) *The Second Report of the Committee: The Seven Principles of Public Life*, London: HMSO.

Confederation of British Industry (CBI) (2013) *Leading the Way: Improving School Governance and Leadership*, London: CBI.

Crick, M. (1996) *Jeffrey Archer: Stranger than Fiction*, London: Penguin.

Cruver, B. (2003) *Enron: Anatomy of Greed*, London: Arrow Books.

Darlington, T., Hinds, T. and Holt, A. (1988) *Skill in Chairing Governing Bodies*, Coventry: AGIT.

Davies, N. (2014) *Hack Attack: How the Truth Caught Up with Rupert Murdoch*, London: Chatto and Windus.

Dean, C., Dyson, A., Gallannaugh, F., Howes, A. and Raffo, C. (2007) *Schools, Governors and Disadvantage*, York: Joseph Rowntree Foundation.

Deem, R., Behony, K. and Heath, S. (1995) *Active Citizenship and the Governing of Schools*, Buckingham: Open University.

Dejevsky, M. (2013) 'Super-Heads are a Super-Huge Mistake', *The Spectator*, 7th December.

Department for Children, Schools and Families (DCSF) (2007a) *The Children's Plan: Building Brighter Futures*, London: The Stationery Office.

Department for Children, Schools and Families (DCSF) (2007b) *Guidance on the Duty to Promote Community Cohesion*, London: The Stationery Office.

Department for Education (DfE) (1992) *School Governor Recruitment Survey: Overview of Findings*, London: HMSO.

Department for Education (DfE) (1995) *Governing Bodies and Effective Schools*, London: HMSO.

Department for Education (DfE) (2010) *The Importance of Teaching – The Schools White Paper, Cm 7980*, London: Department for Education.

Department for Education (DfE) (2012) *Statistical First Release: Schools, Pupils and their Characteristics*, London: Department for Education.

Department for Education (DfE) (2013) *Teachers' Standards*, London: Department for Education.

Department for Education (DfE) (2014a) *The School Governance (Roles, Procedures and Allowances) (England) Regulations 2013: Departmental Advice for School Leaders and Governing Bodies of Maintained Schools and Management Committees of PRUs in England*, London: Department for Education.

Department for Education (DfE) (2014b) *The Constitution of Governing Bodies of Maintained Schools: Statutory Guidance*, London: Department for Education.

Department for Education (DfE) (2014c) *Statistical release: Expenditure by Local Authorities and Schools on Education, Children and Young People's Services: 2013–14*, London: Department for Education.

Department for Education (DfE) (2015a) *Governors' Handbook: For Governors in Maintained Schools, Academies and Free Schools*, London: Department for Education.

Department for Education (DfE) (2015b) *National Standards of Excellence for Headteachers: Departmental Advice for Headteachers, Governing Boards and Aspiring Headteachers*, London: Department for Education.

Department for Education and Employment (DfEE) (1996) *Guidance on Good Governance*, London: HMSO.

Department for Education and Employment (DfEE) (1997a) *Excellence in Schools*, London: HMSO.

Department for Education and Employment (DfEE) (1997b) *Raising Standards for All: The Government's Legislative Plans*, London: HMSO.

Department for Education and Employment (DfEE) (1997c) *From Targets to Action: Guidance to Support Effective Target-Setting in Schools*, London: DfEE.

Department for Education and Employment (DfEE) (1997d) *Setting Targets for Pupil Achievement: Guidance for Governors*, London: DfEE.

Department for Education and Employment (DfEE) (2001) *Schools: Building on Success: Raising Standards, Promoting Diversity, Achieving Results*, London: HMSO.

Department of Education and Science (DES) (1963) *Half Our Future, A Report of the Central Advisory Council for Education (The Newsom Report)*, London: HMSO.

Department of Education and Science (DES) (1967) *Children and Their Primary Schools, A Report of the Central Advisory Council for Education (The Plowden Report)*, London: HMSO.

Department of Education and Science (DES) (1977a) *Education in Schools: A Consultative Document*, London: HMSO.

Department of Education and Science (DES) (1977b) *A New Partnership for Our Schools (The Taylor Report)*, London: HMSO.

Department of Education and Science (DES) (1984) *Parental Influence at School*, London: HMSO.

Department of Education and Science (DES) (1985) *Better Schools*, London: HMSO.

Department of Education and Science (DES) (1988) *School Governors: A New Role*, London: HMSO.

Department for Education and Skills (DfES) (2003) *Performance Management 2003: Support Guide for Governors and Headteachers*, London: DfES.

Department for Education and Skills (DfES) (2004) *National Standards for Headteachers*, London: DfES.

Desforges, C. with Abouchaar, A. (2003) *The Impact of Parental Involvement, Parental Support and Family Education on Pupil Achievements and Adjustment: A Literature Review*, London: Department for Education and Skills.

Dorling, D. (2011) *Injustice: Why Social Inequality Persists*, Bristol: The Policy Press.

Earley, P. (1994) *School Governing Bodies: Making Progress?*, Slough: NFER.

Ellis, A. (2003) *Barriers to Participation for Under-represented Groups in School Governance*, London: Institute for Volunteering Research/Department for Education.

Ellis, T., McWhirter, J., McColgan, D. and Hadow, B. (1976) *William Tyndale: The Teachers' Story*, London: Writers and Readers Publishing Cooperative.

Findlay, J. J. (1923) *The Children of England*, London: Methuen.

Fitzjohn, L. (2014) Letter to David Moran, E-ACT, 25th March.

Freire, P. (1972) *Pedagogy of the Oppressed*, London: Penguin.

Fryer, J. (2014) 'The Toughest and Most Inspiring Head in Britain', *Daily Mail*, 3rd December, http://www.dailymail.co.uk/news/article-2858282/The-toughest-inspiring-head-Britain-sent-40-girls-home-one-day-skirts-short-super-strict-regime-transformed-worst-schools-like-him.html (accessed May 2015).

Gann, N. (1995) *Managing Change in Voluntary Organizations*, Buckingham: Open University Press.

Gann, N. (1999a) *Targets for Tomorrow's Schools: A Guide to Whole School Target-Setting for Governors and Headteachers*, London: Falmer Press.

Gann, N. (1999b) 'The Beacon in Barnstaple', *Teachers' Magazine*, December.

Gann, N. (2002) 'Parents', in G. Reeves (ed.), *The Governor's Handbook: The Complete Guide to Being a Primary School Governor*, London: PFP Publishing.

Gann, N. (2003) 'Don't Be Scared of Challenging Heads', *Times Educational Supplement*, 31st January.

Gann, N. (2005a) 'No More Heroes: Heads Have to Drop the "Super"', *Times Educational Supplement*, 7th January.

Gann, N. (2005b) 'Seven Steps to a Better Body: What Are the Obstacles That Prevent Governors Working Together Well?', *Times Educational Supplement*, 13th May.

Gann, N. (2010a) *INSET in a Box: Managing the New Self-Evaluation Form*, Deddington: Philip Allan.

Gann, N. (2010b) *INSET in a Box: Developing an Effective Governing Body*, Deddington: Philip Allan.

Gann, N. (2011) 'Academy Conversion: A View from the Governing Body', *Forum* 53(3), Oxford: Symposium Books.

Gann, N. (2012a) 'Academies: Stewards or Stakeholders?', *Governing Matters*, January/February.

Gann, N. (2012b) 'Playground Robbery', *The Land* 12.

Gann, N. (2014) 'Educating Ethics: The Probity of School Governance', in Chitty, C. (ed.), *Forum*, 56(3), Oxford: Symposium Books.

Glatter, R. (2013) 'We Need to Talk About the Ownership and Control of Schools', *The Guardian*, 21 March.

Goffman, A. (2014) *On the Run: Fugitive Life in an American City*, Chicago: University of Chicago Press.

Golby, M. and Brigley, S. (1989) *Parents as School Governors*, Tiverton: Fairway Publications.

Golby, M. and Lane, B. (1989) *The New Parent Governors*, Tiverton: Fairway Publications.

Gordon, P. (1974) *The Victorian School Manager*, London: Woburn Press.

Greany, T. and Scott, J. (2014) *Conflicts of Interest in Academy Sponsorship Arrangements: A Report for the Education Select Committee*, London: Institute of Education.

Greenleaf, R. (1977) *Servant Leadership*, New York: Paulist Press.

Greenleaf, R. (1991) *The Servant as Leader*, Westfield, Indiana: The Greenleaf Center.

Grimmer, D. (2012) 'Education Secretary Michael Gove: I'd like to clone Costessey school head', *Norwich Evening News*, http://www.eveningnews24.co.uk/news/education_secretary_ michael_gove_i_d_like_to_clone_costessey_school_head_1_1419255 (accessed May 2015).

Hallgarten, J. (2000) *Parents Exist, OK!? Issues and Visions for Parent–School Relationships*, London: Institute for Public Policy Research.

HarperCollins (2006) *Collins English Dictionary* (6th ed.), Glasgow: HarperCollins.

Harrison, P. (1988) 'The Panic to Complete', *Times Educational Supplement*, 21st October.

Heald, T. (2006) Letter to *The Guardian*, 6th July.

Heckstall-Smith, H. (1962) *Doubtful Schoolmaster*, London: Peter Davies.

Herbert, S. (1989) *Guardian Law Report*, 26th May.

Hill, R. www.mindtools.com/pages/main/newMN_STR.htm (accessed March 2015).

Hill, R., Dunford, J., Parish, N., Rea, S. and Sandals, L. (2012) *The Growth of Academy Chains: Implications for Leaders and Leadership*, Nottingham: National College for School Leadership.

Hirschkorn, U. (2014) 'How Ofsted Destroyed Our School', first published on Parentdish UK and now available at http://www.huffingtonpost.co.uk/2014/11/21/how-ofsted-destroyed-our-school_n_7319758.html (accessed May 2015).

HMSO (1986) *Education (No. 2) Act*, London: HMSO.

HMSO (1988) *Education Act 1988*, London: HMSO.

Holmes, E. (1911) *What is and What Might Be: A Study of Education in General and Elementary Education in Particular*, London: Constable.

Holmes, G. (1952) *The Idiot Teacher: A Book About Prestolee School and its Headmaster E. F. O'Neill*, London: Faber and Faber.

House of Commons (2003) *Every Child Matters*, London: The Stationery Office.

House of Commons Education Committee (2013) *The Role of School Governing Bodies: Second Report of Session 2013–14*, London: The Stationery Office.

House of Commons Education Committee (2015) *Academies and Free Schools, Fourth Report of the Session 2014–15*, London: The Stationery Office.

Hudson, M. (1995) *Managing Without Profit: The Art of Managing Third-Sector Organizations*, London: Penguin.

Humphries, S. (1981) *Hooligans or Rebels? An Oral History of Working-Class Childhood and Youth 1889–1939*, Oxford: Blackwell.

Hurt, J. (1971) *Education in Evolution*, London: Hart-Davis.

Hurt, J. (1979) *Elementary Schooling and the Working Classes 1860–1918*, London: Routledge and Kegan Paul.

Ipsos Mori (2006) *Parent Power*, London: Ipsos Mori.

IQRA Trust (1991) *Participating in School Governing Bodies: Advice for Muslims*, London: IQRA Trust.

Jackson, P. and McKergow, M. (2002) *The Solutions Focus*, London: Nicholas Brealey.

James, C., Brammer, S., Connolly, M., Fertig, M., James, J. and Jones, J. (2011) 'School Governing Bodies in England Under Pressure: The Effects of Socio-Economic Context and School Performance', *Educational Management Administration and Leadership*, 39(4): 414–433.

James, C., Brammer, S., Connolly, M., Fertig, M., James, J. and Jones, J. (2012) *The Hidden Givers: A Study of School Governing Bodies in England*, Bath: University of Bath.

James, C., Brammer, S., Connolly, M., Fertig, M., James, J. and Jones, J. (2013a) 'The Challenges Facing School Governing Bodies in England: A "Perfect Storm?"', *Management in Education*, 27(3): 84–90.

James, C., Brammer, S., Connolly, M., Spicer, D. E., James, J. and Jones, J. (2013b) *The Chair of the School Governing Body in England: Roles, Relationships and Responsibilities*, Reading: CfBT Education Trust.

James, C., Goodall, J., Howarth, E. and Knights, E. (2014) *The State of School Governing in England 2014*, Bath: University of Bath/National Governors' Association.

Janis-Norton, N. (2005) *Could Do Better: How Parents Can Help Their Children Succeed at School*, Edinburgh: Barrington Stoke.

Jefferies, G. and Streatfield, D. (1989) *The Reconstitution of School Governing Bodies*, Slough: NFER.

Johnson, M. and Mansell, W. (2014) *Education Not for Sale: A TUC Research Report*, London: Trades Union Congress.

Jones, O. (2014) *The Establishment: And How They Get Away With It*, London: Allen Lane.

Karpman, S. (2014) *A Game-Free Life: The Definitive Book on the Drama Triangle and Compassion Triangle*, San Francisco: Drama Triangle Publications.

Keys, W. and Fernandes, C. (1990) *A Survey of School Governing Bodies*, Slough: NFER.

MacInnes, T., Aldridge, A., Bushe, S., Tinson, A. and Born, T. (2014) *Monitoring Poverty and Social Exclusion*, York: Joseph Rowntree Foundation.

Mansell, W. and Hackett, J. (2013) 'The Crème de la Crème of Academy Governors?', *The Guardian* 19th March.

Marson, D. (1973) *Children's Strikes in 1911*, London: History Workshop.

May, A. with Berwick, D. (2014) *The School of Freedom: The School Strike, Burston, Norfolk (1914–1939) and its Legacy*, Norwich: David A Berwick.

McChesney, R. W. (1999) 'Noam Chomsky and the Struggle Against Neo-Liberalism', *Monthly Review*, 1st April, http://www.chomsky.info/onchomsky/19990401.htm (accessed May 2015).

McKergow, M. and Bailey, H. (2014) *Host: Six New Roles of Engagement for Teams, Organisations, Communities and Movements*, London: Solutions Books.

McInerney, L. (2011) *The Six Predictable Failures of Free Schools . . . and How to Avoid Them*, Cambridge: LKM Consulting.

McLellan, T. and Gann, N. (2002) *Schools in the Spotlight*, London: Routledge Falmer.

Meek, J. (2014) *Private Island: Why Britain Now Belongs to Someone Else*, London: Verso.

Midwinter, E. (ed.) (1972) *Projections: An Educational Priority Area at Work*, London: Ward Lock Educational.

Millar, F. (2014) 'Are the "Forces of Conservatism" in Retreat?', *The Guardian*, 8th July.

Ministry of Education (1921) *Report of the Departmental Committee on the Teaching of English in Schools (The Newbolt Report)*, London: HMSO.

Ministry of Education (1945) *Model Instruments and Articles of Government*, London: HMSO.

Ministry of Education (1947) *School and Life, A Report of the Central Advisory Council for Education*, London: HMSO.

Murray, N. (1997) *A Life of Matthew Arnold*, London: St. Martin's Press.

National Audit Office (2014) *Academies and Maintained Schools: Oversight and Intervention*, London: NAO.

National Consumer Council (1990) *Minority Ethnic Communities and School Governing Bodies*, London: National Consumer Council.

National Governors' Association and National College for School Leadership (2011) *Leading Governors: The Role of the Chair of Governors in Schools and Academies*, Nottingham: National College for School Leadership.

National Governors' Association and Wellcome Trust (2015) *A Framework for Governance: A Flexible Guide to Strategic Planning*, London: Wellcome Trust.

O'Brien, P. (1992) *Positive Management: Assertiveness for Managers*, London: Nicholas Brealey.

O'Brien, P. (1993) *Taking the Macho out of Management*, London: Sheldon Books.

O'Connell, S., Powell, T. and Gann, N. (2010) *Community Cohesion and Pupil Voice Toolkit*, Hampton: Forum Business Media.

O'Connor, M., Hales, E., Davies, J. and Tomlinson, S. (1999) *Hackney Downs: The School that Dared to Fight*, London: Cassell.

Ofsted (1993) *Handbook for the Inspection of Schools*, London: HMSO.

Ofsted (2013a) School Report: Etz Chaim Jewish Primary School, January 2013, London: Ofsted.

Ofsted (2013b) *Subsidiary Guidance April 2013 No. 110166: Supporting the Inspection of Maintained Schools and Academies*, London: Ofsted.

Ofsted (2013c) School Report: Cardinal Newman Catholic High School, Warrington, December 2013, London: Ofsted.

Ofsted (2014a) *School Inspection Handbook July 2014*, London: Ofsted.

Ofsted (2014b) *School Inspection Handbook September 2014*, London: Ofsted.

Ofsted (2014c) *The Report of Her Majesty's Chief Inspector of Education, Children's Services and Skills 2013/14*, London: Ofsted.

Ofsted (2014d) School Report: Didsbury Road Primary School, Stockport, April 2014, London: Ofsted.

Ofsted (2014e) School Report: Parish Church (CE) Junior School, Warrington Road, Croydon, June 2014, London: Ofsted.

Ofsted (2014f) School Report: Lindsworth School, Monyhull Hall Road, Birmingham, March 2014, London: Ofsted.

Owen, D. (1964) *English Philanthropy 1660–1960*, London: Oxford University Press.

Page, A. and Millar, C. (2009) *School–Parent Partnerships: A Short Guide*, London: Family and Parenting Institute.

Parker, S. (1988) 'Power to Which People?', *Times Educational Supplement*, 30th September.

Paxton-Doggett, K. (2014) *How to Run an Academy School*, London: ICSA Publishing.

Peters, R. (ed.) (1976) *The Role of the Head*, London: Routledge and Kegan Paul.

Poster, C. and Kruger, A. (eds) (1990) *Community Education in the Western World*, London: Routledge.

Punter, A. and Adams, J. (2008a) *Adding Value to Governance*, London: SGOSS.

Punter, A. and Adams, J. (2008b) *Skills Development in School Governor Volunteers: The Experience of Staff from Linklaters and Dresdener Kleinwort Wasserstein in Hackney Schools (Commissioned by Freshfields Bruckhaus Deringer LLP)*, Hatfield: University of Hertfordshire.

Punter, A., Adams, J. and Kraitman, L. (2007) *Adding Value to Governance: An Evaluation of the Contribution made by Governors Recruited by the Governors' One Stop Shop to their Schools' Governing Bodies and to their Own Development*, London: SGOSS.

Putnam, R. (2000) *Bowling Alone: The Collapse and Revival of American Community*, New York: Simon and Schuster.

Ree, H. (1973) *Educator Extraordinary: The Life and Achievement of Henry Morris 1889–1961*, London: Longman.

Reeves, G. (2002) *The Governor's Handbook: The Complete Guide to Being a Primary School Governor*, London: PFP Publishing.

Regan, D. (1977) *Local Government and Education*, London: Allen and Unwin.

Rennie, J. (1990) 'Why Community Education?', in C. Poster and A. Kruger (eds), *Community Education in the Western World*, London: Routledge.

Roche, F. (2014) 'Many headteachers are not going to like this, but . . .', http://insights. thekeysupport.com/author/fergalroche2014 (accessed January 2014).

Royal Commission on Local Government (1966) *The Redcliffe-Maud Report*, London: HMSO.

Sallis, E. (1993) *Total Quality Management in Education*, London: Kogan Page.

Sallis, J. (1977) *School Managers and Governors: Taylor and After*, London: Ward Lock.

Sallis, J. (1992) *Working Together: Rules and Good Practices for School Governors*, Northamptonshire County Council.

Sallis, J. (1993) *Basics for School Governors*, Stafford: Network Educational Press.

Sallis, J. (1994) *Heads and Governors: Building the Partnership*, Coventry: Action for Governors' Information and Training.

Sallis, J. (2001) *Effective School Governors: A Practical Guide*, Harlow: Pearson Education.

Sandel, M. (2012) *What Money Can't Buy: The Moral Limits of the Markets*, London: Penguin.

Savage, K. (2010) 'How Unhappy are Our Children?', *Teaching Times*, 2nd July.

Schattschneider, E. (1960) *The Semi-Sovereign People: A Realist's View of Democracy in America*, New York: Rinehart and Wilson.

Select Committee on Education and Employment (2000) *The Role of Private Sector Organisations in Public Education*, London: House of Commons/HMSO.

Secret Teacher Blog (2014a) 'Why Are We Really Put Through the Pain of Ofsted Inspections?', *The Guardian*, http://www.theguardian.com/teacher-network/teacher-blog/2014/may/24/secret-teacher-ofsted-inspections-education (accessed May 2015).

Secret Teacher Blog (2014b) 'The Culture of Fear in my School Stops us Taking Sick Leave', *The Guardian*, http://www.theguardian.com/teacher-network/teacher-blog/2014/nov/22/secret-teacher-fear-sick-leave (accessed May 2015).

Simon, B. (1965) *Education and the Labour Movement, 1870–1920*, London: Lawrence and Wishart.

Simon, B. (1988) *Bending the Rules: The Baker 'Reform' of Education*, London: Lawrence and Wishart.

Smith, J. (1995) 'The Voluntary Tradition: Philanthropy and Self-Help in Britain 1500–1945', in J. Smith, C. Rochester and R. Hedley (eds), *An Introduction to the Voluntary Sector*, London: Routledge,

Smith, J., Rochester, C. and Hedley, R. (eds) (1995) *An Introduction to the Voluntary Sector*, London: Routledge.

Smith, T. (1980) *Parents and Preschool*, London: Grant McIntyre.

Smithies, F. (1988) 'Governor Power', *Times Educational Supplement*, 9th September.

Southampton Racial Equality Council (1990) *Ethnic Origin of School Governors in Southampton*, Southampton: Southampton Racial Equality Council.

Spicer, D., Crawford, M., Earley, P., James, C., Bubb, S., Furniss, R., Jones, J., Nelson, R. and Wood, E. (2014) *Effectively Managing Headteacher Performance: Research Report*, Nottingham: NCTL.

Stacey, M. (1991) *Parents and Teachers Together*, Milton Keynes: Open University Press.

Sutcliffe, J. and Blackburne, L. (1988) 'Still Some Dud Bulbs on Parent Power Circuit', *Times Educational Supplement*, 21st October.

Sutherland, G. (1973) *Policy-Making in Elementary Education 1870–1895*, Oxford: Oxford University Press.

Times Educational Supplement (1989) 'The Governors' Guide', *Times Educational Supplement*, 7th July.

Troyat, H. (trans. J. Pinkham) (1982) *Alexander of Russia*, New York: E P Dutton Inc.

Van der Eyken, W. and Turner, B. (1969) *Adventures in Education*, London: Allen Lane.

Verhaeghe, P. (trans. J. Hedley-Prôle) (2014) *What About Me? The Struggle for Identity in a Market-Based Society*, London: Scribe Publications.

Walters, J. and Richardson, C. (1997) *Governing Schools Through Policy: A Blueprint for Creative School Governance*, London: Lemos and Crane.

Waterfield, L. (1961) *Castle in Italy: An Autobiography*, London: John Murray.

Watson, L. and Johnston, D. (1979) *Home, School and Community: Report of a Workshop*, Sheffield: Sheffield City Polytechnic Department of Educational Management.

Wells, H. G. (1934) *Experiment in Autobiography*, London: Victor Gollancz.

Wilkins, A. (2014) *Governing Schools: The Role of Community and Professional Volunteers*, https://www.academia.edu/8901867/Briefing_Paper_for_ESRC_SASE_project__findings_and_recommendations (accessed May 2015).

Wilkinson, R. and Pickett, K. (2010) *The Spirit Level: Why Equality is Better for Everyone*, London: Penguin.

Winkley, D. (2002) *Handsworth Revolution: The Odyssey of a School*, London: De la Mare.

Wolfendale, S. and Bastiani, J. (eds) (2000) *The Contribution of Parents to School Effectiveness*, London: David Fulton.

Appendices

Visiting schools
A policy

This is a policy to cover visits to the school by governors. The major purpose of visiting the school is to observe the impact of the policies and procedures the governing body has in place. It is not judgemental – though governors will need to know what to do with the judgements they inevitably make. Governors should also see the agreed protocol on how to conduct a visit.

The governing board and staff of this school have agreed:

1   that all governors should visit the school for at least one half day at least twice during the school year;

2   that governors should visit more frequently if possible, in order to help them carry out their responsibilities on the governing body;

3   that a governors' visit is distinct from any other purpose that the individual may have for being in the school, and that the right to visit the school as a governor is applicable to *all* governors;

4   that the purpose of visiting the school is to observe the impact of the policies and procedures the governing body has in place;

5   that all visits are arranged beforehand with the headteacher and any staff concerned;

6   that staff are informed in advance of all such visits;

7   that a record of visits is made in an agreed format, and that governors report back to the governing board and/or their committees as appropriate.

A protocol for governors' visits

Governors are asked to observe the following protocol in conducting school visits:

Schools are busy workplaces and nobody should expect to just turn up, be shown around or wander around on their own – however informal your relationship with the staff. Governors have no automatic right to visit the school. They only do so on invitation or by governing body decision (for example, within the terms of a visiting policy). The visit must fit in with the needs of the school and its pupils. The primary purpose of a governor visiting a school must be to explore the impact and effectiveness of the school's policies and procedures. This is to enable you as a governor to do your job better.

School visits by governors are

- arranged in advance;
- for an agreed length of time;
- for an explicit and agreed purpose, which the people you are visiting know in advance;
- well-prepared beforehand;
- have an agreed outcome;
- contribute to the monitoring role of the governing board (not of the individual governor);
- to show teachers, parents and children that we are interested in what the school is doing.

Governors visit the school to learn about its ways of doing things, not to make judgements. So, please, when visiting the school:

1 do nothing – and do not carry anything – that might suggest that your visit is an inspection;
2 consider who 'owns' which parts of the school, and behave accordingly;
3 be punctual throughout your visit;

4   if you are invited to a lesson, never arrive late or leave early, unless to do so is an agreed part of the programme;

5   report to the office when you arrive and when you leave;

6   if possible, do not confine your meetings to teachers – talk to children and a range of staff;

7   know beforehand – and tell those who don't know – what the outcome of your visit will be: a verbal report to governors or a committee, a written report available to all, an item in a newsletter;

8   do not quiz people too rigorously unless invited and be careful about raising concerns about matters that may be school policy. If in doubt, don't – but talk to the headteacher;

9   remember you have no authority as an individual governor unless specifically delegated by the governing body;

10   avoid making judgements about matters which are in the professional domain. If anything you see in your visit raises serious concerns, talk to the headteacher in confidence.

A code of conduct for governors of local governing boards

Codes of Conduct must be reviewed and ratified annually.

1 No Governor has individual authority or power by being a member of the Governing Board, unless it has specifically been delegated; only the Governing Board as a whole can take actions or decisions unless agreed otherwise and formally minuted.

2 No Governor should use his or her position to gain advantage in other relationships with the school or community (e.g. as a teacher, employee, or parent).

3 The Governing Board recognises that it administers a public body funded by local and national taxation. It therefore recognises the need to ensure that its proceedings are open to public scrutiny. Minutes of the most recent Governing Board and committee meetings will be displayed in a public part of the school, and requests to observe meetings will be considered with regard to the importance of the accountability of the Governing Board to the local community (while recognising the need to retain confidentiality where individual students, staff and others are under discussion).

4 All Governors, however appointed or elected, recognise that they are individually accountable to certain bodies or constituencies. All Governors, therefore, have a duty to consider the significance of Governing Board decisions for the source of their appointment during discussion on any item. Elected Governors undertake to report to their elective bodies regularly, and to initiate methods of gathering views on matters likely to be brought before the Governors, where these are of a general nature or interest connected with the welfare of the school. Appointed Governors will consider ways in which the reason for their appointment may be reflected in their contributions.

5 No Governor may be mandated by his or her elective or appointing body under any circumstances, although (s)he should report any views expressed by members of that body.

6 All Governors are of equal standing.

7   All Governors are appointed, and should act, for the good of the school, whatever their constituency.

8   Many Governors have other relationships with the school, such as employee or parent. They should be particularly careful to ensure that these relationships are conducted in a proper and ethical manner, and that their standing as a Governor is not compromised or open to misinterpretation.

9   Governors will attend meetings punctually and well prepared as far as possible, having read supporting material and considered the contributions they may make on agenda items.

10   Governors will not use any material learned at meetings for other purposes, and no item designated as confidential will be discussed outside the Governing Board.

11   Governors accept corporate responsibility for the decisions of the Governing Board.

12   Governors will treat other governors, staff, children, parents and anyone else they may come into contact with in the course of their work with respect. There will be no behaviour in the workplace which might be seen as bullying, victimisation or harassment.

13   Governors will consider what individual skills, personal qualities and knowledge they possess, and put them to use for the good for the school. They will be prepared to engage in appropriate continuing professional development throughout their period of office.

Pre-inspection checklist for governing boards

These questions are designed to cover all those that might be raised during an inspection with governors (most likely the chair). It is unlikely you will be asked all of them!

Area	Yes	Partly	No	Action
Contents of a pre-inspection information sheet for governors:				
Progress of all students compared to nationally				
Attainment of all students compared to nationally				
Progress of all students compared to locally				
Attainment of all students compared to locally				
Progress of all students compared to similar				
Attainment of all students compared to similar				
Progress of SEN students compared to others				
Progress of FSM pupils compared to others				
Which groups of students make least progress				
Action to address these issues				
Impact of actions				
How do you know				
3-year trends in progress and attainment				
How do you know				

Areas of weakness				
Actions to reduce gaps in progress				
Impact of actions to reduce gaps in progress				
Governors data dashboards (Ofsted/MAT/FFT)				
Key issues from RAISEonline				
Amount and spending of pupil premium				
Impact of pupil premium				
Amount and spending of sports premium				
Impact of sports premium				
Quality of teaching				
Actions to raise quality of teaching				
Monitoring of quality of teaching				
Location of best teaching				
Staff CPD				
Impact of staff CPD				
Actions on under-performance in teaching				
How appraisal improves quality of teaching				
Percentage of outstanding/good, etc. lessons				
Behaviour policy and its implementation				
Exclusions				
Actions on challenging behaviour				
Safety of students				
Attendance compared to nationally/locally/similar				
Attendance by groups of students				
Actions on attendance				
Safeguarding reports to GB				

(continued)

(continued)

Area	Yes	Partly	No	Action
Bullying and actions				
Parents' view of behaviour				
Performance of leadership and management				
Setting of head's objectives				
Conduct of appraisal of staff, inc. key objectives				
Relationship between teaching performance and pay				
Key priorities in SDP				
Contribution of GB to SDP				
GB monitoring of SDP				
Monitoring of safeguarding procedures				
Strengths and areas of development in SLT				
Strengths and areas of development in GB				
Holding head and SLT to account: examples of challenge				
GB input to format of headteacher's report to GB				
Evidence (e.g. GB minutes)				
GB monitoring of expenditure on and use of resources				
Value for money				
GB training				
GB skills				
GB succession planning				
GB attendance				
GB impact on pupil progress				
GB engagement with stakeholders				
How the school is doing: strengths and weaknesses				
How you rate the school				

What parents and the community think of the school				
How you know				
Regarding the GB				
Members' details are available to parents and others				
Members make themselves available to parents and pupils				
Members' pen portraits and photos are in evidence				
A skills audit is regularly conducted				
Action is taken to fill skills gaps by recruitment/ training				
Action is taken to develop a pool of potential members				
There is competition to fill vacancies				
The GB has its own development plan				
Members have role descriptions				
There is a code of conduct				
Attendance at GB meetings is monitored and reported				
Members' school visits are logged				
There is a visiting policy and protocol				
Visits are reported to GB/Committees				
All training is logged				
Impact of training is recorded				
Whole GB training is planned and delivered				
Other ways of staying up-to-date with GB development				
The GB engages in self-evaluation annually				
The GB knows it has a positive impact on the school				

(continued)

(continued)

Questions for the Chair and Clerk	Yes	Partly	No	Action
Regarding the GB's agenda and minutes as evidence for:				
A relentless focus on school improvement				
Reporting and interrogation of relevant data				
Challenging and holding to account the leadership				
Supporting the leadership				
Key actions identified with named persons responsible				
Timescales for completion/reporting of key actions				
Monitoring of SDP				
Head's report, demonstrating GB and MAT input to format				
Other sources of information about the school				
Knowing what people think of the school				
Professional advice/input from the clerk				
Chairing that enables GB to discharge its responsibilities				
Chairing that develops the GB				
And the GB agenda and minutes are:				
Available quickly to parents and others in hard copy				
Available quickly on the school website				
Referred to in newsletters				

Inspection is providing significant challenge to governing bodies about monitoring and performance management

Main recommendations for governors
September to November 2012

- Communication: better links with pupil and parents
- Attendance/Dealing with parents over absence
- Minutes to clearly reflect work
- Ensure that policies are put into practice or effective
- Own monitoring procedures including regular visits to...
- Monitoring pupil premium
- Monitoring of achievement for different groups
- Performance management and...
- Specifically monitor staff performance/teaching and...
- Govs to use milestones/targets to check progress on...
- Accurate self-evaluation/understanding
- Govs use and understanding of data
- Require senior leaders to present info
- Info presented by HT and SLT understood by govs
- Fill vacancies
- Training for new governors
- Arrange external review of governance
- Know their own roles and responsibilities
- Involvement in improvement planning
- Strategic planning and leadership

Inspection handbook

Inspectors should consider whether governors:

- carry out their statutory duties, such as safeguarding, and understand the boundaries of their role as governors;
- ensure that they and the school promote tolerance of and respect for people of all faiths (or those of no faith), cultures and lifestyles; and support and help, through their words, actions and influence within the school and more widely in the community, to prepare children and young people positively for life in modern Britain;
- ensure clarity of vision, ethos and strategic direction, including long-term planning (for example, succession);
- contribute to the school's self-evaluation and understand its strengths and weaknesses, including the quality of teaching, and reviewing the impact of their own work;
- understand and take sufficient account of pupil data, particularly their understanding and use of the school data dashboard;
- assure themselves of the rigour of the assessment process;
- are aware of the impact of teaching on learning and progress in different subjects and year groups;
- provide challenge and hold the headteacher and other senior leaders to account for improving the quality of teaching, pupils' achievement and pupils' behaviour and safety, including by using the data dashboard, other progress data, examination outcomes and test results; or whether they hinder school improvement by failing to tackle key concerns or developing their own skills;
- use the pupil premium and other resources to overcome barriers to learning, including reading, writing and mathematics;
- ensure solvency and probity and that the financial resources made available to the school are managed effectively;
- are providing support for an effective headteacher;
- monitor performance management systems and understand how the school makes decisions about teachers' salary progression, including the

performance management of the headteacher, to improve teaching, leadership and management;
- engage with key stakeholders;
- are transparent and accountable, including in terms of recruitment of staff, governance structures, attendance at meetings, and contact with parents and carers.

Inspection Handbook, July 2014

Appendix 6

What governing bodies should expect from school leaders and what school leaders should expect from governing bodies

Introduction

This is the second edition of this joint paper between NGA, ASCL and NAHT. It aims to improve the effectiveness of school governance; underpinning it is an expectation that governing bodies and school leaders will jointly develop effective working practices which are mutually supportive and respectful of each others' roles and responsibilities.

Since its first edition in 2008 much has changed in the structure of the school system in England, and in particular increasing autonomy of schools increases the need for effective accountability. Effective governance is essential for the health and success of any organisation. In any sector when an organisation fails there has been a failure of governance. Therefore if we wish to prevent any school failing its pupils, we need to ensure that governance in schools is strong.

Effective governing bodies are prepared and equipped to take their responsibilities seriously. This means they must have:

- the right people round the table;
- an understanding of their role & responsibilities;
- a good chair;
- professional clerking;
- good relationships based on trust;
- a knowledge of the school – the data, the staff, the children, the parents, and the community
- a commitment to asking challenging questions; and
- the confidence to have courageous conversations in the interests of the children and young people.

School leaders in return must have:

- an understanding of governance, including an acknowledgement of the role of the school's accountable body;
- willingness to provide information in the most appropriate way in order that the governing body can carry out its role;
- a willingness to be challenged; and time to devote to ensuring professional relationships are established with governors.

1 Governance and management

Governance is strategic and management is operational. This distinction between governance and management needs to be clearly understood by all, so that governors are not asked to, and do not try to, involve themselves in day to day management.

Governors are there to govern, not to carry out other work on a pro-bono basis. School leaders must not be micro-managed. The governing body should concentrate on matters related to strategy and school improvement, delegating to school leaders those tasks which are operational (for example, drafting policies, making judgements about teaching quality, and recruiting and deploying staff below senior leadership level). The agenda of governing bodies should be driven by the strategic planning cycle.

2 Developing and supporting the governing body

Skills audit: We recommend all governing bodies carry out a skills audit of governors to inform both the training programme and what skills gaps needs to be filled: NGA has a skills audit for schools to use or adapt.

Recruitment: When the school is advertising for new governors, the role and level of commitment and responsibility should be explained along with any skills that the governing body is particularly seeking.

Induction: Governing bodies and school leaders should expect all new governors (including staff governors) to undertake both school based induction and professional induction training paid for by the school. This expectation should be set out in writing in advance of the appointment, and agreed to as part of the Code of Practice signed by each governor.

Continuous professional development (CPD): Governors must be willing to participate in relevant training, both internal and external, and there must be an appropriate budget commitment for training. Governors need to have ways of learning what is good practice, and to meet with governors from other schools; this can also enable collaboration between schools.

Expenses: Governors' out of pocket expenses should be reimbursed as per an agreed policy.

Reviews of performance: A governing body should evaluate its own impact, and also set up a process for reviewing the contribution of individual governors.

3 Effective ways of working

Clerking: The clerk to the governing body must be properly qualified and remunerated, and capable of servicing and advising the governing body with independence. S/he should be employed to carry out this role with a separate job description and a specific contract, with sufficient time to manage the

business of the governing body and CPD to ensure s/he is able to advise governors of forthcoming changes in legislation.

Chairing: The headteacher and the chair of the governing body should communicate regularly at mutually convenient times, while understanding that the chair is unable to take decisions on behalf of the governing body (except in very limited situations). The chair should seek external support when necessary and be encouraged and prepared to join the National College for School Leadership's development programme for chairs of governing bodies, paid for by the school. It is considered good practice for a chair to serve no more than six years in the role at one school (under normal circumstances).

Code of practice: We recommend each governing body adopts a code of practice which sets out the expectations placed on governors and is signed by governors. This code includes the expectation on confidentiality of sensitive or personal information. NGA has a model code for schools to adapt.

Size and composition: Over the past two years more flexibility on the composition of governing bodies has been introduced, and the structures, including the remits of committees, should be reviewed to ensure effective ways of working are in place.

Meetings: It is the joint responsibility of school leaders and the governing body to ensure that meetings are well planned, at appropriate intervals, with manageable agendas that are appropriate to the remit and driven by school improvement. Papers must be provided seven days in advance of meetings. The headteacher is present or is represented at full governing body meetings. Governing bodies must have regard to the work-life balance of school leaders when arranging meeting times, and school leaders should have regard to governors' work and other commitments.

Delegation: Governing bodies have considerable freedom regarding the delegation of work to committees or individuals, and should delegate as many tasks as required to ensure full governing body meetings focus on strategic priorities. Business should not be repeated in different forums, and matters discussed by committees should be consistent with their terms of reference.

Policies: Governing bodies should only decide the principles guiding school policies and should delegate drafting of the remainder of policies and all procedures to school leaders. Governing bodies must ensure school leaders have the expertise or access to the relevant expertise externally to carry out these responsibilities and other delegated to them.

Appraisal of the headteacher: The governing body must appoint an external adviser to support the governors carrying out the appraisal and ensure they are fully prepared.

Duty of care: The governing body must remember that it has a duty of care to the headteacher, including ensuring that the head has a reasonable work-life balance. The governing body's role is both to support and challenge as a critical friend to the headteacher.

4 Understanding the school and engaging with stakeholders

The governing body monitors the work of the school and holds the headteacher to account for the performance of the school. It is vital that it receives the information required to carry out that role promptly; the governing body is primarily reliant on school leaders to provide this, but should also seek external advice and verification where possible.

School self-evaluation: Governing bodies must be centrally involved in all stages of the strategic planning cycle, the review of the previous year and the setting of the priorities for the coming year. It can be very useful for a governing body and senior leaders to hold an annual joint strategic planning session.

Attainment data: The RAISEonline summary report of the previous year's attainment should be discussed by governors, and access to the full data given to at least one governor. NGA provides a briefing for governors on understanding RAISEonline.

Current information: Senior leaders should provide the information necessary to monitor progress against annual development priorities, targets and budgets: this will include information on progress of groups of students, quality of teaching, staff performance and financial information.

Surveying pupils, staff and parents: The governing body has to understand the needs of these three groups, and must make every effort to obtain their views. This can be done in a number of ways including parent and student councils, written surveys, or focus groups.

Visiting the school: Visits during the school day provide important opportunities for governors to better understand the school and the learning environment and to undertake their monitoring role. School leaders should welcome governors to visit the school, both formally to monitor agreed priorities and developments, and less formally to broaden their knowledge of the school. Visits should be arranged in accordance with an agreed protocol which is communicated in advance to governors and school staff involved in visits. All parties need to be sensitive to the pressures of the school calendar and governors' other commitments.

Feedback from Ofsted: Recognising that Ofsted inspections take place at very short notice governors should make every effort to be available at the school and as many governors as possible should attend the feedback sessions at the end of an inspection. School leaders will support governors' requests that these sessions are held at the end of the working day to enable governors to attend.

Reporting to the community: The governing body must ensure it reports to interested parties and the wider community. This can be done in large part through the school's website, but other forms of communication should be considered. 📖

Self-evaluation

The headteacher and the governing board

Does our headteacher:	Always	Mostly	Sometimes	Rarely	Never
1 ensure that the governing board is fully involved in strategic planning from beginning to end?					
2 ensure that the governing board is fully involved in formulating school policies (being in at the beginning and the end of the process)?					
3 help the governing board to operate a strategic cycle of development?					
4 ensure that the governing board directly hears views about the school other than his/her own?					
5 share with the governors all the information that helps us to identify the strengths and weaknesses of the school?					
6 always support any assertions (s)he makes about the school's performance with evidence?					
7 invite governors (and teaching staff and support staff and pupils and parents and others) to share what they think is right and wrong with the school?					
8 show that (s)he values the contributions of all governors?					
9 help governing board meetings to be creative and dynamic?					
10 welcome governing board meetings that are challenging and sometimes uncomfortable for her/him?					

11	ensure that the governing board collectively leads on setting the school's ethos and development?				
12	help the governing board to organise itself so as to maximise its own performance, although that may sometimes conflict with her/his own preferences?				
13	ensure that the governing board meets its statutory responsibilities?				
14	ensure that the governing board has clear aims and policies for the school, and reviews them regularly (for example, every three years)?				
15	help the governing board to meet its obligations for performance management, both in reviewing his/her own performance and in receiving information and advice on the quality of teaching and performance management throughout the school?				
16	encourage and enable *all* governors to visit the school *as governors*, (including governors who work in the school), so that we can learn about the whole school's operation?				
17	enable and encourage the governing board to hold him/her to account for the performance of the school?				
18	enable and encourage the governing board to explain its decisions and actions to the staff, pupils, parents and the press, as well as to the LA or trustees?				
19	offer a range of actions and solutions to the governing board, so that we are not obliged to choose only between accepting or rejecting her/his advice?				
20	ensure that the governing board carries out all the functions it should and enable us to do so by giving us the necessary information and support?				

Responding to parents

Notes for governors

Parents have not always been welcomed into schools, so there are some historical barriers to be broken down. Also, many parents have less than pleasant memories of their own schooldays. These circumstances mean that, even in the most welcoming schools (such as ours), there are obstacles to free communication between parents and teachers.

All governors (but especially parent governors) should act as a channel of communication, interpreting the school to its parent community and the parent community to the school.

Some parents – especially those who have got used to other schools – expect schools to blame them when things go wrong. Some schools claim that when parents don't turn up to parents' meetings and other events, it's because they are *completely* satisfied with the school, or because they are 'apathetic'. It is probable that the answer lies more in the historical obstacles created by schools. Blaming parents is unlikely to help the school to work more closely with them. The following points are worth remembering:

- Parents are the first teachers of their children.
- Children spend less than 15 per cent of their year in school.
- Children's first loyalty is always to their parents.
- It is very difficult for a school to make a difference to a child's life chances without the support of the parents.
- When parents have different expectations of their children from the school's, they are not necessarily wrong!
- Parents' principal relationship with a school is through their own child – their interest in how the school organises itself will always be secondary to that.
- Schools and parents need to work together for the good of the child – schools know a lot about teaching and learning, but parents are the experts in their own children.

If you are approached by parents about an issue in school:

- always refer them first to the headteacher – she is responsible for all organisational matters and for personnel;
- if they are reluctant to speak to the head, offer to accompany them if you can;
- if there is an issue about the headteacher, refer them to the chair of governors (again, offer to accompany them if they are reluctant);
- always listen sympathetically and carefully to the issue raised, but do not take sides – say that you can only listen at this stage and then investigate. Remember there will always be another side to the story;
- promise that someone (if not you) will come back to them by a certain date;
- if necessary, point out that they can make a formal written complaint to the governors and/or to the local authority, but that this should be a last resort;
- whether or not you believe the complaint or problem is not important. Any issue needs to be addressed – the parent is almost certainly expressing his or her concern in the only way they know how (although the real problem is sometimes hidden under other stuff);
- when people shout, it's probably because they don't think anyone is listening (and sometimes they're right!). But do not accept aggressive behaviour – always tell the aggressive parent that you will ask the chair or headteacher to contact them.

Appendix 9

Some assertive things for school governors to say

How will the final decision be made on this – and who will make it?

What outcome is needed from this item?

What evidence is there to support that claim?

I'd like to hear from (the teacher/staff/parent/LA governor/s) on this issue – perhaps they have a different perspective.

Is there a limit (or a structure) on talking about this item?

Could the chair summarise the decision briefly?

What is expected of individual governors in connection with this item/issue?

Who can I share this decision with – and when?

Who needs to know this?

Who should know this?

I would like more time to think about/consult/hear other views before I decide.

I believe what's best for the children is . . .

I believe what's best for the school is . . .

I believe what's best for the governing board is . . . (on making unpalatable/uncomfortable decisions – e.g. proposing a new chair)

Since we carry the ultimate responsibility/accountability for shaping the future direction of the school . . .

I want to congratulate . . .

I am very pleased that . . .

I believe . . .

What other alternatives/options are there to the action proposed?

Will this action (How will this action) help the school to meet its aims/mission/objectives/raise standards?

What have we done at this meeting to make things better for the children?

All Party Parliamentary Group

Twenty questions (2nd edition) 2015

20 questions every governing board should ask itself

Governing board effectiveness

Right skills: do we have the right skills on the governing board?

1 Have we completed a skills audit which informs the governor specification we use as the basis of governor appointment and interview?

Effectiveness: are we as effective as we could be?

2 How well do we understand our roles and responsibilities, including what it means to be strategic?
3 Do we have a professional clerk who provides legal advice and oversees the governing board's induction and development needs?
4 Is the size, composition and committee structure of our governing board conducive to effective working?
5 How do we make use of good practice from across the country?

Role of the chair: does our chair show strong and effective leadership?

6 Do we carry out a regular 360° review of the chair's performance and elect the chair each year?
7 Do we engage in good succession planning so that no governor serves for longer than two terms of office and the chair is replaced at least every six years?
8 Does the chair carry out an annual review of each governor's contribution to the board's performance?

Vision, ethos and strategy

Strategy: does the school have a clear vision and strategic priorities?

9 Does our vision look forward three to five years, and does it include what the children who have left the school will have achieved?

10 Have we agreed a strategy with priorities for achieving our vision with key performance indicators against which we can regularly monitor and review the strategy?

11 How effectively does our strategic planning cycle drive the governing board's activities and agenda setting?

Engagement: are we properly engaged with our school community, the wider school sector and the outside world?

12 How well do we listen to, understand and respond to our pupils, parents and staff?

13 How do we make regular reports on the work of the governing board to our parents and local community?

14 What benefit does the school draw from collaboration with other schools and other sectors, locally and nationally?

Effective accountability

Accountability of the executive: do we hold the school leaders to account?

15 How well do we understand the school's performance data (including in-year progress tracking data) so we can properly hold school leaders to account?

16 Do governors regularly visit the school to get to know it and monitor the implementation of the school strategy?

17 How well does our policy review schedule work and how do we ensure compliance?

18 Do we know how effective performance management of all staff is within the school?

19 Are our financial management systems robust so we can ensure best value for money?

Impact: are we having an impact on outcomes for pupils?

20 How much has the school improved over the last three years, and what has the governing board's contribution been to this?

Index

1870 Education Act 13–16
1918 Education Act (Fisher) 19
1944 Education Act (Butler) 19, 24, 154
1986 Education Act (No. 2) 7, 27, 28, 29–30, 35, 52, 81
1988 Education Reform Act 27–8, 29, 30
1989 Local Government and Housing Act 33
1996 Employment Rights Act 107
1998 Education Act 40–1
2010 Academies Act 43, 46

academies 4, 39, 186; accountability 170, 192; changes in academisation 183–4; community-based charities 193–4; establishment of 42–4; finance 42, 52, 84, 179–80; governance 45–6; impact of 179; inspection 145–7; regulations 175; single academies 45; standards 46–7; teachers' pay 176; umbrella trusts 46, 145; see also academy chains; free schools; Studio Schools; University Technical Colleges
academy chains 46, 171, 184, 190, 192, 200–1; multi-academy trusts 46, 145–6
accountabilities 86, 91, 170, 192, 197
Adonis, A. 39, 40
advisers 135
Advisory Centre for Education 25
Agnew, R. 116
aided schools 41
Alexander, R. 201–2
All Party Parliamentary Group (APPG) on Educational Governance 168–9, 171, 200, 239–40

Allott, N. 84
Ambrose, P. 16
appraisal 126–7; of clerk to the board 97; of headteacher 126–7; of staff 130–2
Archer, J. 32
Ark Academies Trust 177
Arnold, M. 12, 134–5
assertiveness 102, 238
Association of County Councils 21–2
Association of Education Committees 21–2
attachment to classes, departments, etc 75
Auld, R. 24–5
awe and wonder 2–3, 156

Bacon, W. 22
Baginsky, M. et al. 33, 37
Bailey, H. 120–1
Baker, D. et al. 201
Baker, K. 31
Balfour, A. J. 18
Barber, M. 142
Baron, G. 20–1
Barrowford Primary School, Nelson 199–200
Bastiani, J. 158, 162
Benn, M. 42
Benn, T. 192
Bennett, N. 185
Bennis, W. 123
Blair, T. 40, 84, 117, 185
Blunkett, D. 40, 41, 118
Board of Education 18
board of governors see governing boards
boards of trustees 10–11
Brighouse, T 129

Brigley, S. 35
British and Foreign Schools Society 11
British Gas 36
British values 56–8, 144, 177, 197
Brougham, Lord 92
Burston Village School 110–11
'business governors' *see* co-opted governors
business model of governance 83–7, 191
Butler, M. 87

Callaghan, J. 26–7, 185
Cameron, D. 185
Campaign for the Advancement of State
    Education (CASE) 25
Carmichael, N. 168–9
Carver, J. 64–5, 71
Casals, P. 172
Caudrey, A. 50
CBI (Confederation of British Industry)
    106
centralisation of state-controlled activities
    175
chairing the board 35, 93–5, 96f
Chapman, C. 190
charity schools 11
charter schools 8, 87
Children's Commission on Poverty 195–6
children's services 44, 165–6
children's wellbeing, mental health and
    experience 136, 165, 203
Chitty, C. 41, 42
Church of England Multi Academy Trusts
    57
church schools 10, 44–5, 46
City Academies *see* academies
city technology colleges 4, 29
Cladingbowl, M. 85
Clark, P. 118
Clegg, A. 39
clerk to the governors 95, 96–7
co-opted governors 35–7
coalition government (2010–15) 4, 43, 46,
    52, 77, 134, 154–5, 181
codes of conduct: for governors 91–2,
    222–3; school behaviour policy 61–2;
    for staff 129–31
Coles, J. 84
collaboration 190, 200–1

Commission for Local Government 23–4
committees 70–2, 93
community cohesion 167
Community Development Foundation 38
community education 157–8, 165
community engagement 166–7
community representation 80–3, 124
community schools 40, 41, 43, 44
community–school relationship 48–51
competition 147, 174, 177, 188, 190
comprehensive system 39–40, 42
Confederation of British Industry (CBI)
    106
continuing professional development
    (CPD) 126
Cook, M. C. 84
cooperation 190, 200–1
Cowper, W. F. 14
Creighton Comprehensive School,
    Haringey 23
Crick, M. 32
critical friends 89
curriculum 13, 16, 20, 22, 28, 30, 182

Darlington, T. *et al.* 102
De Souza, R. 176
Dean, C. *et al.* 166–7
Deem, R. *et al.* 35
Department for Children, Schools and
    Families (DCSF) 77, 165, 167
Department for Education (DfE) 38, 52,
    118; *Governing Bodies: Statutory Guidance*
    44, 50, 70, 80–1, 182; *Governors'
    Handbook* 52, 53, 68–9, 106, 112; *School
    Governance Regulations* 7, 59, 69, 95, 96,
    114; *Teachers' Standards* 58, 62, 68, 84,
    90, 129–31, 144
Department for Education and
    Employment (DfEE) 41–2, 90–1
Department for Education and Skills
    (DfES) 126
Department of Education and Science
    (DES) 21–2, 26, 27, 35, 52, 153
Desforges, C. 161

Earley, P. 35
Education Action Zones 41
education administration 9–10

education as national issue 185

Education Development Plans 65

Education Funding Agency (EFA) 42, 45, 146, 187

Education Office 11

Eland, Rev. 110

Ellis, A. 166

ethos 55–6, 125

evaluating governance 168; accountabilities 170; best governing boards 171–2; governor development 170–1; obstacles to effective governance 103–5; self-evaluation models 168–70

evaluation of the school 58, 76–9; effectiveness of governing boards 78–9, 230–1; expectations 66, 74, 77, 136, 162, 177–8; self-evaluation 76–7

Every Child Matters (ECM) 77, 165–6

federated maintained schools 45, 85, 145, 190

Fernandes, C. 35

finance: academies and free schools 42, 52, 84, 179–80, 184; fundraising by parents 151, 152; the future 186–7; history 14, 18, 22, 28, 29, 30; managing in austerity 202; Payment by Results 134–5; Private Finance Initiative 43, 180; staff pay 132, 176, 180; *see also* Education Funding Agency

Findlay, J. J. 19

Finland 188

Fitzjohn, L. 146

Forster, W. E. 13, 14

foundation schools 40, 41, 43, 44–5

Fraser, C. 84

free schools 4, 183, 186; community-based charities 193–4; competition 190; curriculum 182; establishment of 43; finance 179–80, 184; governance 46, 153

Freire, P. 156

Fryer, J. 183

the future: dominant trends in schools 180–8; key issues 189–94; neoliberalism 173–80; predicting the unpredictable 173; strategic checklist 194–204

Future Perfect 54

Gann, N. 42, 43, 65, 66, 77, 83, 84, 88, 114, 121–2, 153, 164, 171, 181, 187

Gladstone, W. E. 13

Glatter, R. 200–1

GLC (Greater London Council) 32

Godfrey, M. 84

Goethe 65

Goffman, A. 177

Golby, M. 35

Gordon, P. 12, 15, 17

Gove, M. 43, 84, 88, 119, 134, 176

governance 3–4, 9; of academies 45–6; business model 83–7, 191; conservative model 48; contribution of lay governors 48–51; effective governance 127; evaluating governance 168–72; external reviews 140; framework 99–100; of free schools 46, 153; 'inadequate' governance 143–4; inspecting governance 138–44, 224–9, 230–1; meetings 101–3, 101f, 102f; obstacles to effective governance 103–5; 'outstanding' governance 142; radical model 48; skills-based model 44, 48, 50–1, 81, 191; as social capital 190–1; stakeholder model 26, 37, 44, 48, 80–1, 87–8; strategic governance 191–2, 203–4; strategies for school improvement 47–8

governing board and the headteacher 78–9, 109; 'antihero' headteachers 119–22; appointing the head 127–8; appraisal of head 126–7; Burston School 110–11; challenges 117; good relationship 125–6, 232–3; interfacing with the head 114; leading and managing 123; national standards for headship 117, 123–4, 162; position of headteacher 109–11; responsibilities 232–3; self-evaluation 234–5; strategic/operational issue 111–13, 114–15; 'superheads' and 'hero heads' 117–19; support and development 115–17

governing board and the staff: conduct of staff 129–31; responsibilities for staff 131–3

governing boards: accountabilities 86, 170; best governing boards 171–2; expectations of 52–3, 232–3; history and

context 4–5; self-evaluation 108,
168–70, 239–40; shared mission 133;
strategic checklist 194–204; strategic
direction 58–79, 100, 100*f*; strategic
functions 47–8, 53–79; terminology
7–8, 44; types of boards 88–9; *see also*
governing board and the headteacher;
governing board and the staff; inspection
governing bodies: history of school
governing bodies 9–31; following 1988
Act 28, 29–31; terminology 7; *see also*
governing boards
governing of schools 4
Government Education Office 11
Governor Charter Mark 171
governors 1–2; accountabilities 86, 170;
assertiveness 102, 238; behaviour 89–92,
124–5, 222–3; co-opted governors
35–7; contribution of lay governors
48–51; development and training
170–1; headteacher governors 38;
headteachers' concerns 124–8, 203–4;
history of 3, 17; induction of 98–9; legal
responsibilities 105–6; local authority
appointments 32–3, 35; minority ethnic
communities 38–9; parent governors 27,
33–5, 153; recruitment of 32–9, 97–8;
representativeness 80–3, 124; responding
to parents 236–7; responsibilities 80–8,
105–6, 232–3; retention of 97–8; rights
106–8; roles of governors 35, 92–7, 125,
140–1; self-evaluation 108, 168–70, 239–
40; teacher (staff) governors 27, 37–8
Governors' Handbook 52, 53, 68–9, 106, 112
grant maintained schools 28, 29, 37, 82–3,
109
Graves, A. 135
Graves, R. 135
Greater London Council (GLC) 32
Greener, A. 84
Greenleaf, R. 120
Grimmer, D. 119
The Guardian 90, 148, 181, 185, 199
Guidance for Inspectors (1840) 12

Hackett, J. 84
Hallgarten, J. 162
HarperCollins 55

Harrison, P. 36
headteacher governors 38
headteachers: 'antihero' headteachers
119–22; appointment 127–8; appraisal
126–7; as chief executive 124–8, 203–4;
following 1988 Act 30; host leaders
120–1; leading and managing 123;
national standards for headship 117,
123–4, 162; self-evaluation 234–5;
servant leaders 120; shared mission 133;
'superheads' and 'hero heads' 117–19; *see
also* governing board and the headteacher
headteacher's report 68–9
Heald, T. 84
Heckstall-Smith, H. 122
Her Majesty's Inspectors of Schools (HMI)
27, 134–5
Higdon, A. 110–11
Higdon, T. 110–11
Hill, R. *et al.* 54, 190
Hirschkorn, U. 182
history of school governing bodies 9–10;
1839–1870 11–12; 1870 Education
Act 13–16; 1970s onwards 20–8; 1976
great debate 26–8; 1988: new governing
bodies 28, 29–31; Dark Ages to Victorian
times 10–11; local government 18–20;
politicians 22–4; professionals 21–2, 26;
role of governors 24–5; school governors
17; Taylor Report (1977) 22, 26
HLHS Academy Trust Ltd 111
HMI *see* Her Majesty's Inspectors of
Schools
Holmes, E. 53
Holmes, G. 53
honesty 91
House of Commons Education Committee
47, 85
Howell, D. 20–1
Hudson, M. 85
Humphries, S. 155, 156
Hurt, J. 14, 17, 18

IEBs *see* interim executive boards
The Independent 28
Independent Academies Association 119
individualism 175–6
induction of governors 98–9

Industry Matters 36
Inner London Education Authority (ILEA) 32–3
inspection: before 1992 134–5; advisers 135; awe and wonder 2–3, 156; changes 184–5; external reviews of governance 140; focus 138; future of inspection 145–7; of governance 84, 138–45, 203, 224–9, 230–1; 'inadequate' governance 143–4; international measurements 147–8, 201; 'outstanding governance' 142; overall judgements on schools 144, 144t, 145t; the point of inspection 148–9; pre-inspection checklist for governing boards 224–9; pupil attainment and achievement 136; quality assurance 136, 137; quality control 136–7; role of governors 140–1; see also Ofsted
integrity 91
interim executive boards (IEBs) 44, 90
international measurements 147–8, 201
Ipsos Mori 166

Jackson, P. 54
James, C. et al. 70, 78, 94–5, 126, 191
Jamieson, I. 89
Janis-Norton, N. 162
Jefferies, G. 34, 35
Jessel, T. 23
Johnston, D. 152
Jones, O. 175, 191

Karpman, S. 118
Kay-Shuttleworth, J. 14
Kennedy, J. F. 57
Kent, M. 112
key issues from 2015 189, 193–4; cooperation and collaboration 190, 200–1; democratic accountability 192; governance as social capital 190–1; probity 191; school improvement 189; thinking strategically 191–2; see also strategic checklist
Keys, W. 35

Labour education policy 4, 26–7, 40–1, 43, 65–6, 153, 165, 180
Lansbury, G. 111

leadership 91; leading and managing 3, 123
legal responsibilities of governors 105–6
local authorities (LAs) 9, 18, 29–31, 39, 43, 171, 185–6; see also Regional Schools Commissioners
local authority governors 32–3, 35
local education authorities (LEAs) 4, 9, 10, 18, 19–20, 21, 22, 23, 27; following 1988 Act 30, 41
Local Education Boards 193
Local Government Association 202
Local Management of Schools (LMS) 37, 50, 83
London Oratory School 84
Lowe, R. 16

McChesney, R. W. 173
McKergow, M. 54, 120–1
maintained schools 43, 47; accountability 170, 192, 197; community schools 40, 41, 43, 44; duties of governing bodies 29–30, 130; federated maintained schools 45, 85, 145, 190; governors 23, 26, 32, 33, 81, 90, 192; grant maintained schools 28, 29, 37, 82–3, 109; headteachers 68, 109; inspection outcomes 184; legal responsibilities 105, 107; regulations 175; safeguarding 136; school performance 184, 201; see also city technology colleges; community schools; foundation schools
managers and management 7, 12–13, 14–15, 16, 17, 18–19
managing and leading 3, 123
Mansell, W. 84
Mason, S. 39, 157
Meek, J. 174
meetings 101–3, 101f, 102f
Meetings Charter 102, 103f
meritocracy 176
Midwinter, E. 157, 158
Millar, C. 162–3
Millar, F. 182
Miller, F. F. 14
Ministry of Education 19–20, 151
minority ethnic communities 38–9, 155, 166, 203

mission 133
mission statements 56–7
monitoring 58, 67, 76; attachment
  to classes, departments, etc 75;
  committees 70–2; headteacher's report
  68–9; stakeholder surveys 75–6;
  understanding the data 69–70, 85–6;
  visiting the school 72–5, 107–8, 219,
  220–1
Morris, H. 39, 157
multi-academy trusts 46, 145–6
Mundella Code (1880) 17
Murray, N. 134–5

Nash, Lord 82, 101
National Association of Governors and
  Managers (NAGM) 25, 36
National Association of Headteachers 91
National Audit Office (NAO) 184
National College for School Leadership
  53–4, 165
National College for Teaching and
  Leadership 93, 108, 119, 165
National College's National Leaders of
  Governance 171
National Commission on Education 110
National Confederation of Parent Teacher
  Associations (NCPTA) 151
National Coordinators of Governors'
  Services 171
National Curriculum 28, 30
National Education League 14
National Education Union 14
national government 9–10
National Governors' Association (NGA)
  21, 38, 91, 108, 112, 169–70, 171
National Professional Qualification for
  Headship 125, 203
National Society 11
National Standards for Headteachers 117,
  123–4, 162
National Teaching Awards 171
National Union of Teachers 22, 34
neoliberalism 173–4; competition 177;
  diminution of social capital 178–9;
  diminution of worth of public sector
  178; impact on schools 179–80;
  individualism 175–6; key elements

174–5; probity at risk 179; results focus
  176; shifting expectations 177–8; target-
  setting 176–7
Newsom, J. 129
Newsom Report (1963) 151–2
NGA see National Governors' Association
Nicol Mere Community Primary School,
  Wigan 56
Norris, Rev. 12–13, 17
Northern Ireland 8, 135
Norton-sub-Hamdon CofE Primary
  School, Somerset 163

objectivity 91
O'Brien, P. 103
The Observer 176
O'Connor, M. et al. 117–18
Ofsted 11–12, 65, 134, 135–8, 184–5; and
  academies 42, 43, 145–7; inspecting
  governance 84, 138–9, 141, 142, 143,
  203; reports 42, 49, 66, 70, 182–3;
  School Inspection Handbook 74, 130,
  136, 138–9, 169, 230–1; school self-
  evaluation 76–7; school visits guidance
  72–4
openness 91
Owen, D. 11

Page, A. 162–3
parent governors 27, 33–5, 153
parents and schools: access 160, 161f;
  community cohesion 167; community
  education 157–8, 165; community
  engagement 166–7; Every Child Matters
  77, 165–6; expectations of parents
  158; history 17, 19, 23, 150–4; models
  of engagement 160, 161–2; notes
  for governors 236–7; parent–teacher
  conversations 159–60; problems of
  engagement 154–7; rights and roles 186;
  school–parent partnerships 162–6
parent–teacher associations 151, 152
parent–teacher conversations 159–60
performance management see appraisal
Peters, R. S. 109–10
Phillips, A. 182
PISA (Programme for International Student
  Assessment) 147–8, 176–7, 201–2

planning 58, 59–60; governing by target-
setting 65–7, 67*f*; governing through
policy 60–5
Plowden Report (1967) 152
policy 60–2; defined 62–4; governors'
role in policy-making 64–5; role of
committees 71; school behaviour policy
61–2; *see also* coalition government;
Labour education policy
politicians 22–4
population change 202–3
poverty 195–6
pre-inspection checklist for governing
boards 224–9
pre-schools 153
primary schools: academies and free schools
4; British values 56; character of the
school 199–200; co-opted governors 36;
engagement of parents 150, 154, 159,
161, 163–4; evaluation 78; governors 7,
12, 23, 25, 29, 33; inspection outcomes
144, 145*t*, 146–7, 189; monitoring
69, 73; outstanding governance 142;
parent governors 34; planning 60, 66;
privatisation 175; teacher governors 37;
trends 181, 183, 186, 187; vision 55
Private Finance Initiative 43, 180
private sector deregulation 175
privatisation 41–4, 174
Privy Council Office 11
probity 179, 191
professionals 21–2, 26
public sector 178
Putnam, R. 178–9

Qualifications and Curriculum Authority
(QCA) 65, 84

RAISE Online (Reporting and Analysis
for Improvement through school Self-
Evaluation) 86, 107, 136
Ramsey, A. 57
Rawlinson, Lord 84
reading list 206–8
recruitment and training of governors 32;
co-opted governors 35–7; headteacher
governors 38; local authority
appointments 32–3, 35; minority ethnic

communities 38–9; parent governors
33–5; recruitment and retention 97–8;
teacher (staff) governors 37–8
Rée, H. 23, 129
Regan, D. 153
Reggio Emilia approach 162
Regina v ILEA, ex parte Brunyate 32–3
Regional Schools Commissioners (RSCs)
183–4
religious instruction 11, 13; *see also* church
schools
Rennie, J. 157
responsibilities of governors: legal
responsibilities 105–6; promoting the
business model? 83–7; representing the
community? 80–3; and school heads
232–3; stewards or stakeholders? 87–8
results focus 176
Richardson, C. 64
rights of governors 106; information 107;
resources 107; role description 108; self-
evaluation 108; time 36, 106–7; training
and development 93, 108; visiting 107–8
Roche, F. 115
roles of governors 96*f*, 125; 1944–86
24–5; chair 35, 93–5, 96*f*; clerk to the
governors 95, 96–7; committees 93;
individual roles 92; in inspection 140–1;
role description 108; vice-chair 35, 93,
95, 96*f*
Royal Commission on Local Government
(1966) 21
RSCs (Regional Schools Commissioners)
183–4
Russell, B. 122

safeguarding 136
Sahlberg, P. 188
Sallis, J. 22, 23, 25, 51, 71, 72, 82, 137
Schattschneider, E. 34, 82, 155
School Attendance Committees 16, 187
school behaviour policy 61–2
The School Board Chronicle 16
school business managers 83
school character 199–200
School Governors' One-Stop Shop
(SGOSS) 191
school leadership 3

school management 3
school performance data 69–70, 85–6, 107, 184, 187, 201–2
school self-evaluation 76–7
schooling in England: since 1988 39–41; privatisation of schooling 41–4
schools in England in 2015: changes in academisation 183–4; changes in inspection 184–5; disruption innovation 181; dominant trends 180–8; education as national issue 185; hardening of attitudes? 182–3; impact of neoliberalism 179–80; improvement in schools 47–8, 185–6, 189; pegging back? 181–2; standards 46–7; see also academies; community schools; evaluation of the school; foundation schools; key issues from 2015; maintained schools; voluntary aided schools; voluntary controlled schools
Scotland 8, 135
secondary schools: academies 4, 37, 42, 43, 190; co-opted governors 36; engagement of parents 150, 151–2, 159, 160; evaluation 78; governors 25, 29, 33; inspection outcomes 144, 144t, 189, 201; outstanding governance 142; parent governors 34; planning 63, 66; privatisation 175; teacher governors 37; trends 186–7, 189
Secret Teacher Blog 148, 182
Secretary of State for Education 11, 42, 43, 45, 90, 175, 176; see also Baker, K.; Blunkett, D.; Gove, M.
self-evaluation: of governing board 108, 168–70, 239–40; of headteacher 234–5; of school 76–7
Self-Evaluation Form (SEF) 76–7
selflessness 90
SGOSS (School Governors' One-Stop Shop) 191
Simon, B. 15, 28
skills-based model of governance 44, 48, 50–1, 81, 191
Smith, J. 11
Smith, T. 153
Smithies, F. 31
social capital: governance as 190–1; in neoliberalism 178–9

Society of Education Officers 17
Southampton Racial Equality Council 38
Specialist Schools and Academies Trust 188
Spicer, D. et al. 126, 127
Stacey, M. 159–60
staff 186; appraisal 130–2; conduct 129–31; as governors 27, 37–8; morale 182; pay 132, 176, 180; shared mission 133; staff supply 187, 198; staffing structure 131; wellbeing 132, 198–9; see also governing board and the staff
stakeholder model of governance 26, 37, 44, 48, 80–1, 87–8
stakeholder surveys 75–6
stakeholders 55, 60, 87
standards: for headship 117, 123–4, 162; of schools 46–7
statements of aims 57–8
stewards 87, 88, 89
strategic checklist 194–5; accountability 197; being strategic 203–4; character of the school 199–200; children's wellbeing, mental health and experience 165, 203; collaboration and governing groups of schools 190, 200–1; managing in austerity 202; performance 201–2; population change 202–3; poverty, hardship and inequality 195–6; staffing and wellbeing 198–9
strategic direction 58–9, 79; annual cycle 100, 100f; evaluating 58, 76–9; monitoring 58, 67–76; planning 58, 59–67
strategic functions of governing boards 47–8, 53; British values 56–8; ethos 55–6, 125; strategic direction 58–79; vision 53–5, 125
strategic governance 191–2, 203–4
Streatfield, D. 34, 35
Studio Schools 46
Sunday School movement 11
'superheads' 117–19
support staff 37–8
Surrey County Council 41
Sutherland, G. 15
Swindon academy 83–4

target-setting 65–7, 67f, 176–7
Taylor Report (1977) 22, 26
teacher (staff) governors 27, 37–8
teachers *see* staff
Thatcher, M. 28
time 36, 106–7
The Times 84, 88
Times Educational Supplement (*TES*) 32, 34, 36, 83, 112
Trades Union Congress (TUC) 36, 180
training of governors 93, 108
'Trojan Horse' episode 52, 56, 138, 146–7, 187

umbrella trusts 46, 145
United States 8
University of Bath 21
University of the Third Age 156
University Technical Colleges (UTCs) 46

Verhaeghe, P. 174, 178
vice-chair of the board 35, 93, 95, 96f
vision 53–5, 125

visiting the school 72–5; governors' rights 107–8; policy 219; protocol 220–1
voluntary aided schools 44–5, 105, 170
voluntary controlled schools 44, 170
vouchers 27

Wales 8, 18, 39, 65, 135
Walters, J. 64
Waterfield, L. 12
Waters, M. 89
Watson, L. 152
Wedgwood, C. V. 92
Wells, H. G. 13
Wenham, J. G. 17
Wild, E. 168–9
Wilkins, A. 192
William Tyndale Junior School, Islington 24–5
Wilshaw, M. 83–4, 85, 134, 187
Winkley, D. 118
Wood, C. 181

Young, M. 176

Printed in Great Britain
by Amazon

50807673R00151